Reliability on the Move:
Safety and Reliability in Transportation

ESRA
IChemE
IEE
INucE
IP
IQA
IMechE

SARSS '89

Proceedings of the Safety and Reliability Society Symposium 1989, held at Bath, UK, 11–12 October 1989

Organised by
The Safety and Reliability Society, Clayton House, 59 Piccadilly, Manchester M1 2AQ, UK

Co-sponsors
The European Safety and Reliability Association
The Institution of Chemical Engineers
The Institution of Electrical Engineers
The Institution of Nuclear Engineers
The Institute of Petroleum
The Institute of Quality Assurance
The Institution of Mechanical Engineers

Organising Committee
Dr G. B. Guy (Chairman)
Mr D. W. Heckle (Secretary)
Mr R. F. Cox
Mr N. J. Locke
Ms B. A. Sayers
Dr M. H. Walter
Mr A. O. F. Venton
Mr R. M. Vote
Mr A. C. C. Burton
Mr N. De Bray
Mr J. V. Skene
Mr R. C. Short (IEE Representative)

Reliability on the Move:
Safety and Reliability in Transportation

Edited by

G. B. GUY

BNFL Engineering, Risley, Warrington, UK
and
Safety and Reliability Society, Manchester, UK

ELSEVIER APPLIED SCIENCE
LONDON and NEW YORK

ELSEVIER SCIENCE PUBLISHERS LTD
Crown House, Linton Road, Barking, Essex IG11 8JU, England

Sole Distributor in the USA and Canada
ELSEVIER SCIENCE PUBLISHING CO., INC.
655 Avenue of the Americas, New York, NY 10010, USA

WITH 30 TABLES AND 69 ILLUSTRATIONS

© 1989 ELSEVIER SCIENCE PUBLISHERS LTD
© 1989 CROWN COPYRIGHT—pp. 1–10
© 1989 CHARTER TECHNOLOGIES LTD—pp. 11–28
© 1989 UNITED KINGDOM ATOMIC ENERGY AUTHORITY—pp. 109–125

British Library Cataloguing in Publication Data

Safety and Reliability Society. (Symposium: 1989:
  Bath, England)
  Reliability on the move: safety and reliability in
  transportation.
  1. Transport. Safety aspects
  I. Title II. Guy, G. B.
  363.12

ISBN 1-85166-425-4

Library of Congress CIP data applied for

Printed in Great Britain by Galliard (Printers) Ltd, Great Yarmouth

PREFACE

The development of transportation has been a significant factor in the development of civilisation as a whole. Our technical ability to move people and goods now seems virtually limitless when one considers for example the achievements of the various space programmes. Yet our current achievements rely heavily on high standards of safety and reliability from equipment and the human component of transportation systems. Recent failures have highlighted our dependence on equipment and human reliability, notably the Clapham Junction rail crash, the M1 air crash, the Kings Cross fire and the Zeebrugge ferry capsize, taken at a purely national level. The Paris (Orly) air crash and the Siberian pipeline failure are examples taken arbitrarily at the international level.

In fulfilment of its several aims, the Safety and Reliability Society provides an organisation to stimulate and advance safety and reliability technology and provides a forum for the exchange of information on such matters. Past symposia have dealt with a variety of Safety and Reliability issues but recent losses in human life, goods and capital from transportation incidents have highlighted the need for the interchange of ideas on safe and reliable transportation. This book represents the proceedings of the 1989 Safety & Reliability Society Symposium held in Bath on the 11th and 12th of October on that topic.

The structure of the book represents the structure of the symposium itself and the papers selected represent current thinking in the wide field of transportation. Inevitably, a two day symposium can only present selected areas within such a wide field, nevertheless, the areas of rail, air, road and sea are well represented.

The response to the Call for Papers produced more papers than could be included in the Symposium and I must thank all of the authors for their interest and enthusiasm. I must also thank the presenters, the reviewers, the organising committee and the Co-sponsors for their support. Through the hard work and dedication of all of these people an interesting and instructive Symposium has been achieved and this book compiled.

G B GUY

CONTENTS

Preface   v

List of Contributors   ix

Hazard Analysis - A Standardised Approach   1
  K. Geary

Application of Formal Methods to Railway Signalling   11
  W. J. Cullyer, J. W. Wise

Fault Tolerance for Railway Signalling - VOTRICS in
Practice   29
  G. Wirthumer, H. Lutnik

An AI/Real Time Solution for Expert Scheduling of
Underground Rail Traffic   47
  C. Horellou, C. Rossi, G. Sissa

Just a Slip of the Cursor: Methods for Identifying
Potential Problem Areas in the Use of a VDU Based
System for the Signalling of Trains   58
  D. A. Lucas

A Knowledge-Based Assistant for Real-Time Planning and
Recovery in Automatic Train Protection Systems   78
  E. Lamma, P. Mello

Safety and Reliability Analysis of the Hermes Crew
Escape Module   95
  I. Jenkins

A Study of Severe Air Crash Environments with
Particular Reference to the Carriage of Radioactive
Materials by Air   109
  H. L. Wilkinson

The Use of Risk Analysis in the Formulation of Policy
for the Transport of Dangerous Goods through Tunnels   126
  M. McD. Grant

Modes and Consequences of the Failure of Road and Rail
Tankers Carrying Liquefied Gases and Other Hazardous
Liquids   136
  V. C. Marshall

Should Dangerous Goods be Moved by Rail Rather than
by Road?   149
  D. Beattie

TREMEX: Transport Emergency Expert System   160
  J. E. Lycett, D. Maudsley, D. L. Milner

Human Reliability and Risk Management in the
Transportation of Spent Nuclear Fuel   169
  S. Tuler, R. E. Kasperson, S. Ratick

Pipelines Once Buried Never to be Forgotten   195
  R. Bolt, T. Logtenberg

LBL - A Computer Simulation Program for Risk
Evaluation of Lifeboat Evacuation   208
  H. S. Soma, K. H. Drager

Monte Carlo Simulation to Assessing the Risk
Associated to the Navigation in Channel-Port   222
  R. Santucci, P. Vestrucci

Reliability Assessment of the Propulsion Machinery,
Steering Gear, Electrical Supply and Fire Systems of
Irradiated Fuel Ships   241
  R. Cheshire

POSTER SESSION

Bayesian and Time Series Modelling Techniques in
Transportation Reliability   260
  N. Davies, J. C. Naylor, C. McCollin

LIST OF CONTRIBUTORS

D. Beattie
Transport Engineering Section Manager, ICI Engineering,
Branches Lane, Runcorn, Cheshire WA7 4JE, UK.

R. Bolt
Technical Operations Department, N.V. Nederlandse Gasunie,
PO Box 19, Groningen, The Netherlands.

R. Cheshire
Transport Approvals and Safety Manager, British Nuclear
Fuels PLC, Fleming House, Warrington, Cheshire WA3 6AS, UK.

W. J. Cullyer
Department of Engineering, University of Warwick, Coventry
CV4 7AL, UK.

N. Davies
Department of Mathematics, Statistics and Operational
Research, Trent Polytechnic, Nottingham, UK.

K. H. Drager
A/S Quasar Consultants, Munkedamsveien 53B, 0250 Oslo 2,
Norway.

K. Geary
Sea Systems Controllerate, Ministry of Defence, Foxhill,
Bath BA1 5AB, UK.

M. McD. Grant
W. S. Atkins Engineering Sciences, Woodcote Grove, Ashley
Road, Epsom, Surrey KT18 5BW, UK.

C. Horellou
CISI Ingénierie, Pont des 3 Sautets, 13100 Aix en
Provence, France.

I. Jenkins
MBB GmbH Space Communications and Propulsion Division,
Munich, Federal Republic of Germany.

R. E. Kasperson
Center for Technology, Environment and Development, Clark
University, 950 Main Street, Worcester, Massachusetts 01610,
USA.

E. Lamma
DEIS - Università di Bologna, Viale Risorgimento 2, 40136
Bologna, Italy.

M. Th. Logtenberg
Department of Industrial Safety, Technology for Society TNO,
PO Box 342, Apeldoorn, The Netherlands.

D. A. Lucas
Human Reliability Associates Ltd., 1 School House, Higher
Lane, Dalton, Wigan, Lancs. WN8 7RP, UK.

J. E. Lycett
Division of Instrumentation and Control Engineering, School
of Information Engineering, Teesside Polytechnic,
Middlesbrough, Cleveland TS1 3BA, UK.

H. Lutnik
Alcatel Austria, Elin Research Center, Ruthnergasse 1-7,
A-1210 Vienna, Austria.

C. McCollin
Department of Mathematics, Statistics and Operational
Research, Trent Polytechnic, Nottingham, UK.

V. C. Marshall
Disaster Research Unit, Department of Industrial Technology,
University of Bradford, Bradford, UK.

D. Maudsley
Division of Instrumentation and Control Engineering, School
of Information Engineering, Teesside Polytechnic,
Middlesbrough, Cleveland TS1 3BA, UK.

P. Mello
DEIS - Università di Bologna, Viale Risorgimento 2, 40136
Bologna, Italy.

D. L. Milner
ICI Chemicals and Polymers, PO Box 90, Wilton, Middlesbrough,
Cleveland, UK.

J. C. Naylor
Department of Mathematics, Statistics and Operational
Research, Trent Polytechnic, Nottingham, UK.

S. Ratick
Center for Technology, Environment and Development, Clark
University, 950 Main Street, Worcester, Massachusetts 01610,
USA.

C. Rossi
Ansaldo Trasporti, Corso Perrone 25, 16161 Genova, Italy.

R. Santucci
NIER, Via S. Stefano 16, Bologna, Italy.

G. Sissa
Ansaldo Trasporti, Corso Perrone 25, 16161 Genova, Italy.

H. S. Soma
A/S Quasar Consultants, Munkedamsveien 53B, 0250 Oslo 2,
Norway.

S. Tuler
Center for Technology, Environment and Development, Clark
University, 950 Main Street, Worcester, Massachusetts 01610,
USA.

P. Vestrucci
Laboratorio Ingegneria Nucleare, Via dei Colli 16, Bologna,
Italy.

H. L. Wilkinson
Safety and Reliability Directorate, UKAEA, Wigshaw Lane,
Culcheth, Warrington, Cheshire WA3 4NE, UK.

G. Wirthumer
Alcatel Austria, Elin Research Center, Ruthnergasse 1-7,
A-1210 Vienna, Austria.

J. W. Wise
VIPER Project Director, Charter Technologies Ltd.,
Room 83/84, U Building, RSRE, St. Andrews Road, Malvern,
Worcs WR14 3PS, UK.

HAZARD ANALYSIS - A STANDARDISED APPROACH

KEVIN GEARY
Sea Systems Controllerate
Ministry of Defence
Foxhill, Bath BA1 5AB

ABSTRACT

There is little in the way of existing standardisation for hazard analysis of mobile systems to establish the safety criticality of a system and to identify which particular elements of that system are safety critical. The discussions in this paper disclose the background experience and debate which led to work on drafting Interim Defence Standard 00-56. Although the paper is set in the context of issues relevant to the safety certification of weapon systems on-board Naval military platforms, the issues raised are of a generic nature.

INTRODUCTION

We are experiencing an increasing rise in the number of systems with embedded software at the heart of their control mechanisms. Demands for greater efficiency, functionallity, speed of response and cost effectiveness are forcing systems designers away from the electrical and mechanical control mechanisms that have traditionally been used in mobile systems to date. This is particulaly true of military systems, which often lead the field in application of new technology.

When one thinks of transport systems, the obvious equipment that springs to mind for military applications is the category of manned platforms, such as battleships, aircraft and tanks. However, military equipment involved in transportation covers not only platforms driven by military personnel, but also automated delivery systems for transporting the active components for military missions to their targets. Examples of military systems that may contain embedded potentially safety critical software for control are given in table 1.

TABLE 1

The following types of system are examples of military equipment that may contain safety critical computing components.

Weapons fire control (ie launcher systems)
Platform autopilots
Aircraft flight control
Nuclear reactor protection
Gas detectors
Missile guidance
Radar direction control
Fusing and arming devices
Weapon safety firing arcs
Aircraft stores management
Alarm systems
Weapon targeting
Hazardous and heavy load transfer
Engine control
Command and control (C2 and C3)
Weapon command systems
Engine order telegraph
Radiation detectors
Digital communications
Simulators

The former category of manually controlled transportation systems may involve automated operator assistance of some form. Examples include sub-systems for power plant control and direction and stability control of the platforms themselves, such as fly-by-wire aircraft and the naval equivalent in ships and submarines (which might be described by the term "steer-by-wire").

The latter category of automated or robotic systems with a degree of intelligence built into their control mechanisms, includes both those that are intentionally destructive and those that have passive missions. Examples of intentionally destructive automated systems are as missiles and torpedos (which are effectively underwater missiles), whereas an example of a passive automated transport system is a pilotless reconnaissance vehicle (operating either above or below water). The obvious potentially hazardous control sub-system within these automated systems is the guidance control mechanism. However, potentially hazardous systems should be considered in the context of the whole system, and this includes their initiation or launch mechanisms.

BACKGROUND

The use of complex computer technology adds a new dimension to the process of hazard analysis. When the lay person thinks of hazard assessment, images of Flixborough, Bopal and North Sea oil rigs may spring to mind. This is not surprising as such disasters are most news-worthy and have thus contributed to the general concept of what hazard assessment is all about. During initial efforts to gather material that might contribute to the development of a standard for hazard analysis of military systems, it was notable that this public image is reflected in the maturity of hazard assessment practices in the commercial world. The technologies with the most advanced hazard analysis procedures and supporting infrastructure appear to be those of the chemical, oil and gas industries.

Involvement with certification of military systems for operational safety has revealed that there is little in the way of existing applicable standards or defacto procedures for hazard analysis of computer controlled transport and delivery systems. The need for hazard analysis of equipment control mechanisms has been focused by the advent of software based systems and the need to identify safety critical software. Sea Systems Controllerate requirements for the identification of safety critical software and the application of mandatory safety assurance practices were first formally defined in NES 620, in 1986 [1][2]. However, the application of these requirements has proved variable. Some developers of potentially hazardous equipment just do not believe that they have safety critical software embedded in their systems.

In the Sea Systems Contollerate, a weapon system needs to be supported by a safety paper which must be approved before embarkation of the weapon is permitted. The procedure for development of a safety paper calls for a hazard analysis to be carried out but does not, at the time of writing, prescibe any preferred methodologies or format for presentation of the safety case. In some cases assessment of the safety paper has proved difficult because the hazard analysis has been conducted without the application of a fully auditable methodology and has been presented with limited supporting evidence. An incomplete safety paper results in delays and extra expenditure due to the rework necessary to present a satisfactory safety case. A subjective declaration that a system does not contain any safety critical software, for example, is not unknown. When the project is asked for the documented hazard analysis to back up this statement, the supporting evidence may be meagre. The declaration may have been formed, in consultation with the equipment developer, based on hasty subjective judgement and may have been strongly biased by the desire to avoid the procedures associated with safety critical software [3].

The lack of methodical hazard analysis runs a high risk of incurring significant delays and extra costs, through a need to carry out expensive rework at a late stage in the project, when final safety certification is conducted. The view has also been expressed that war is a hazardous activity and therefore weapon systems are exempt from consideration of operational hazards because the military personnel are knowingly going into a dangerous situation anyway. All this would be of little comfort to the military personnel involved if such a view were allowed to prevail. Furthermore, the act of scoring an own goal during a battle would not only provoke severe criticism of those in charge, it could also hand a strategic advantage to the enemy thereby resulting in many more deaths.

This of course is not the norm; it is a worst case approach, but serves to illustrate an extreme, demanding expensive rectification, that fortunately is rarely encountered. However, hazard analyses can vary between giving very little effort to the exercise to presenting a well considered case. The task of the certification authority would naturally be made easier if there were some consistency and methodology of approach which might be achieved by invoking a standard. However, it very rapidly became apparent that outside of the established basitions of safety in the chemical, oil and mining industries [4], there is very little in the way of standards for hazard analysis. The two main existing documents containing some guidance on hazard analysis of systems containing embedded software are MIL STD 882B [5] and the HSE Guide [6].

Another problem that became apparent was that hazard analysis was being applied in the latter stages of development or at acceptance. When such an analysis is likely to reveal that some system components (eg software) are safety critical, there are moves to devise arguments as to why they are not critical. Identification of safety criticality of design at a post design stage is too late to have any influence on the design of the system without significant and costly retrospective work to the appropriate standard. Thus there is the temptation to pass over existing methods [7][8] in favour of less methodical and sometimes novel approaches that do not contradict the assumed safety critical status of components. With no definitive policy or mandatory standard, hazard analysis may be progressed by subjective judgement exercised by a committee. This practice may have been very successful with the relatively simple technology of mechanical or analog control mechanisms. However, such an approach is not sufficiently effective when applied to modern complex technology involving high functionality systems controlled by embedded software executed by VLSI electronics.

Software based technology undoubtably has many advantages in terms of design flexibility, development cost reduction, enhanced equipment performance, reduced physical size and weight, and enhanced safety. It is therefore here to stay. However, the methods of safety assessment and the certification procedures must keep pace with design technology in order to prevent it becoming uncontrolled. It is not possible to guarantee that a complex design, such as software or a VLSI component, will be risk free but that is no reason to spurn the use of such technology. Policies that advocate the use of simpler technology for safety critical functions on the grounds that project management becomes easier may not be practical if high performance demands are to be met.

ACCEPTABLE RISK

Considerations of safety criticality inevitably lead to the question "What is an acceptable risk?". Deciding on the acceptability of risk is unfortunately not a quantitative judgement; it is strongly biased by emotions. It is the public opinion, albeit strongly influenced by what constitutes a good news story, and the resulting political opinion that will have most influence on what is an acceptable risk. For example, we accept a probability of death by road accident of 1 in 10000, but a risk of death of 1 in 1000000 for an uncontrolled nuclear release from a power station [9] can cause reactions resulting in expensive public enquiries, mass demonstrations, and Parliamentary questions. There have been attempts to raise public awareness of risks due to road accidents, but there seems to be a general apathy when the inevitable result will be greater restrictions on public freedom, such as stricter speed limits or the total abolition of alcohol for drivers.

Decisions on what represents an acceptable risk in the military field tend to be aligned with traditional safety assessment practices based on assessing simple control technology. Until relatively recently weapons did not possess any form of intelligent control. They were directly under human control where, barring tangible hardware failure, the human operator could predict potentially hazardous situations and take appropriate evasive action. Reliance was vested in the human operator and the issue of human fallibility was not of great concern. Although many notable disasters are directly attributable to human failure, we still seem to be prepared, under many circumstances, to rely on the human operator that we are all familiar with and show lack of trust in automated systems, especially those that we do not have an understanding of.

Another legacy from simple control technology is the domain of what should be assessed. Military considerations are still polarised to a large extent around the safety of the launch platform. When missile delivery systems are effectively ballistic or under human operator controlled wire guidance, it is up to the operator to identify potential hazards and to take the appropriate action. The human operator can be trained and has the intelligence to interpret his training in the context of what his senses perceive and to act accordingly. The potential hazard of hitting a friendly platform should be easily recognised and evasive action taken. If an accident did occur, it was comparatively easy to modify operational procedures and training to accomodate the situation. However, when there are many automated delivery systems, all alike, it may cost many millions of pounds to develop and refit new software.

The problem of deciding what is an acceptable risk is hampered by the need to attribute a metric to risk in the form of probability of accident per unit of entity. But, what is the unit of entity to be? It could be units of time, which are used to quantify hardware reliability, units of activity, such as number of projectiles fired, or units of demand. The latter is a combination of the former two units, for example the units of time for the duration that an activity is taking place. Metrics based on the unit of time are most understood as they are derived from hardware availability and reliability quantification, procedures for which are laid down in Def Stan 00-41 [10]. Such calculations are based on statistically quantifiable data for random failure distributions which are a measure of physical degradation. However, these calculations are not readily transferable to design errors that may or may not manifest themselves in an unsafe way, depending on the operational circumstances. This can lead to the subjective conclusion that the consequent system failures are random with respect to time, whereas they are predetermined with respect to specific operational circumstances immediately preceding the incident.

POLICY

Policy inevitably revolves around the question, "What constitutes a Safety Hazard in the context of the operational use of the system?". Discussions lead to questions about what risks are reasonable, what risks can be tolerated, and how to balance safety requirements with the impact on design, operations and costs. These are questions which are still to be fully answered, and therefore any standard produced must necessarily take a generic approach concerning acceptable risks.

A policy lays down the overall requirements for the application of standards, procedures and supporting infrastructure. Work towards the development of a hazard analysis standard brought to light a number of policy issues that had been causing problems for safety certification, but which until recently had been overcome by improvisation through subjective judgement applied to individual projects at the appropriate time, or sometimes later, and by invoking operational constraints. Such action inevitably leads to lack of consistency in decision making and lack of coordination and focusing of exprience.

Before decisions can be made as to what constitutes a hazard, policy must be formed on the severity of accident that is being addressed. The term "accident", used in the general sense, has a wide meaning which can refer to any unintended event that may or may not cause damage or harm. An unintended event that causes damage could range from a minor scratch on some paintwork to large scale destruction of property. The prime consideration for MOD is the class of accidents that risk human life.

The draft MOD(PE) Policy for Safety Critical Software [11] defines Safety Critical Software in terms of risk to human life. In taking this line, MOD has deviated from former definitions used in the military world which also include damage to non-human objects. Some of these definitions inlcude damage to the launch platform, some include damage to the environment, and some include damage to property in their definitions of safety criticality.

However these generic terms still have an air of ambiguity. What constitutes damage to the launch platform? What constitutes damage to property? What constitutes damage to the environment?

Such problems in trying to classify the kind of accident, damage or harm that is unacceptable lead on to the use of the adjective "major". This helps to some extent, but it is still a subjective term that means different things to different people. When it comes to the grey area of deciding whether a system is in one category or another, arguments occur between those that have economics as their prime objective and those concerned with prevention of what the safety assessors consider to be unacceptable accidents.

The subjectivity that surrounds what is an unacceptable accident in terms of non-human objects is also parallelled by similar controversy over what constitutes injury to humans. The occasional minor scratch is part of every day life and could be regarded as insignificant, provided the victim is not a haemophiliac and is up to date with tetanus injections. The loss of limbs is clearly unacceptable, but that refers to the whole limb. What do we do about part of a limb? Loss of the leg below the knee is also unacceptable, but can the loss of the end of a toe be tolerated, provided it does not happen too often? Then, what is meant by "too often"?

In drawing up the draft MOD Policy for Safety Critical Software [11], MOD found itself involved in such discussions which turned out to be very lengthy and showed little sign of converging to a timely and definitive conclusion. To break out of this dilemma it was decided that safety criticality would be expressed in terms of risk to human life. It was considered that any system that could cut off somebody's arm could just as easily cut off their head.

It is clear that software by itself is not a hazard; it is only when software is used in such a way that it controls or influences some physical entity, for example a submarine or a missile, that it becomes potentially dangerous. It is not therefore possible to consider system components, such as software, in isolation when deciding what is safety critical. The safety criticality of a component can only be determined by analysis which first considers the system and its actions as a whole. For a missile system to be fitted to a ship, for example, consideration must be given to all activities which effect dockside delivery, through embarkation, stowage and launch, to target aquisition and warhead detonation. It is therefore envisaged that a system oriented safety policy will be developed.

It is also anticipated that such a policy will need to be backed by an infrastructure. The issue is not just a MOD problem, it needs to be tackled on a national basis. The difference between civil considerations and military ones is that the military makes use of systems that are designed to be hazardous, but only to an enemy and only when intended. Although the MOD is currently giving a great deal of attention to the safety of systems that could kill, it must also take into account the additional considerations pertinent to the Health and Safety at Work Act [12] and the Consumer Protection Act [13], which are of major concern in the civil sector. The two activities are complementary in that current MOD priorities should equate to the class of civil safety considerations for systems that are potentially lethal.

STANDARD

The need to introduce consistency, clarity and methodical argument to justifications for safety criticality of system elements, or rather to the justifications of non-criticality, inevitably lead to the need for a standard. Although work on a draft standard was initiated and managed by the Sea Systems Controllerate, the MOD committees responsible for progressing work on safety critical software standardisation took an interest. Instead of generating a Naval Engineering Standard, it was decided that the work would be promulgated as draft Interim Defence Standard 00-56 [14].

Any policy regarding safety needs to be sure that safety critical systems and components are identified at an early stage. Furthermore, in order that projects for non-critical systems are not overburdened unnessarily with hazard analysis overheads, such systems should be exempted from policy requirements as early as possible in their lifecycle. This implies the need to carry out an early hazard analysis of all systems in order to identify those that are not safety critical. For this reason there is a simple preliminary hazard analysis stage defined in Interim Def Stan 00-56 as being required at the feasibility study stage.

Safety assessment requires demonstration that safety management has been properly applied. This is accomplished by documentary evidence. In the draft Standard there is a requirement for all systems to have a Hazard Log to record safety criticality status and, where relevant, the safety management activities carried out throughout the lifecycle of the system. This is an important concept because it is central to the documentary evidence that would be required by a safety assessor. For non-critical systems, this Hazard Log should impose an insigificant overhead, sufficient to show that safety had been properly considered.

When carrying out a hazard analysis of a system, it is necessary to include in any such exercise the operational scenario in which the system will be used. Hazard analysis for the identification of safety critical components cannot be performed by analysing the system in isolation; it must include relationships with the world [15]. It is not valid to analyse systems by considering them as detached from the way in which they will be used. For missile systems, for example, the siting on a ship and the arc of fire from the launcher must be evaluated. A missile system fitted to a particular location on a particular platform may not present a hazard to that platform when the missile is fired, and therefore any elements of the missile system such as software could be regarded as non-safety critical. However, when sited on a different platform, the arc of fire could pass over part of the ship and present a potential hazard. The argument that if a system component such as software has been shown to be non-critical in the original role implies non-criticality for any role is not valid. Similarly, if the siting of other equipment or the structure of a ship, say, were altered it could affect the hazard assessment of that platform and its weapon systems.

CONCLUSIONS

Experience has shown that hazard analyses can be variable in the depth, completness and timeliness of application and therefore there was a need for a standardised approach. This led to the work on drafting Interim Defence Standard 00-56. When finally published, this Standard will represent a significant step forward in Ministry of Defence procedures to introduce engineering disciplines to an area that has hitherto been addressed, for both MOD and civil projects, by a large degree of subjectivity.

There is however more work to be carried out before a framework for safety certification is completed. This new Standard does not in itself provide all the answers, but it has served to focus minds on the issues of acceptable risk and the infrastructure necessary for the application of engineering thoroughness to safety management.

Disclaimer
Any views expressed are those of the author and do not necessarily represent those of the Department.

REFERENCES

1. Ministry of Defence, Naval Engineering Standard 620 Requirements for Software for use with Digital Processors, issue 3, MOD Controllerate of the Navy, 1986, pp. 8-10.

2. Geary, K., Beyond Good Practices – A Standard for Safety Critical Software. In Achieving Safety and Reliability with Computer Systems, ed. B.K. Daniels, Elsevier Applied Science, London, 1987, pp. 232-241.

3. Ministry of Defence, Ordnance Board Proceeding 42413 Principles of Design and Use for Electrical Circuits Incorporating Explosive Components, MOD Ordnance Board, London, 1986.

4. Nimmo, I., Nunns, S.R. and Eddershaw, B.W., Lessons Learned from the Failure of a Computer System Controlling a Nylon Polymer Plant. In Achieving Safety and Reliability with Computer Systems, ed. B.K. Daniels, Elsevier Applied Science, London, 1987, pp. 189-206.

5. US Department of Defense, Military Standard 882B System Safety Program Requirements, DOD, Washington DC, 1984.

6. Health and Safety Executive, Programmable Electronic Systems in Safety Related Applications, HMSO, London, 1987.

7. Nuclear Regulatory Commission, NUREG-0492 Fault Tree Handbook, NRC, Washington DC.

8. US Department of Defense, Military Standard 1629A Procedures for Performing a Failure Mode Effect and Criticality Analysis,, DOD, Washington DC.

9. Health and Safety Executive, The Tolerability of Risk from Nuclear Power Stations, HMSO, London, 1987.

10. Ministry of Defence, Defence Standard 00-41 MOD Practices and Procedures for Reliability and Maintainability. Part 4: Reliability Engineering. Directorate of Standardization, Glasgow, 1983.

11. Ministry of Defence, Draft MOD Policy Statement for the Procurement and use of Software for Safety Critical Applications, MOD, 1988.

12. The Health and Safety at Work Act, 1984.

13. The Consumer Protection Act, 1987.

14. Ministry of Defence, Draft Interim Defence Standard 00-56 Requirements for the Analysis of Safety Critical Hazards, Directorate of Standardization, Glasgow, 1989.

15. Pyle, I.C., Designing for Safety Using Ada Packages. In Achieving Safety and Reliability with Computer Systems, ed. B.K. Daniels, Elsevier Applied Science, London, 1987, pp. 29-43.

APPLICATION OF FORMAL METHODS TO RAILWAY SIGNALLING

PROFESSOR W.J. CULLYER
Department of Engineering,
University of Warwick,
Coventry   CV4 7AL, UK

JONATHAN W. WISE
VIPER Project Director,
Charter Technologies Ltd.,
Room 83/84, U Building, RSRE,
St. Andrews Road, Malvern, Worcs   WR14 3PS, UK

ABSTRACT

At the moment, railway signalling systems are designed in a manner which is based on concepts of interlocking and signalling which have grown up over the last 150 years. Considerable use is made of "relay diagrams" and tables to define interlocking and routing. The excellent safety record of railways worldwide is due to a large extent to the rigour of the regulations which have been evolved by generations of signalling and telecommunications engineers.

With the increasing use of microelectronics and computing in railway signalling, it is reasonable to ask if the rules promulgated by the UK Institute of Railway Signalling Engineers can be formulated in a mathematical way, which will suit the development of computer-controlled interlocking and routing. In particular, this paper considers the application of the specification language HOL and computer languages such as Pascal.

1. INTRODUCTION

Computers and software are beginning to be used in railway signalling. To support these developments it is important to express the safety rules and the specifications for particular systems in modern mathematical form. This paper is based on the current signalling rules imposed by British Rail (BR) in the UK, but is a fair representation of the standards in use across the rest of the developed world.

The standards adopted by BR are described in the textbook "Railway Signalling", published by the UK Institute of Railway Signalling

Engineers (IRSE). All designers of railway signalling equipment in the UK and all of the senior staff concerned with installation and maintenance must have passed stringent examinations set by the IRSE. The regulation of safe design and operation of signalling and associated telecommunications equipment in the UK is in the hands of BR, with overall national supervision being the responsibility of the Railway Inspectorate, UK Department of Transport.

There is a sense in which the rules and regulations which are now in force grew from the early accidents and mishaps in Victorian times. Those who wish to learn more details of this evolution are advised to read L T C Rolt's book "Red for Danger", [1] which is written for the general reader and does not assume any previous technical knowledge. The early railway signalling engineers had to cope with the ever increasing speeds of trains over the years 1850 to 1920, with limited electrical technology.

With the advent of four-aspect colour light signalling in 1922, the various railway companies in Europe moved progressively towards the standards which are now accepted. Mechanical interlocking gave way to electrical techniques. In the UK, by the time BR was formed, the disciplines of the Signalling and Telecommunications Engineers were a complex yet rigorous subject, albeit with some regional variations over details. In the 1980s various railway authorities have done innovative work on the use of microelectronics in signalling and telecommunications and the resulting is thoroughly proven in operational use. Despite these advances in technology the fundamental rules remain the same. Routes must not conflict. In all circumstances drivers must be given warnings to reduce speed when approaching a signal at danger. The signalling system must "fail safe" in the event of electrical or mechanical malfunction.

The introduction of computers into this highly regulated domain calls for the highest standards of specification, design and certification. The consortium of UK companies involved, together with the University of Warwick Department of Engineering, will be pursuing the techniques described in this paper. This paper introduces some of the key concepts.

2. FORMAL METHODS FOR CLOSED-LOOP CONTROL

Over recent years a great deal of experience has been built up in the aviation industry on the use of formal methods for establishing the correctness of the design of "Level 1" systems, i.e. those deemed to be "critical" to the safe flight of an aircraft [2]. This paper considers the possibility of using such techniques in the very different world of railway signalling. Both communities of engineers have the same objective; the travelling public must be protected from the consequences of malfunction in equipment and rare but significant errors by operational staff.

A number of formal spec languages have been invented for example HOL [3], Z [4], OBJ [5], VDM [6]. Following the authors' experience with the application of formal methods to aircraft, the following tools and languages are discussed in this paper:

*   Top level specifications - Gordon's Higher Order Logic (HOL);

*   Design decomposition - HOL, hence software and hardware specifications;

*   Operational software - Pascal subset, with a formal definition;

In order to keep this paper to a reasonable length, it has been assumed that readers will have at least a limited acquaintance with these techniques and languages. For those who have not met the concepts of the specification language HOL, a brief introduction is given in Section 4.

The methods listed above have been proved to be effective in computer-based systems which have to implement digital filters of the type found in closed-loop control [7]. It is interesting to reflect that a railway signalling system is an example of a "closed-loop", in that the positions of trains are detected by track circuits, routes are interlocked based partly on the occupancy of these circuits and signals indicate to the driver that it is safe to proceed (or otherwise). Only in the unusual case when no speed reduction is made by the driver may the loop be "closed" electrically and mechanically, by an Automatic Warning System (AWS). A sound view of modern railways is to regard the automatic signalling, interlocking and permitted routes as a high integrity inner control loop, surrounded by a less critical loop which contains the drivers, signalmen and other operational staff.

3. FUNDAMENTAL MECHANISMS

There are many ways of introducing the underlying rules of railway signalling but the view taken here is that the system is driven by the "sensors" on the track and in the signals themselves and that the "actuators" drive points into the required positions and set signals to the required aspects. As noted above, no attempt is made to include the driver in the mathematical definition of the "closed-loop".

Most railways in the world obtain their primary protection from "track circuits" and multi-aspect colour light signals. This type of signalling is assumed in the rest of this paper. The principle is shown in Figure 1. Any axle bridging the running rails will produce a short-circuit and will prevent current flow through the sensor, hence indicating "circuit occupied". Equally, if the power supply fails or a conductor is broken the remote indication will be "occupied". The system is inherently "fail-safe". Insulating joints separate the track into distinct sections. Some of these may be very short physically, for example the length of the arms of a "diamond crossing".

In this elementary analysis the track circuit sensors will be assumed to have one of two states:

* FALSE - indicating no current in the track circuit detector, ie either the track is occupied or the detector is faulty;

* TRUE - indicating current flow in sensor, ie track is free of obstruction.

It is fundamental to safe operation that the passage of a train must set the signal it has just passed to RED. This is done using a track circuit to control the setting of the signal, in a manner which overrides any selection in the Control Centre. Figure 2 shows the principle. It would not be safe to place the relevant track circuit joint precisely at the signal. Although it is rare, it is possible in adverse weather for a train to overshoot a signal at danger and stop some tens of metres past the signal post itself. For this reason the critical track circuit joint is placed some 180 metres past the signal. The track between the signal and this insulating joint is called the "OVERLAP" and many other safety rules rely on the margin provided by staggering the signals and these overlap joints.

The signals are the primary means of controlling the speed of each train. The number of aspects which the signal displays is a function of the overall design of the system, taking account of the speeds of traffic and the density of working over the line in question. On rural lines, two aspect signals are adequate, on main lines away from major conurbations three aspects may be used and in the approaches to large cities four aspects are required, (Figure 3).

The system does not assume that the signals are alight simply because remote logic is producing the correct output. All signals have internal detection circuits to determine if the double filament bulbs which are used are working. If one filament fails, an auxiliary filament is switched in and a warning is issued electrically to the supervising Control Centre. Drivers will not be aware of any problem. If subsequently this auxiliary filament fails as well, the signal will not be "proved" to be alight and selection of the failed aspect will cause the preceding signal to be set to RED. This is a major defence against drivers arriving at a signal and finding no visible indication.

Leaving aside, for the moment, the issue of failed bulbs, the elementary coding used in this paper for the "state" of any signal is:

* 0 - Signal is GREEN, train may proceed;

* 1 - Signal is 2 - YELLOW, train may proceed (advance warning);

* 2 - Signal is YELLOW, train starts brake application ready to halt;

* 3 - Signal is RED, train must stop, (a few metres before the signal).

Obviously not all these states apply to all classes of signals. For example, a "two-aspect stop signal" can only be in states 0 to 3.

It is important to understand the concept of a signal being "ON" or "OFF", as viewed from the Control Centre responsible for that signal. Using the proving circuits which determine the state of the bulb filaments, the definitions are:

*   A signal is ON if the RED aspect is selected and is alight;

*   A signal is OFF if any other aspect is selected and is alight.

In the event of a failure of both of the relevant filaments in the signal, the signalman will observe that the signal is not ON or OFF and that urgent maintenance action is needed. As noted in the description of the logic for each bulb, this fault condition has the collateral requirement that the preceding signal must be held at RED whenever the offending aspect is selected in its successor along the route in question.

Dealing with the setting of points is a more complicated matter, since the mechanical mechanisms introduce time delays and sequential behaviour into the system. Whereas a signal may be assumed to switch from one aspect to another in a very short time, it may take some 5 to 10 seconds to change the state of points. The sequence of operations for the individual points machine is UNLOCK, THROW, RE-LOCK. The locks concerned are mechanical "dogs" which make sure that the points blades cannot move under a train. These mechanical locks have an exceptionally high integrity. Obviously there are electrical contacts which "prove" that the moving blade is in contact with the correct running rail and that the corresponding mechanical lock is engaged.

The nomenclature used for the setting of points is that "NORMAL" describes one setting and "REVERSE" the other. In any installation the application of these terms is arbitrary but there is a preference for using NORMAL to apply to the "main line" and REVERSE to denote a path to a "branch line", probably requiring some reduction in speed at the junction. Allowing for the finite time for points to move from NORMAL to REVERSE or vice versa, this paper uses the following elementary notation to describe the state of points:

*   0 - Points NORMAL and locked;

*   1 - Points moving from NORMAL to REVERSE;

*   2 - Points moving from REVERSE to NORMAL;

*   3 - Points REVERSE and locked.

It might be thought that the only sequence of states which occur in practice are (0 -> 1 -> 3) and (3 -> 2 -> 0). In practice, transitions from (2 -> 3) or (3 -> 2) are possible, if the selection of position is changed whilst the points are unlocked and moving. It will be clear that points must be in either state 0 or state 3 before signals can be cleared to permit movement over the path in question. In addition, if a train is approaching the points and the protecting signals are OFF, there must be interlocking to make sure that no movement is initiated. In many systems, such locking is provided by track circuits on the approach side of the points in question, but on lightly worked lines such locking may be controlled from an approaching locomotive.

4. THE LANGUAGE HOL

If specifications for railway signalling systems are to be written in an unambiguous manner, a mathematical discipline is needed which covers all the aspects of behaviour described above, including the sequential nature of the setting of routes due to the movement of points. After many years of research, the Computer Laboratory, University of Cambridge, has devised a very powerful system for specifying, designing and verifying the design of digital systems. The method is described in the literature [3] and is supported by a very good set of computer tools, produced by a team led by Dr. M. Gordon. It was this "HOL" system which was central to the original development in the UK of the 32-bit VIPER microprocessor, intended for use in safety-critical systems.

The language HOL and much of the power of its tools is derived from the concept that all digital systems rely on n - bit numbers, as stored and manipulated in computers. The names of the associated "types" are:

word1   The set of all 1-bit computer words (#0, #1)

word2   The set of all 2-bit computer words (#00, #01, #10, #11)

.....

word8   The set of all 8-bit computer words (#00000000, #00000001,..)

In addition the language recognises the existence of the natural numbers;

num   The set {0,1,2,3.......}

and the obvious definition of the Boolean type;

bool   The set {F, T}

To make up the types of more complicated entities, the basic types listed above may be bound together, as in (word2#bool), which defines a type with two fields. When it is necessary to examine the individual components of the composite object, two operators are supplied in the HOL system to pick out the first and second elements, as shown later. Also, "lists" may be formed which are like arrays of data in a programming language.

The HOL system comes with a well-established library of functions for manipulating the various types listed above. Written out for a word-width of two bits, some of these library functions perform the following transformations:

    VAL2 :word2 -> num   WORD2 :num -> word2

    NOT2 :word2 -> word2   BITS2 :word2 -> bool list

Similar definitions apply for all the other word-widths used in the problem in question.

To write a specification in HOL, the user defines functions which express the underlying safety rules and then proceeds to create the description of the system to be designed. At all stages, the interactive HOL tools keep track of the evolving specification to make sure that no function conflicts with previous definitions. This is a powerful method for preventing a number of the types of errors which tend to creep in at this first stage of engineering design.

Once a consistent specification exists, other designers can set to work to decide how best to implement the signalling (or other digital control system). Often the route from the top level specification in HOL to detailed hardware and software designs is too long to be attempted in one design step. In such cases, HOL may be used in several layers of documentation, each giving greater visibility of the ultimate design.

5. SAFETY RULES IN HOL

The HOL type used for the state of track circuits will be defined as 'word1', in the sense that #1 represents "circuit clear" and #0 represents "circuit blocked". The mapping between this elementary type and 'bool' is:

    BIT :word1 -> bool (w) = (VAL1 w = 1)

Hence the pair of definitions of a track circuit, t, being clear or blocked;

    CLEAR t = BIT t

    BLOCKED t = NOT(BIT t)

The state of signals is expressed in this paper using the compound type (word2#word4), where the 'word2' element indicates which aspect of the signal should be alight and the 'word4' element is a map of filaments which are sound and can draw current. A binary '1' in the word4 map indicates that either the main or auxiliary filament can be "proved" to draw current. For a signal with current state s;

    ASPECT :(word2#word4) -> word2 (s) = FST s   {First field}

    FILAMENTS :(word2#word4) -> word4 (s) = SND s   {Second field}

The aspect currently being requested by the Control Centre can be deduced from the state table given in Section 3 and the four definitions are;

GREEN s = VAL2(ASPECT s) = 0

TWO_YELLOW s = VAL2(ASPECT s) = 1

YELLOW s = VAL2(ASPECT s) = 2

RED s = VAL2(ASPECT s) = 3

In the Control Centre the "proof" that an aspect is displayed as required is deduced by sensing the state of the signal based on which bulb filaments are intact. As described above a bulb is capable of drawing current if the relevant bit in the four word map is TRUE.

BULB(n,s) = EL n (BITS4(FILAMENTS s))   {Index into map}

The coding adopted in this paper for the bulb index n is;

0   RED bulb

1   Lower YELLOW bulb

2   GREEN bulb

3   Upper YELLOW bulb

In other words, the bulbs are numbered from the bottom of the signal post upwards. Given the functions defined above, the requirement for the signal being ON or OFF, as displayed in the Control Centre, can be defined as:

ON s = (RED s) AND BULB(0,s)

OFF s =

((YELLOW s) AND (BULB(1,s))) OR

((TWO_YELLOW s) AND (BULB(1,s)) AND (BULB(3,s))) OR

((GREEN s) AND (BULB(2,s)))

From these definitions for ON and OFF, the overall condition for recognising a faulty signal (a double filament failure) in the control centre becomes;

SIGNAL_FAULT s = NOT((ON s) OR (OFF s))

The logic for automatic signals can be specified by creating the set of inputs which the signal receives and defining the resulting outputs. For lengths of track protected by four-aspect signals a reasonable statement of the functions required is:

FOUR_ASPECT(control, path_proved, ahead) =

```
(let green = #00 in        )
                           )
let two_yellow = #01 in    )
                           )  (local variables)
let yellow = #10 in        )
                           )
let red = #11 in           )

let ahead_faulty = SIGNAL_FAULT ahead in

(control => red |              {manual control}

((NOT path_proved) => red |   {auto control}

(ahead_faulty => red |        {error case}

((RED ahead) => yellow |

((YELLOW ahead) => two_yellow | green))))))
```

This more complicated function has three parameters:

> control Input from Control Centre to hold signal at RED

> path_proved Input showing that signal may be set to OFF

> ahead Input showing state of next signal

A similar function expressing the logic for three-aspect signals can be derived easily from the text above;

```
THREE_ASPECT(control, path_proved, ahead) =

(let green = #00 in

let yellow = #10 in

let red = #11 in

let ahead_faulty = SIGNAL_FAULT ahead in

(control => red |

((NOT path_proved) => red|

(ahead_faulty => red|

((RED ahead) => yellow | green)))))
```

Note that this function is valid for the situation when a three-aspect signal proceeds a four-aspect signal, since a TWO_YELLOW aspect at the latter will force a GREEN aspect at the former. The reverse situation, of a three-aspect signal following a four-aspect is catered for as well.

The state of points can be expressed using the type (word2#word1) which the first field expresses the position of the points using the table given in Section 3 and the second field expresses whether or not these points are "approach locked" at present. As with the projection operators for the type (word2#word4) used for signals, it is convenient for points to define:

POSITION :(word2#word1) -> word2 (p) = FST p

APPROACH :(word2#word1) -> word1 (p) = BIT(SND p)

Hence the two statements of the points being mechanically locked can be written:

NORMAL p = VAL2(POSITION p) = 0

REVERSE p = VAL2(POSITION p) = 3

These basic safety functions are used to "prove" that routes through the points and other trackwork are safe. The concept of proof depends on the logical AND of a number of sensor inputs. In HOL these sensor inputs may be thought of as applications of the functions CLEAR, BLOCKED, ON, OFF, NORMAL and REVERSE to "lists" of the states of track circuits, signals and points, respectively. The types involved for each component are:

Track circuits CLEAR or BLOCKED   :word1 list {1-D array}

Signals ON or OFF   :(word2#word4) list

Points NORMAL or REVERSE   :(word2#word1) list

The concept of proof can be defined recursively as;

PROOF = (PROOF SENSE [] = T) AND

(PROOF SENSE (CONS head tail) = ((SENSE head) AND (PROOF SENSE tail)))

This function is a multiple input AND, whose inputs are the list elements concerned, with the function SENSE applied to each. That is, the function SENSE is one of the set (CLEAR, BLOCKED, ON, OFF, NORMAL, REVERSE).

The commonly occurring verb in "Railway Signalling" to indicate that sensor inputs must be taken into account is "requires", as in "route S701 requires track circuits a,j,h and signal S702". To follow this nomenclature, it is sensible to define six individual functions, based on the global definition of proof given above;

REQ_CLEAR track_list   = PROOF CLEAR track_list

```
REQ_BLOCKED track_list      = PROOF BLOCKED track_list

REQ_ON signal_list          = PROOF ON signal_list

REQ_OFF signal_list         = PROOF OFF signal_list

REQ_NORM points_list        = PROOF NORMAL points_list

REQ_REV points_list         = PROOF REVERSE points_list
```

These six functions are used in the examples in Section 6.

In practice, many other rules have to be declared and checked by fully qualified signalling engineers, including those for junction signals, before any such set of functions can be regarded as sound enough for use in practical signalling projects. Suppose that this step has been taken and the bulk of the diagrams in the textbook "Railway Signalling" have been documented in HOL. Then it should be possible to take a given section of track and write the specification for the local signalling based on this underlying formulation of these "absolute" safety rules.

6. EXAMPLES OF SIGNALLING PROBLEMS

Taking a very simple example, the plain track shown in Figure 3 could have the automatic signalling requirements defined for the four signals as follows:

```
S504(c504,e,ahead) = FOUR_ASPECT(c504, REQ_CLEAR [e], ahead)

S503(c503,d,s504) = FOUR_ASPECT(c503, REQ_CLEAR [d], s504)

S502(c502,c,s503) = FOUR_ASPECT(c502, REQ_CLEAR [c], s503)

S501(c501,b,s502) = FOUR_ASPECT(c501, REQ_CLEAR [b] s502)
```

Each signal is represented by a separate HOL function, the first parameter being the selection of ON or OFF in the Control Centre (c501, c502, etc), the second parameter being the "path_clear function" and the third the designation of the following signal.

Figure 4 shows a crossover between two tracks, the routing depending on the setting of the pair of points P100. For running along the slow line, (points P100 NORMAL), signal S601 will be controlled by track circuits A, B, C and D. For running on the main line, Signal S602 will be controlled by track circuits E, F, G and H. The presence of the two "extra" track circuits (B and F) and extra insulating joints needs explanation. These extra track-circuiting sections are inserted so that the position of points P100 can be changed immediately after a train has passed, rather than being locked until C and/or G are clear.

If the points P100 are set to REVERSE, signal S601 will be controlled by track circuits A,B,F,G and H, plus track circuit E. The latter is included in the list to provide "flank protection" to the train moving from the slow to the main line, ie to guard against a second train overrunning signal S603. The required logic can be expressed in HOL as;

S601(c601,a,b,c,d,e,f,g,h,s602,s604,p100) =

(let slow_to_main = REQ_REV (p100) in

let slow = (REQ_CLEAR [a;b;c;d]) AND (REQ_NORM [p100]) in

let cross = (REQ_CLEAR [a;b;f;g;h;e]) AND (REQ_REV [p100]) in

(slow_to_main => THREE_ASPECT(c601,cross,s604) |

THREE_ASPECT(c601,slow,s602)))

The corresponding specification function for signal S603 becomes;

S602(c602,e,f,g,h,s604,p100) =

(let main = (REQ_CLEAR [e;f;g;h]) AND (REQ_NORM [p100]) in

THREE_ASPECT(c603,main,s604))

The final example concerns a double junction, with the "branch line" diverging to the left, Figure 5. Consider the specification function for signal S701. For this signal to be OFF with points P100 set to the branch, track circuits A,B and C must be clear and as a precaution so must D, to prove that a preceding train has cleared the junction. However, as a simultaneous movement of a train from the branch line to the main line must be possible, the use of track circuit D must be predicated on P101 being NORMAL. This is an example of conditional interlock. Therefore, the specification for signal S701 is:

S701(c701,a,b,c,d,e,p100,p101,ahead_up_main,ahead_branch) =

(let set_main = REQ_NORM [p100] in

let main = (REQ_CLEAR [a;b;d;e]) AND (REQ_NORM [p100]) in

let cond_d = (REQ_CLEAR [d]) AND (REQ_NORM [p101]) in

let branch = (REQ_CLEAR [a;b;c]) AND (REQ_REV [p100]) in

let branch_with_d = branch AND cond_d in

(set_main => THREE_ASPECT(c701, main, ahead_up_main) |

(cond_d => THREE_ASPECT(c701, branch_with_d, ahead_branch) |

THREE_ASPECT(c701, branch, ahead_branch)))

Equally interesting is the logic for signal S702, which permits movement from the branch to the DOWN main line. For this signal to be

OFF requires F,D,H and J to be clear to prove the path, G to be clear for flank protection and points P100 to be REVERSE to provide flank protection at the diamond crossing. Note that this latter form of flank protection removes the need for any locking with signal S701. Hence the specification for S702:

S702(c702,f,d,h,j,g,p100,p101,ahead_down_main) =

(let proved = (REQ_CLEAR [f;d;h;j;g]) AND (REQ_REV [p100;p101]) in

THREE_ASPECT(c702, proved, ahead_down_main))

7. IMPLEMENTATION IN SOFTWARE

It is a straightforward matter to provide an implementation of the above logic in a subset of a well-disciplined language, such as Pascal.

Starting with the type declarations;

TYPE word1 = 0..1;

TYPE word2 = 0..3;

TYPE word4 = 0..15;

TYPE signal = RECORD aspect :word2; proved :word4;

END;

TYPE points = RECORD position :word2; approach :word1;

END;

From these definitions the elementary functions needed to express the state of track circuits can be written down directly from the HOL specifications;

FUNCTION BIT (w :word1) :boolean;

BEGIN BIT := (w = 1) END;

FUNCTION CLEAR (w :word1) :boolean;

BEGIN CLEAR := BIT(w) END;

FUNCTION BLOCKED (w :word1) :boolean;

BEGIN BLOCKED := NOT(BIT(w)) END;

Turning to rules for signals, the functions can be implemented as follows:

```
FUNCTION GREEN (s :signal) :boolean;

BEGIN GREEN := (s.aspect = 0) END;

FUNCTION TWO_YELLOWS (s :signal) :boolean;

BEGIN TWO_YELLOWS := (s.aspect = 1) END;
```

....

and so on for the other aspects. The derivation of the rules for an aspect being proved to be alight follows from the definition:

```
FUNCTION BULB (n :word2; s :signal) :boolean;

BEGIN CASE n OF

    0: BULB := odd(s.proved);        1: BULB := odd(s.proved DIV 2);

    2: BULB := odd(s.proved DIV 4);  3: BULB := odd(s.proved DIV 8)

        END

END;
```

Therefore the functions for ON, OFF and SIGNAL_FAULT become:

```
FUNCTION ON (s :signal) :boolean;

BEGIN ON := RED(s) AND BULB(0,s) END;

FUNCTION OFF (s :signal) :boolean;

BEGIN OFF := (YELLOW(s) AND BULB(1,s)) OR

                (TWO_YELLOWS(s) AND BULB(1,s) AND BULB(3,s)) OR

            (GREEN(s) AND BULB(2,s))

END;

FUNCTION SIGNAL_FAULT (s :signal) :boolean;

BEGIN SIGNAL_FAULT := NOT (ON(s) OR OFF(s)) END;
```

By now the derivation of these functions in Pascal should be clear. To complete the derivation of the fundamental rules for multi-aspect signalling:

```
FUNCTION FOUR_ASPECT(control, path_proved :boolean; ahead :signal)
                                                        :word2;

VAR c_green, c_two_yellow, c_yellow, c_red :word2;
```

```
BEGIN c_green := 0; c_two_yellow := 1; c_yellow := 2; c_red:= 3;

     IF control THEN FOUR_ASPECT := c_red

     ELSE IF NOT path_proved THEN FOUR_ASPECT := c_red

     ELSE IF SIGNAL_FAULT(ahead) THEN FOUR_ASPECT := c_red

     ELSE IF RED(ahead) THEN FOUR_ASPECT := c_yellow

     ELSE IF YELLOW(ahead) THEN FOUR_ASPECT := c_two_yellow

     ELSE FOUR_ASPECT := c_green

END;

FUNCTION THREE_ASPECT(control,path_proved :boolean; ahead :signal)
                                                   :word2;

VAR c_green, c_yellow, c_red :word2;

BEGIN c_green := 0; c_yellow := 2; c_red := 3;

     IF control THEN THREE_ASPECT := c_red

     ELSE IF NOT path_proved THEN THREE_ASPECT := c_red

     ELSE IF SIGNAL_FAULT(ahead) THEN THREE_ASPECT := c_red

     ELSE IF RED(ahead) THEN THREE_ASPECT := c_yellow

     ELSE THREE_ASPECT := c_green

END;
```

Given this type of foundation, it is feasible to program the examples shown in Figures 3,4 and 5, to establish the logic for the interlocking for each.

CONCLUSIONS

Starting from the rules defined in the textbook "Railway Signalling", this paper attempts to describe a little of the safety logic, using the specification language HOL. As regards the implementation of a signalling system, it appears to be feasible to use a subset of Pascal.

Although the research is still in progress, sufficient knowledge has been gained to feel confident in the formulation of the basic safety rules. In collaboration with railway authorities and contractors, it is intended to adopt these methods in the development of practical systems.

26

ACKNOWLEDGEMENTS

HOL has been developed by Dr. Michael Gordon and his team in the Computer Laboratory in the University of Cambridge.
The adoption of these methods in collaboration with Teknis Systems, Adelaide, is being led in the UK by Charter Technologies Ltd. with support from Warwick University. The implementation of the system being based on the use of the VIPER microprocessor.

REFERENCES

1. Rolt, L.T.C., <u>Red for Danger</u>, Pan, 1982.

2. RTCA, Software Considerations in Airborne Systems and Equipment, DO-178A, March 1985.

3. Gordon, M., Specification and design of VSLI circuits, Calgary 1986.

4. Suffrin, B., Z Handbook, draft 1.1, Oxford University Programming Research Group.

5. Goguen, J.A., Meseguer, J., and Plaisted, D., "Programming with Parameterised Abstract Objects in OBJ", Theory & Practice of Software Technology, North Holland, 163-194.

6. Jones, C.B., <u>Systematic software development using VDM</u>, Prentice Hall, 1986.

7. Cullyer, W.J., Hardware Integrity, The Aeronautical Journal of the Royal Aeronautical Society, August/September 1985.

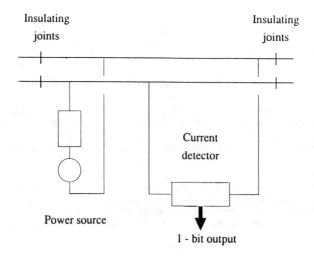

Figure 1 Track circuit

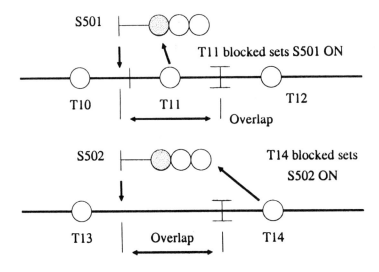

Figure 2 Protection of train

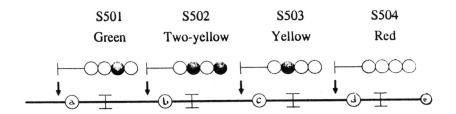

Figure 3 Four aspect automatic signals

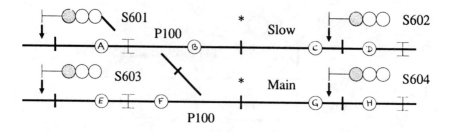

* Extra joints to allow P100 to be replaced quickly

Figure 4 Slow to Main line crossover

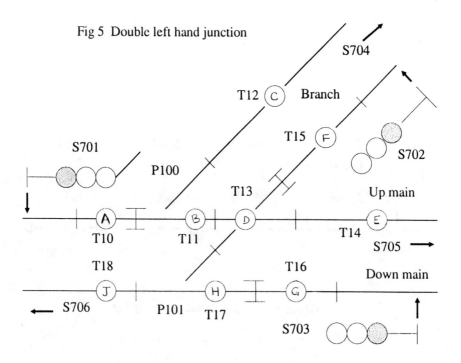

Fig 5 Double left hand junction

FAULT TOLERANCE FOR RAILWAY SIGNALLING – VOTRICS IN PRACTICE

GUNTER WIRTHUMER, HUBERT LUTNIK

Alcatel Austria – Elin Research Center
Ruthnergasse 1–7, A–1210 Vienna, Austria

Keywords: Fault Tolerance, Reliability, N–Modular Redundancy, Distributed Software Voting, Railway Signalling.

ABSTRACT

The increasing reliability requirements of computerized process control systems, such as railway signalling systems, have to be met by fault–tolerant architectures. The mechanisms for achieving fault tolerance have to be clearly separated from the normal functionality of the system and, in particular, from the safety measures included in the system. These requirements can be met by using a new architecture for fault tolerance.

The new architectural features of VOTRICS (Voting Triple–modular Computing System) include arbitrary application scheduling (not periodic), flexible configuration to different degrees of redundancy in the application's network, fault tolerance mechanisms – in particular recovery – transparent to the application, and independence of the underlying hardware.

These benefits are obtained by applying a clear hierarchical concept to the fault–tolerant system structure and functions at the application's message handling level, such that different properties can independently be configured to the application's actual needs.

This layered structure is discussed in the paper. The fault tolerance mechanisms are implemented in software, and also executed in redundancy, such that no single point of failure may affect the system's reliability.

The generic interfaces to the application's message handling system allow for flexible configurations of the application's network structure.

Experiences from the integration with a railway signalling application are presented.

INTRODUCTION

In a wide field of application areas, such as railway control or telecommunication, already today many process control systems consist of a network of processing nodes, which contain computers of varying complexity and inportance for the system. This trend to distributed processing will continue also in future developments of such systems, leading to larger structures of system controllers, subsystem and peripheral controllers.

Depending on the influence of the reliability of the individual processing node on the availability of the network, i.e. of the complete system, these nodes may be classified according to their actual importance for the total reliability.

In order to improve the overall availability of the system, some measures for tolerating hardware faults have to be taken. These fault tolerance measures should be tailored to the user requirements on the availability, ranging from a minimal redundancy concept, e.g. with only vital components being duplicated (e.g. central process controllers), up to highly reliable systems, where more redundancy is employed in the network.

These requirements are met by a new "modular" fault tolerance architecture and system developed at the Alcatel Austria – Elin Research Center. Its name VOTRICS derives from "**V**oting **T**riple–**M**odular **C**omputing **S**ystem", as it was named in the initial design stages as a threefold redundant system [1].

In the meantime, our system has been developed further and implemented to cover different degrees of redundancy for improving the reliability and availability of various process control systems [2]. Its mechanisms are realized in software, they do not need any special hardware developments for their execution.

The architecture supplies two– or threefold redundancy to selected nodes of the control network, leading to flexible strategies for employing hardware fault tolerance precisely in those nodes where it is required.

Presently, our architecture has been integrated and tested within its first application, the electronic interlocking system "ELEKTRA" [3], [4] of Alcatel Austria. Further use for projects in the fields of process control and of telecommunication are under discussion.

The mechanisms to manage and synchronize the various degrees of redundancy in such a control network, as well as the fault tolerance mechanisms, are transparent to the application's software and network structure, and they are independent of the application as well as of the hardware and the operating system on which the application and the fault tolerance mechanisms are executed. They thus allow enhancement of existing computer equipment with fault tolerance mechanisms in a way transparent to the application software.

First, some basic issues concerning hardware fault tolerance and n–modular redundancy are considered. In the next chapter the central ideas and principles of our architecture are discussed. An overview on the functions of the fault tolerance mechanisms in normal operation and in case of fault is given. Then the fundamental structures of our architecture are presented, and how the fault tolerance mechanisms are realized. Some experiences from the integration of VOTRICS with its first application, the electronic interlocking system ELEKTRA, conclude the chapter. A summary constitutes the final chapter.

BASIC CONSIDERATIONS

For the following a clear distinction of the concepts *fault* and *failure* is important. However, the consideration and effect of a defective part of a system as fault or failure depends upon the observer's point of view. To achieve a clear definition, we adopt the hierarchical system view presented in [5], [6].

Fault tolerance then is the ability of a system to continue its operation as specified, i.e. it does not fail, even in the presence of faults in the system. Obviously, with this definition, the occurrence of system failure depends on the specification of the expected service. This point should be kept in mind when analyzing the system reliability and when classifying the relative importance of individual components for the overall system reliability (see below).

Tolerate Hardware Faults

There exists a wide variety of faults, which are liable to lead to system failure.

One large class are the systematic or design faults, such as software faults, configuration faults, or systematic hardware faults, which are due to "human errors" during the design, production or maintenance of the system, i.e. a failure of a human as part of the system's lifecycle. For the detection of faults of this class, with the aim of tolerating them or of guaranteeing the system's safety by entering a safe state, there exist a variety of different approaches and measures, which are beyond the scope of this presentation.

Our system concentrates on the tolerance of the other large class of faults, namely the random hardware faults or physical faults due e.g. to aging effects of the computer's components or to external interference. These faults may affect the behaviour of the computer under consideration in an arbitrary way, i.e. it does not only simply stop operation ("crashed computer"), but it may even produce wrong results and behave in a way which is often called "malicious".

Active Redundancy

In order to achieve fault tolerance some form of redundancy is necessary. *Redundancy* is defined as the provision of more resources than absolutely necessary to provide a specified service.

Apart from the variety of measures on component level for detecting and tolerating faults, such as cyclic redundancy checks or error correcting codes, frequently n–modular redundancy is used for the tolerance of random hardware faults.

N–modular redundancy is the provision of n identical resources. In the following, we consider this form of redundancy on the level of central and peripheral processing nodes in the control network. The software executing on these computers and controlling the process is designated as *application*.

In many systems, the redundant computer operates in standby mode (*cold* or *warm redundancy*), waiting to start operation in case of failure of the active computer. Faults in the active computer are detected by some self–checking means, such as memory tests or watchdog timers.

However, there always exists the possibility that a yet undetected fault in the active computer leads to its failure in a way which seriously affects the controlled system, e.g. by wrongly issuing a critical command. Further, if a fault is detected in time and control of the system is switched over to the standby, it takes some time for the standby to enter a fully functional state, e.g. it has to boot. During this time provision of service is interrupted, and data may be lost.

A way to reduce this time needed for switch–over is to update the standby's data from the active computer. However, this introduces the problem that a yet undetected fault in the active computer may lead to the corruption of both the active and the standby computer's databases, thus again requiring a complete reboot of the system.

So the more efficient way of using the redundant computers is to operate them in parallel (*hot* or *active redundancy*), thus achieving better fault detection and tolerance.

In addition to the usual and well–proven techniques applicable also in standby systems, the outputs of the actively redundant computers are continuously compared. Therefore, any fault leading to wrong outputs is detected. If the actively redundant computers are coupled loosely, there exists also the opportunity to prevent a fault in one computer from corrupting data in the other computers.

Further, with active redundancy there is no need to switch over to a standby system in case of failure of the active computer, since all two or more redundant computers have equal and complete knowledge of the actual process state. This enables the system to continue operation without any interruption of service.

The architecture presented here provides fault tolerance to selected nodes of process control networks by operating them in *two– or threefold active redundancy*. Consider one control node, which is important for the availability of the complete system. This node, again considered as a system, is supplied with active redundancy, i.e. it consists of two or three identical computers operating in parallel.

If one of these redundant components of the node becomes faulty and possibly fails, the node contains a fault. However, owing to the redundant components, the node can continue to provide its service, thus tolerating the fault.

Mixed Redundancy

For the design of our fault tolerance architecture, the continually increasing requirements on present and future process control developments have been taken into account.

These control systems should have the possibility to control a high number of peripheral elements, they should provide an ever higher functionality and number of different services. In addition, they should offer the possibility to interconnect process control systems to form larger networks, and they should also be able to connect to other equipment, such as high level control or network management on external computers, or to existing peripheral equipment for reuse of previous developments.

Fulfilling all these requirements leads to ever more complex control structures. The way to master this complexity is to decentralize control wherever possible. This leads to distributed, and possibly hierarchical, networks of control processors.

An additional requirement, which arises naturally with the increasing size and complexity of the control network, is to increase the availability and reliability of the system. Some measures for tolerating hardware faults have to provided in the system.

The obvious way to achieve this goal is to employ redundancy (apart from quality assurance, which is assumed to be a natural thing). Redundancy implies the provision of additional resources. With our system, the control computers are replicated and operated in parallel, i.e. in active redundancy.

This provision of additional hardware in a process control system immediately leads to an economic trade—off:

* The indirect cost of products with low reliability and/or availability (reduced market possibilities) has to be weighed against the immediate cost of supplying the process control system with redundant hardware in order to increase its reliability.

The goal is therefore twofold:

* Minimize the cost of faults (leading to system failures), and

* minimize the cost of redundancy.

In order to achieve this goal, the importance of each node of the control network has to be evaluated with respect to its influence on the overall availability and reliability of the system. As a rough guide—line, the following classification of nodes can be given:

* *Vital nodes* must not fail in case of a fault, or at least they should continue operation with a very high probability. In addition, they might contain sensitive data which must not be corrupted or lost. Therefore these nodes should be provided with threefold redundancy, or at least with twofold redundancy with the addition of proficient self—diagnosis mechanisms.

* *Non—vital nodes* are allowed to fail in case of a fault, although this may be a nuisance (e.g. only a small part of the periphery or services of minor importance are affected). The provision of redundancy to these nodes cannot be justified economically.

* *Semi—vital nodes* are of an intermediate importance. They should continue operation in case of a fault with a good probability, however an occasional failure does not lead to total system failure. These nodes should be supplied with twofold redundancy, or provision of redundancy can be optional.

After this evaluation the individual control nodes are supplied with the appropriate redundancy, for an example see fig. 1. This will result in control networks of *mixed redundancy*, where nodes with various degrees of redundancy (ranging from one to three) are interconnected in some way.

The example in fig. 1 shows a possible structure of two interconnected process control systems, one large and one small. The large system contains intermediate levels of control.

The (vital) system controller of the large control network is supplied with threefold redundancy, whereas the subsystem controllers and the system controller of the smaller system are supplied with only twofold redundancy. The peripheral controllers are considered non—vital in this example.

The redundant components interact only via separate I/O–processors, which perform all communication between the nodes as well as the mechanisms for achieving fault tolerance.

An essential point of the architecture presented here is the independence of the mechanisms ensuring the management and synchronization of redundant computers for achieving fault tolerance from the process control software and from the network structure.

It is not necessary to decide in advance the redundancy of the individual control nodes, or to include corresponding mechanisms in the process control software. On the contrary, it is possible to upgrade, if it should turn out necessary, the redundancy of individual nodes after completion of the application software.

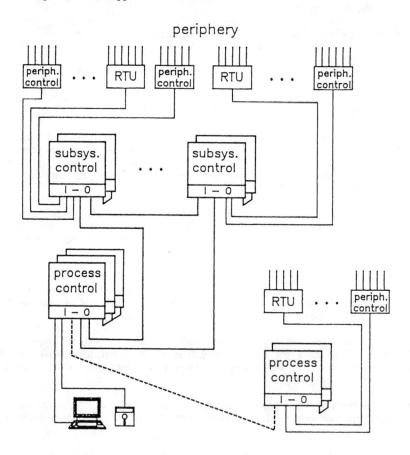

RTU: Remote Terminal Unit

Figure 1. Example of a process control network with computers of different degrees of redundancy. The fault tolerance mechanisms are executed at the I/O–interfaces.

GENERIC FAULT TOLERANCE MECHANISMS

Goals

VOTRICS is a fault tolerant system architecture intended to provide various control systems with high availability and reliability. The goal is to provide the application with various services and mechanisms for:

*   The management of nodes with different degrees of availability requirements, resulting in different degrees of redundancy. This redundancy ranges from non-redundant over twofold to threefold active redundancy.

*   Supporting the communication between application nodes in distributed control system with high connectivity in a highly reliable way.

*   Supervision of the correct operation of the individual units in redundant nodes. This is achieved through the comparison of redundant messages. Detected HW faults can then be tolerated and masked.

*   On-line maintenance and recovery. A defective computer can be serviced while the other continues normal operation. After maintenance the serviced computer is reintegrated into full operation without disturbance of normal system services.

Further requirements are:

*   The structure and operation of our system are such that the application software and the fault tolerance mechanisms are independent of each other.

*   Our architecture shall support application software which is driven by incoming messages communicating events, i.e. it need not be cyclic.

*   For the execution of the application software as well as of the fault tolerance mechanisms off-the-shelf process control computers may be chosen.

*   The application units and the VOTRICS computers may communicate among each other with different means and protocols.

*   The generic fault tolerance mechanisms are dynamically configurable at system boot time and during operation after system extensions.

Assumptions on Application Behaviour

In order to realize the above goals, our system operates on the message streams exchanged by the application in the various processing nodes. For operation in active redundancy, and for providing the possibility of recovery by VOTRICS, the application software has to satisfy some assumptions on its behaviour.

These considerations may apply individually to each of a set of jobs in the application computer, if the jobs are strictly separated (e.g. different users), i.e. they do not interact with each other.

The application operating on a message stream has to be "*deterministic*" in the following sense: If redundant application computers, which do not contain a fault, are provided with identical input streams, the outgoing message streams from the redundant application computers have to be equal.

This means that the logical behaviour of the application software must not (randomly) depend on timing variations or on the local scheduling by the operating system. Timeouts for the application software must not be derived from local clocks, they are inserted synchronously into the normal message stream by our system.

The one input stream may be separated into several logical input streams, each one corresponding to one of the independent jobs in the application unit.

A different view to describe these assumptions is the concept of a "*task set*":

An input message may only be received after all internal activities of the job have ceased. This input message will then start a new task (set of processing steps), which, by internal communication, may start further tasks in the job. As long as internal messages or activities are pending to be performed, no further input messages may be processed by this job. This sequence of tasks which are triggered by one input message, and then only by further internal activities, is called a "task set". The task set is completed when all internal activities again have ceased. Only then the next input message may be received, triggering the next task set.

From the view of our fault tolerance mechanisms, a task set is considered as an atomic action. It is similar to the concept of a transaction used in other fault–tolerant systems, such as Mars [7].

Principles

The goals are realized through the use of N–modular active redundancy. The degree of redundancy can be chosen for each application node according to the actual system requirements:

* VOTRICS nodes may execute in 2– or 3–fold redundancy.

* Application computers may execute in 1–, 2– or 3–fold redundancy.

The redundant application computers do not have direct interconnections. They communicate via our system with other application nodes, peripheral processors, etc. The redundant computers of a VOTRICS node are coupled loosely to each other, i.e. there is no microsynchronization, thus reducing the probability of common mode failures through external interferences.

The fault tolerance mechanisms operate on a message handling level below the application software, and transparently to the application software. The synchronization of the software in redundant application units is performed through the synchronization of redundant message streams. In normal operation, all actions are performed on messages exchanged in the applications control system.

Distributed software voting algorithms operate on these synchronized redundant message streams. To this end messages, which are redundant to each other, are collected and compared.

A message stream may enter our system with a degree of redundancy different from the degree of redundancy with which it should be sent to the destination. Our system transforms these degrees of redundancy as required.

These actions are transparent to the application software, i.e. it need not know the actual redundancy of individual application computers. This opens the possibility to upgrade, according to actual or future requirements, individual control nodes from no redundancy to 2–fold redundancy to 3–fold redundancy without impacts on the application software.

The central principles can be summarized as follows:

*   *n–modular redundancy*, with n ranging from one to three. If n is greater than one, the two or three replicated components operate in parallel, i.e. in active redundancy.

*   The decision which input or output message is the correct one is also performed in active redundancy by *distributed software voting*.

*   The replicated components of one node are *coupled loosely*.

*   All mechanisms for managing and synchronizing redundant components and for achieving fault tolerance are performed on a message handling level below the process control software, in a way *transparent to the application* and *independent of the application*.

*   The application software may execute on existing *off–the–shelf computers*, using standard or proprietary operating systems.

*   The fault tolerance mechanisms are of a *generic nature*, i.e. they are independent of the application and can be parameterized to conform to the actual needs of the application.

*   Maintenance of a faulty replicated computer can be done during undisturbed operation of the other computers. The serviced component is automatically reintegrated in the system in a way transparent to the application (*on–line maintenance and recovery*).

*   The individual nodes of the network may be interconnected by a network containing different communication means and protocols.

*   Nodes of different degrees of redundancy may be connected to each other.

Regular Operation

A number of different processing nodes and computers (1–, 2– or 3–fold redundant) are connected among each other via nodes (2– or 3–fold redundant) executing our fault tolerance mechanisms, resulting in a so–called VOTRICS network (see also fig. 1).

Any two application units may communicate with messages (of different redundancies) along routes. From the application's view, a route is a direct connection from sender to destination.

The routes are defined paths through the VOTRICS network. Our system handles the communication to the destination, the redundancies of the messages and the fault tolerance mechanisms. The properties of the routes, which our system has to know, are configurable at system boot time, and may be expanded later after system upgrades.

The correlation of a message to a route is derived from the message header. The structure of the message header, and how to interpret it within VOTRICS, constitutes one of the interfaces from our system to the application (see below). From this header then not only the destination of the message is derived, but also information relevant for the message's treatment within the fault tolerance mechanisms, such as expected redundancy or applicable voting mode, which may be 2 out of 3, 2 out of 2, or 1 out of 2 with some variations.

The correct operation of redundant computers is continually supervised, concurrently to the normal operation. If a HW fault occurs in one of the redundant application units, this fault can be detected by comparison of redundant messages, or through the detection of a lacking message.

Exceptional Operation

After a fault has been detected through the comparison of redundant messages, the fault location can, in the case of twofold redundancy, be diagnosed with the help of self checks, time–outs, diagnosis routines, decision algorithms. In the threefold redundant case, fault detection, masking and localization are easily achieved by the 2 out of 3 voting scheme.

If one of the redundant application units is faulty, this fault is masked from the rest of the system. The system continues operation without intermediate loss of service. A "switch over" to a stand–by unit is not necessary, because the redundant units have operated in active redundancy.

The results of the fault diagnosis are reported to an operations and maintenance entity in one of the application computers, which then may issue a maintenance request to the operating personnel.

After maintenance of a faulty computer, it has to be reintegrated into normal operation, i.e. it has to be resynchronized with the other one, which has continued operation in the meantime.

This process of recovery can be performed with different methods, the goal being to allow the application to continue providing its service. Recovery of application history is another interface between the application and our system. Control and execution of recovery is performed by the fault tolerance mechanism at the message handling level, together with a local extension of our system to the application computer. For this local extension, the definition of the application's history to be recovered, and access methods to this history, have to be defined.

REALIZATION

These functions, together with the required independence of the application software and the fault tolerance mechanisms, are achieved by placing all synchronization and fault tolerance mechanisms at a message handling layer below the application software proper, i.e. at the I/O–interfaces connecting the nodes among each other.

The fault tolerance mechanisms are realized in software. They are executed on separate I/O–processors, thus relieving the application's processors from a large part of the message handling load. Only the fault tolerance mechanisms on these I/O–processors are aware of the fact that there exist redundant components in some nodes. The application software may execute in the same way as in systems without any redundancy.

Initially, VOTRICS (Voting Triple–Modular Computing System) has been intended to realize threefold redundancy in a way transparent to the application [1], [8]. It has been developed further such that it can now be applied also for twofold active redundancy, leading to systems of mixed redundancy [2].

Physical Structure

An example of the physical structure of a twofold redundant node with fault tolerance mechanisms, and some of its possible connections to other nodes, is shown in fig. 2. The entity to be replicated is an application computer with an independent processor for I/O–handling. The fact of redundancy in the present node, as well as the redundancy of the other nodes, is visible only to the I/O–processors, which connect, manage and synchronize the redundant components.

Fig. 2 shows that nodes with different degrees of redundancy, either with or without fault tolerance mechanisms, may be interconnected freely. Redundant components of a node interact only via the fault tolerance mechanisms executing on the I/O–processors, in a way transparent to the application.

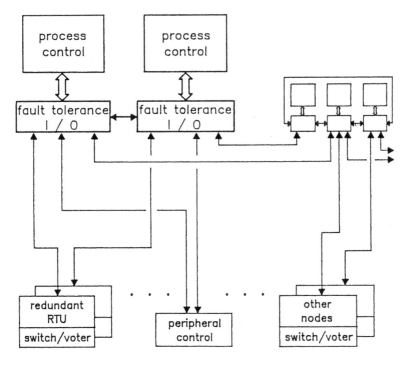

RTU: Remote Terminal Unit

Figure 2. Nodes with different degrees of redundancy, either with or without fault tolerance mechanism, may be interconnected freely.

The outputs to the periphery from redundant nodes without fault tolerance mechanisms may either be voted by some other mechanisms (e.g. in hardware), or they may be switched from one component to the hot standby without loss of service at switch over.

Fig. 2 also shows several options for supplying redundancy to each of the nodes in the network. The main variations are as follows:

* Nodes may be established with two- or threefold redundancy, which is managed and synchronized by supplying also the corresponding fault tolerance mechanisms to the node.

* Nodes without redundancy, or also with two or threefold redundancy, may be operated without fault tolerance mechanisms in the I/O-layer of this node. If such a node A is supplied with redundancy, it has to be attached to a VOTRICS node B with fault tolerance mechanisms, which then manage also the redundancy of node A.

* The redundancy of the interconnection of two nodes may differ from the redundancies of the nodes. In particular, a non-redundant node may be attached to a redundant VOTRICS node by redundant links. This serves to decouple the availability of the non-redundant node from possible faults in the I/O-processors executing the fault tolerance mechanisms in the redundant node.

When deciding on the redundancy to be supplied to each node, the persistent trade-off between hardware cost and reliability has again to be considered:

* Maximum reliability of a control node can be obtained by two out of three voting, i.e. with a threefold redundant VOTRICS node. In addition, threefold redundancy allows for an easy and reliable fault diagnosis, helping in maintenance.

* Still high reliability can be achieved with twofold redundant systems, which operate completely in parallel. For the purpose of fault diagnosis the redundancy management mechanisms should be supplemented by effective self-diagnosis mechanisms in the application computers. In the ideal case they would be self-checking or fail-stop components.

* Good availability is reached with twofold redundant nodes without fault tolerance mechanisms. The two replicated components still operate in hot redundancy, and their outputs may be selected by a switch. If the "on-line" computer becomes faulty (may be detected by the fault tolerance mechanisms of a VOTRICS node to which the present one is attached), switch-over to the hot standby may be performed without any loss of data or service.

Logical Structure

The redundancy management, synchronization and fault tolerance mechanisms executing on the I/O-processors act in the same way on all messages entering or leaving a node equipped with these mechanisms. From a logical point of view, all messages enter the fault tolerance layer below the application software via different IMH's (Incoming Message Handler), which administer the links leading to other nodes, as well as the data paths to and from the application computers of the present node, cf. fig. 3.

Since a network global time is not a requirement for the operation of the fault tolerance mechanisms (in contrast to other fault tolerance concepts, [7], [9]), messages from different nodes may arrive within the VOTRICS layer at the same time, and the arrival times of redundant messages from different nodes may be overlapping and interleaved. Therefore the IMH's on the two, respectively three, redundant I/O–processors operate independently of each other and asynchronously.

In order to arrive at a synchronized operation of the redundant application computers, our architecture is structured into sub–layers. The consistency & synchronization layer on top of the IMH's serves to synchronize the redundant components and to establish a global view on all messages which have entered the fault tolerance mechanisms. A protocol similar to the one in [10] has been developed in order to achieve a consistent view on all messages also in case of fault [11].

This global and consistent view on all messages provides the basis for achieving fault tolerance. All further processing is done in a synchronous way in the two respectively three redundant components of the node, such that the remaining fault tolerance mechanisms can be considered as executing on a single logical machine.

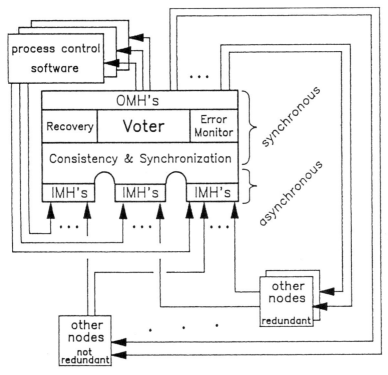

IMH : Incoming Message Handler
OMH : Outgoing Message Handler

Figure 3. Internal logical structure of the fault tolerance mechanisms for the threefold redundant case.

The voter collects and compares redundant messages, and determines which message should be forwarded as the correct one. It performs its task according to the redundancy, which has been configured for the actual message to be treated.

This configuration of different voting schemes for various classes of messages and redundancies (2 out of 3, 2 out of 2, 1 out of 2, and variations of these) leads to high flexibility in various types of networks of mixed redundancy, such that the applications requirements can be fulfilled as closely as possible.

The functionality of the system is continually supervised by an error monitor, which diagnoses faulty components and informs the application, thus supporting maintenance of the system.

After a faulty component has been serviced, it is reintegrated into the system by the recovery task. The recovery actions are performed concurrent to normal operation of the system. In applications with indeterministic load distribution, phases of low load are used for recovery, such that the continuous provision of service is not disturbed.

The decision where to route messages, and on the redundancy with which the messages have to be sent, is performed by the OMH's (Outgoing Message Handler), which also have some knowledge on the network topology visible to this node.

An essential advantage of this structured approach is the large independence of the fault tolerance mechanisms from the actual degree of redundancy of the messages to be acted on, and of the redundancy of the VOTRICS node itself.

Comparing fig. 4 to fig. 3 shows that the logical structure of our architecture in a twofold redundant node is the same as for threefold redundancy. The only difference lies in a different number of input and output message handling interfaces, which actually see the redundancy of nodes and of the links leading to these nodes.

Interfaces to Application

The fault tolerance mechanisms of our architecture are of a generic nature, they are independent of and transparent to the application software controlling the process.

However, some interface definitions obviously are indispensable for the operation of our system and for some actions in case of fault. These interfaces are:

* Definition of the application's message format. In particular, our system needs to know the contents of the message header, in order to derive from it the information necessary for the operation of the fault tolerance mechanisms on the message.

* Information on the application's network structure and topology, and on the fault tolerance mechanisms to be executed on the messages exchanged in the network. This information is loaded down to our system at boot time, thus parametrizing the actual operations of the fault tolerance mechanisms.

* These configuration parameters contain also the information, how to inform the application's maintenance entity on the results of fault diagnosis done by our system. The format and content of this information has to be defined between our system and the application.

* Definition of the application's history to be recovered after service of a faulty computer, and of the access methods to this history. With the help of these definitions, the local VOTRICS extension on the application computer can perform recovery in a way transparent to the application.

Apart from the interface to the maintenance entity for reporting diagnosis results, these interfaces do not have any impact on the application software at runtime. Also the diagnosis and maintenance interface influences only this single entity, it is independent of the main part of the application software controlling the process.

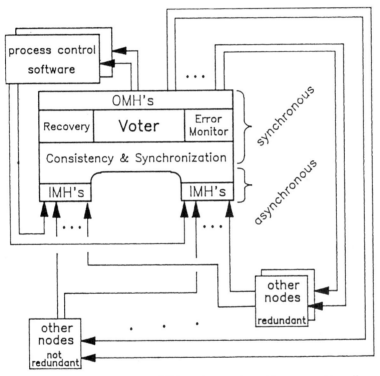

IMH : Incoming Message Handler
OMH : Outgoing Message Handler

Figure 4. Internal logical structure of the fault tolerance mechanisms for the twofold redundant case. It is identical to threefold redundancy.

Integration with Railway Interlocking

The first application of our architecture is in the safety critical field of railway interlocking. VOTRICS is used to supply the required reliability to the electronic interlocking system ELEKTRA, developed at Alcatel Austria [4].

The architecture of this interlocking system strictly separates the mechanisms controlling the railway station, from the mechanisms ensuring safety, and from the mechanisms supplying reliability [3]. It consists of two diverse software channels in the system control, each executing on independent computers. One of the channels performs the operational control of the railway station, the other, diverse channel executes an expert system continuously checking the safety aspects of the process.

These two central processing nodes, in particular the integrity of their databases, are of vital importance for the operation of the system. Therefore they are realized as threefold redundant nodes operated with our architecture for achieving fault tolerance. For the control of peripheral equipment, such as sensors, actuators and human interfaces, high availability is achieved through twofold redundancy, thus realizing a network of mixed redundancy.

During the development phase, there have been occasional meetings for the definition of the interfaces listed above. Apart from these meetings, the two systems, ELEKTRA and VOTRICS, have been developed independently, by different companies at different locations. For the ease of testing the functionality, the ELEKTRA system was first realized and validated as a non−redundant system, and also our system was tested on its own.

Only in the final integration step, the planned redundancy, together with the fault tolerance mechanisms, were installed in the processing nodes of the ELEKTRA system. The only impacts on the application software concerned the operations and maintenance process, which supplies our system with its configuration parameters at boot time, and which receives the diagnostic informations sent by our system.

There have been two issues, which could only be tested in this last integration step. The one point was the final check on the correctness of the configuration parameters to be supplied to the fault tolerance mechanisms. The other issue was the fine tuning of some internal parameters of our system to the actual load profile of the ELEKTRA system, in order to achieve optimum performance.

Apart from these two points, this integration test was a clear demonstration that the strict independence of control software and fault tolerance mechanisms are feasible and can be realized. This separation even led to savings in the development costs, since smaller systems, each with less complexity, have been developed and tested independently.

SUMMARY

The fault tolerance architecture presented here allows for a flexible provision of reliability and availability to process control networks for a wide range of applications in traffic control, telecommunication, industrial automation, etc.

The following selection of features summarizes the main advantages of applying this technology in future process control developments:

* Management of different degrees of redundancy according to the actual reliability requirements.

* Transparency to the application allows for the decoupling of control software and fault tolerance mechanisms. In addition, the degree of redundancy to be supplied to a particular node is irrelevant to the application software.

* An additional advantage of our system is the possibility to expanded two–fold redundant application units to three–fold redundancy without any effort for adapting the application software.

* Independence from the hardware, on which the application and the fault tolerance mechanisms are executing, allows the use of standard computers.

* Due to the open architecture, the generic fault tolerance mechanisms can be supplemented with different message handling interfaces, allowing for a flexible extension of this architecture in order to communicate via different control networks.

* On–line maintenance of faulty components, and automatic and transparent reintegration leads to high system availability and reliability without disruption of service.

Our system has been integrated in its first application, the electronic railway interlocking system ELETKRA, containing two threefold redundant VOTRICS nodes. Process control and telecommunication projects using two– and/or threefold redundant VOTRICS nodes are under discussion.

The integration phase of VOTRICS with ELEKTRA, which has been performed at the very latest stage before putting the interlocking system ELEKTRA into operation in the field, has demonstrated the feasibility and advantages of the approach to strictly separate the fault tolerance mechanisms from the operational and safety functions of the control system.

REFERENCES

1. Theuretzbacher, N.: "VOTRICS: Voting Triple–Modular Computing System", Proc. FTCS–16, Vienna, Austria, July 1986, pp.144–150.

2. Wirthumer, G.: "A Fault–Tolerant Control Concept for PABX's", Alcatel N.V. Technology Review, Stuttgart, FRG, Nov. 1987.

3. Theuretzbacher, N.: "ELEKTRA: A System Architecture that Applies New Principles to Electronic Interlocking", Proc. IFAC Conf. on Control in Transportation Systems, Vienna, Austria, July 1986.

4. Erb, A.: "Safety Measures of the Electronic Interlocking System ELEKTRA", Proc. SAFECOMP'89, Vienna, Austria, Dec. 1989, to be published.

5. Avizienis, A., Laprie, J.C.: "Dependable Computing: From Concepts to Design Diversity", Proc. IEEE, vol.74, nr.5, May 1986, pp.629–638.

6. Laprie, J.C.: "Dependable Computing and Fault Tolerance: Concepts and Terminology", Proc. FTCS–15, Ann Arbor, MI, USA, June 1985, pp.2–11.

7. Kopetz, A.H., Merker, W.: "The Architecture of MARS", Proc. FTCS–15, June 1985, pp.274–279.

8. Wirthumer, G.: "Fault–Tolerant Computing Technology", ITT International Research Review, Stuttgart, FRG, Oct. 1986.

9. Weinstock, C.B.: "SIFT: System Design and Implementation", Proc. FTCS–10, Kyoto, Japan, Oct. 1980, pp.75–77.

10. Lamport, L., Melliar–Smith, P.M.: "Synchronizing Clocks in the Presence of Faults", J. ACM, vol.32, nr.1, Jan. 1985, pp.52–78.

11. Lamport, L., Shostak, R., Pease, M.: "The Byzantine Generals Problem", ACM Trans. on Prog. Langu. and Systems, 1980.

AN AI/REAL TIME SOLUTION FOR EXPERT SCHEDULING OF UNDERGROUND RAIL TRAFFIC

Horellou C., Rossi C., Sissa G.
CISI INGENIERIE/ANSALDO TRASPORTI
CISI INGENIERIE - Pont des 3 Sautets - 13100 Aix en Provence - France
ANSALDO TRASPORTI - Corso Perrone, 25 - 16161 Genova - Italy

ABSTRACT

This paper presents the PETRUS system (Pianificazione Esperta Traffico Urbano e Simulazione : Urban traffic scheduling and simulation), which is a high level system for scheduling and controlling underground rail traffic.
We begin by presenting the expert traffic management issue and then describe the precepts of the artificial intelligence approach we have chosen. This is followed by a description of the functioning of the system and its installation in the existing network.

1. THE PROBLEM

1.1. Introduction.

In traffic management of an underground rail network, the basic aim is to keep constant headway of trains by using management of delays and perturbations (disturbances). Figure 1 represents the abnormalities and perturbances the expert has to consider.

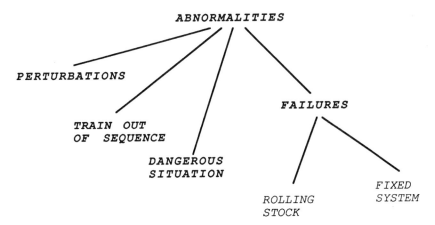

Figure 1. Classification of abnormalities

The information coming from plants and trains is available in the Central Traffic Office, where the Traffic Controller (TC) continuously analyzes the line situation, plans actions to solve system perturbations and puts into practice pertinent strategies.

At times of major disruptions to the system the TC's task is extremely complex and his decisions and susbsequent actions must be taken in very short time intervals.

It is therefore appropriate to supply the traffic controller with systems able to advise and drive him in his choices of action.

In order that such support can be effective it is necesary to equip the system with the same "intelligent" characteristics as those of the TC activity. For underground or overground rail traffic scheduling systems, algorithmic approaches are rigid and not very effective. They are time-consuming as far as the computation is concerned, and provide only limited semantics, especially when the network is complex and the traffic heavy. There are a large number of recorded anomalies and an equally large number of action plans for bringing the situation back to normal. The precepts of the expert's activity are not algorithm-related. They are empirical rules based on the experience acquired over many years' practice.

In this context, AI techniques can provide the necessary solutions, particularly in terms of knowledge representation and implementation. The expert's knowledge and reasoning processes can be very accurately modelled and the end system is capable of formulating solutions which reproduce case by case the sequence of actions involved when the expert puts his expert knowledge into practice.

1.2 The system

PETRUS is an action plan generator. The plans it generates are those most likely to restore normal running conditions in the event of a disruption. In the final version of the system, which will be connected to the real world, the user will be able to analyse the line configuration at any given moment. At present, this functionality is simulated with a graphic configuration interface. By means of this interface the user can place trains on the network, generate anomalies, define the time of day, etc.. Once the configuration phase is over, he can then request an expert analysis of the situation he has just generated. The system uses the configuration of the knowledge base describing the network to interpret the situation and then goes on to reproduce the expert's reasoning and provide one or more action plans to rectify the situation.

These plans are in fact advice to the user in the form of fully described actions, which make it possible to restore normal running conditions.

2. THE METHODOLOGICAL PRINCIPLES UNDERLYING OUR APPROACH

From the outset PETRUS was clearly defined as an artificial intelligence project. Indeed, the control of the modelled underground network and the safety guarantee depend on the strategies of an expert, in this case the traffic controller (TC). Traditional approaches to this type of problem have proved unsatisfactory in that they generate far too great a combination. What is more, scheduling systems must necessarily include a diagnosis phase and the advantages of using artificial intelligence technology in this area are no longer questioned.

As with any other AI project, a knowledge elicitation methodology was required for the specification phase of PETRUS. KOD™ (Knowledge Oriented Design), CISI Ingénierie's in-house methodology was used. Since it is not the objective of this paper to present the methodology in detail, we will simply outline the basic principles.

The KOD™ methodology stems from a resolve to describe in full the expert's area of expertise and reasoning models. Experience and observation have shown that the expert's utterances are working material for the knowledge engineer since they enable him to identify the entities, or objects, manipulated by the expert, the actions he is capable of carrying out and ultimately the schemas or rules he uses in his reasoning processes.

The transcriptions of the interviews with the expert constitute the input of the method. The output is composed of the following :
  - the list of objects in the area of expertise,
  - a well-structured classification of these objects,
  - the dependency graphs installed on the objects,
  - the methods or procedures attached to the specified objects,
  - the rules or schemas describing the reasoning.

These data can all be directely modelled and implemented in an object oriented programming environment.

3. KNOWLEDGE AND REASONING PROCESS MODELLING

The KOD™ methodology can be used to model the various types of knowledge that the expert manipulates, once this knowledge has been elicited. The reasoning processes used by the expert can be identified by means of the case studies examined with him during the interviews.

3.1 Knowledge modelling

3.1.1 The objects : The object formalism means that the area of expertise can be described in its entirety. In the PETRUS project, the underground line is described by means of the objects in the knowledge base. These include the classes of trains, rails and signals, with every physical object in the installation being described as the instance of a class. A mesh of relationships is then built on these classes which describes the dependency graphs establishing the connections between the objects. We thus see that a semantic network is used to described the area of expertise.

Example :

If we want to model the following :

"Signal S2 controls rail R10, which is a simple rail, train T1 is on rail R10. Its doors do not function".

The following facts emerge from the reformulation of this statement :
- S2 is a signal,
- R10 is a simple rail ,
- S2 controls R10,
- T1 is a train,
- T1 occupies R10,
- T1 's doors do not function.

The modelling method adopted is shown in Fig 2.

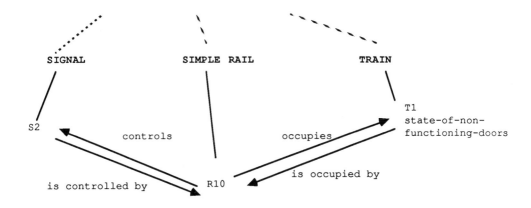

Figure 2. Classification and dependency graph

Figure 3 describes the identified objects and their attributes. The first column shows the objects, the second the attribute names and the third the attribute values.

S2	is-a	signal
	controls	R10
R10	is-a	rail
	is controlled by	S2
T1	is-a	train
	occupies	R10
	state of doors	malfunctioning

Figure 3. Illustration of the attributes

The knowledge base modelled for the PETRUS system contains 2500 objects with their dependency graphs. The number of objects is high because the description of the network is very detailed ; it goes right down to the level of the physical rail.

3.1.2 The actions : Once all the objects have been described, the actions carried out by the expert must be modelled. The purpose of the actions is to control the underground line. They are marked in the expert's utterances by a verb of action.

Example : "... *in this case, we must stop the train. We do this by closing the signal which controls the rail the train is on, i.e. by switching the signal to red."*

In this example the actions "STOP" and "CLOSE" can be found. "stopping a train" is an action which can be carried out by "closing the signal which controls the rail the train is on".

The SADT (Structured Analysis and Design Technics) formalism is used to model the actions. An action will therefore be described by a sequence of "sub-actions" , that is changes in state of one or more of the objects in the base effected by an agent.

For the signal closing example, the SADT form of the action is shown in figure 4 .

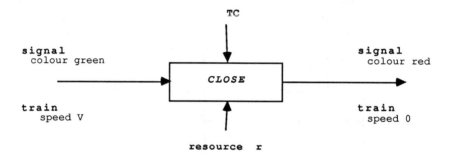

Figure 4. Example of an action

This description is essential for modelling the action plans used by the expert to regulate a disruption. The plans are represented in the form of action sequences. Approximately 200 plans were modelled for the PETRUS application. Each plan also includes a very thorough audit, describing the sequences of actions to be carried out with varying degrees of precision.

3.2 Reasoning process modelling

In the preceding paragraph we described the modelling options adopted for the knowledge the expert manipulates. We are now going to examine the reasoning mode and the rules employed by this reasoning.

3.2.1 Presentation of the PETRUS behavioural cycle : The inference engine used in this application functions according to a three level behavioural cycle which is described in figure 5.

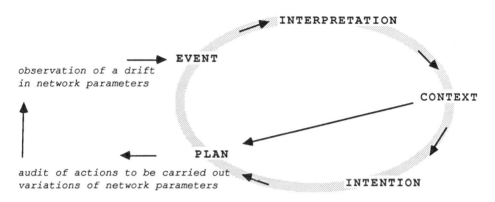

Figure 5. The behavioural cycle

The left hand side of the diagram corresponds to the real world. The facts existing at the beginning of the cycle, i.e. events on the network, undergo an initial interpretation. Once the interpretation is finished the situation is diagnosed, that is, a particular context is recognized. There are few contexts. On the basis of the context, the system generates one or more regulating intentions. Finally, for each intention, an action is generated according to the context.

If we reason in terms of simulation, the generation and carrying out of actions introduces new facts which modify the network situation, thereby completing the behavioural cycle.

The PETRUS engine follows the cycle we have just described. It is composed of two functional modules :

- a hypothetical-deductive engine
- a plan generator.

The hypothetical-deductive engine works by induction (generation of hypotheses) and deduction (creation of new facts) in saturation mode. It generates an interpretation of the situation followed by one or more regulating intentions. The plan generator works by deduction only. It provides the first action plan to be triggered for each of the intentions generated, and then executes this plan.

The working mode we have just described induces several types of rules. These rules, which we call schemas, are presented in the following paragraph.

3.2.2 The PETRUS system rules : For each level described in the presentation of the behavioural cycle, there is a corresponding type of rule or schema. The system thus includes :
- interpretation schemas,
- intention schemas,
- action schemas.

The PETRUS schemas were modelled according to a grammar established for the purposes of the application.

There are few interpretation schemas and they are mainly used for classifying the disruptions recorded.

Example
"a delay is a disruption of the network",
"any halt outside a station is a danger on the network".

Intentions are generated using intention schemas. Within the set of premises which compose an intention schema, there is a context the system recognizes.

Example
"if there is a delay on the network, the intention is to reduce this delay",
"if a train has broken down, it must be replaced by another one".

Action plans are generated using action schemas. All action schemas have an intention in their premises. The only conclusion for an action schema is an action plan.

Example
"if train T must be replaced and if T is near to station S and if there is a train T' in the station depôt, then plan < SUBSTITUTION (T, T') > .

Plan <SUBSTITUTION (T,T')> is composed of a sequence of actions which result in T being removed from the network and replaced by T'.

4. HOW THE SYSTEM FUNCTIONS

When the system is activated, the graphic interface displays the complete line and it is possible to carry out a certain number of operations :
- creation of a new train,
- modification of train parameters,
- creation of train anomaly,
- positioning of the conditions of the network and its components,
- positioning of anomalies on the network

The result of these configuration operations is a modification of the state of the knowledge base (creation of new objects, modification of attribute values on the objects, ...) The modification of a set of attributes which are recognized as relevant corresponds to the detection of an anomaly and automatically triggers the "primary level interpretation" of the situation.

The interpretation is carried out well before the rule base schemas are set off. It corresponds to a phase of enhancement of the network data. At the end of this phase, the PETRUS engine reproduces the sequence of the traffic controller's reasoning rules. First of all the hypothetical-deductive engine produces one or more regulating intentions. The plan generator then provides one or more action plans. The audit of all the schemas used is displayed on the screen so that the system's reasoning processes can be followed step by step. The audit of the plans which are triggered may be listed on the screen as a resumé or in detail. In resumé form, the plan audit provides the principle actions to be carried out.

If the user so requires, he can list out the action plan in detail. This gives him access not only to the broad outlines of the strategies necessary for rectifying the situation but also to the complete list of elementary actions to be carried out, right down to the opening or closing of the signals on the line. This is the level of the network automatisms.

5. INSERTION OF THE PETRUS SYSTEM IN
THE EXISTING INSTALLATION

The PETRUS expert system is to be connected to the Rome underground installation. It will act on the central traffic supervision and management system. The final version of the system will be capable of gathering traffic data and putting forward the solutions which are considered to be the most appropriate.

An interface chain between the expert system and the "Train Describer" will be developed for data acquisition purposes. This chain will filter and process the line-related data.

The expert system output will provide the user with strategic elements of a varying degree of precision, according to the option selected. This means that during the decision or action phases, the user will rapidly have a general idea of the situation which will allow him to make strategic decisions, or alternatively, during the action phases, he will be given very precise advice. In particular, the system will be able to produce an overall audit , and then, if the user so desires, a list of all the elementary actions required for the execution of the selected strategy. The system and acquisition chain will have a sufficiently low response time to ensure that they can be used on line by the traffic controller in time intervals which are compatible with the controller's real time constraints.

6. CONCLUSION

The PETRUS system was developed in two work phases. The first full-scale mock up runs on Macintosh II and was developed in "I", an object environment produced by CISI Ingénierie. It requires a memory of 8 Mo to run. The industrial prototype was developed on a SUN 3.260 workstation with 16 Mo of memory, in the KEE programming environment (Intellicorp).

This application illustrates the value of artificial intelligence technology for solving complex problems such as the scheduling and control of an underground rail traffic network. The system will be operational on the real line in 1990. As it is completely human-oriented, it will give the traffic controller powerful assistance and at the same time be easy to handle. The system's graphic configuration facilities make it a useful tool for training new staff.

Including a system of this kind in the expert's decision loop represents a major step forward in passenger transport line management. On-line use of the system will make it possible to assess its effectiveness on all possible network configurations.

The results obtained during the validation phase indicate that the adjustment of the regulating solutions put forward by the system will not be a lengthy process. The expert will then be able to rely on the results provided by the system to carry out his traffic control tasks. The project demonstrates the incorporation of a considerable mass of expert knowledge in a high level computer system which should in time lead to a valuable gain in terms of cost and reliability.

BIBLIOGRAPHY

Borning, A.
1988   "Constraint-Oriented Programming", in K. Nygaard and P. Wegner, Eds, *Object-Oriented Programming*, Addison-Wesley
Doukidis, G.I., Paul, R.J.
1986   "Experiences in automating the formulation of discrete event simulation models", in E.J.H. Kerckhoffs, G.C. Vansteenkiste, B.P. Zeigler, Eds, *AI applied to Simulation*, Simulation Series, Vol. 18, N°1, pp 79-91
Fox, M.S.
1983   *Constraint-directed Search: A Case Study of Job-Shop Scheduling*, PH.D., Computer Science Department, Carnegie-Mellon University
Stefik, M.
1981   "Planning with constraints", *Artificial Intelligence* 16, pp 111-14O
Vogel, C.
1988   *Génie Cognitif*, Masson, Paris

KOD™ : KOD is a trademark of CISI Ingénierie

Just a slip of the cursor: Methods for identifying potential problem areas in the use of a VDU based system for the signalling of trains.

Deborah A. Lucas, Ph.D.
Human Reliability Associates Ltd.,
1 School House, Higher Lane,
Dalton, Wigan,
Lancs. WN8 7RP, UK

ABSTRACT

A case study is presented concerning the human factors and human reliability aspects of the Integrated Electronic Control Centre (IECC) system. This system is currently being introduced into some power signal boxes in the UK by British Rail. The IECC system involves the signalling of trains using visual display units (VDUs) and a "trackerball" control. This represents a significant departure from existing equipment in power boxes. Given the critical nature of the task of signalling trains potential operational problems needed to be identified and rectified in advance of its implementation.

This paper describes the use of available methods for identifying areas where operational difficulties may arise in routine and non-routine situations. Each method is illustrated using the IECC system as a case study and possible solutions to the problems identified are suggested.

INTRODUCTION

It was inevitable that information technology (IT) would have a major impact on control systems in the transportation industry. For the signalmen on the British railway network the most significant aspect of the introduction of such new technology is the implementation of the Integrated Electronic Control Centre (IECC) which, at the time of writing, is already installed in Liverpool Street and York. The IECC system represents a considerable departure from the existing NX control panels (currently used in large power signal boxes) in that it involves the signalling of trains using visual display units (VDUs) with a trackerball and keyboard as the controlling devices.

The introduction of new technology has always raised issues of human reliability (see Rasmussen et al, 1987) and the implementation of IT on the railways is no exception to this. Human factors engineering stresses the need for a user-centred design which will lead to a more productive system which is both easy to use and more error tolerant. To achieve such a design is not simple. However, there are a number of data sources and methods of analysis which can be used to assist the designer. Figure 1 lists some of these methods and sources. These techniques may also be used to evaluate a design to ensure that usability and human reliability requirements have been met. This paper illustrates the use of such methods through a case study of the IECC system.

OBJECTIVE OF STUDY

This case study involved the human reliability implications of introducing the IECC system, a VDU based system for the task of signalling trains. Human Reliability Associates were commissioned by the National Union of Railwaymen to conduct an independent review of a prototype of this system prior to its introduction and to consider a number of issues including:-

a. Are the Health and Safety Executive (HSE) guidelines on the use of visual display units applicable to the IECC system? Are there any omissions in these guidelines with respect to the VDU based system?

b. What effect will the introduction of the IECC system have on the ability of signalmen to efficiently handle both routine and non-routine tasks?

It is not possible to give full details of the results of this study here. Instead, the aim of this paper is to illustrate how data sources and analysis techniques can be used together to provide an effective method of evaluating a prototype system to identify human reliability problems and to produce effective recommendations.

Human Factors Engineering

General design
guidelines → ← Analysis of users
and tasks

Experience of
other systems → ← Analysis of
existing systems

Theories of user
behaviour → ← User involvement
in testing design

User-centred design

Benefits

- *safer/reliable design*
- *more productive system*
- *easier to use equipment*

FIGURE 1
Methods, information sources and benefits of user-centred design

KEY DIFFERENCES BETWEEN EXISTING AND VDU BASED SYSTEM

In order to provide the necessary background information for the reader a brief comparison of the existing NX system and the IECC system is given below. This list illustrates the magnitude of the changes for the signalman who will use the new system.

Mode of control:
The NX panel contains push/pull route setting buttons whilst the IECC system makes use of a trackerball and associated push buttons.

Nature of control:
The present system employs manual route setting, whereas the availability of automatic route setting is a predominant feature of the IECC system.

Information display:
Wall mounted NX panel and desk control versus 3 VDU screens on a workstation. The VDU screens will typically show 2 overview maps and 6 associated detailed maps.

Reminder devices:
The NX panel system uses physical collars and button covers, the IECC system will use coloured information on the screens. The information shown on the VDU screens is also held in the signal interlocking as additional protection.

Alarms:
Audible alarms and lights on NX wall and control panel versus audible alarms and verbal messages on a "general purpose" screen in the IECC system.

Layout of signalbox:
Current NX panels have many positions with adjacent and overlapping control and wall areas between different control areas. In the IECC system there will be separate workstations for each area covered by power box.

DATA SOURCES

In the design or evaluation of a new system there are a wide range of sources of information which should be consulted. In designing or evaluating a system it is important that information is gathered from as many of these sources as possible. In addition, it must be stressed that the involvement of the end users of the system is crucial. Such involvement may occur through interviews, discussions, questionnaires and user trials of prototypes. On occasion a formal working party arrangement may be a useful way of securing user involvement and acceptance of a new system. The data sources which were used in this case study are described briefly below.

Field observation

Visits were made to three power signalboxes. Detailed observations of the use of the NX panel system were made at two boxes. An early version of Automatic Route Setting was observed at one of these. The visit to a third power box was made to observe the use of an early VDU and trackerball system installed in a power box but not currently used to control the movement of trains.

Interviews, discussions and questionnaires

At each of the three signalboxes visited signalmen were interviewed. In addition, at the third box (with the early VDU system) a questionnaire was given to the signalmen. This questionnaire is reproduced in the appendix to this paper. It enabled the operational problems of a similar system to be collected and fully documented.

Review of documentation

The specification document for the design and operation of the proposed IECC system was reviewed together with the initial draft of the operating manual.

Viewing a demonstration of the IECC system

A prototype workstation was examined. In addition, a demonstration of the software for the new VDU system was viewed.

METHODS OF ANALYSIS

A variety of analytical methods were used to analyse the impact of the VDU system on the task of signalling trains. As with data sources, it is important to use as many of these techniques as possible in order to develop a comprehensive understanding of the task requirements and information processing demands imposed on users. A brief outline of each of the methods used to evaluate the IECC system is given below.

Task analyses of routine tasks

Task analysis is the process of determining what users of a system currently do with the system to accomplish their goals. It is the analysis of operator behaviour and goals (not an analysis of the system to be designed). Task analysis provides clearly documented evidence of the task steps, plans, goals, decisions, and information requirements necessary to successfully carry out a given task.

Task analyses of nine routine events were constructed for the operation of the NX panel. The nine events studied were:-

- Control timetabled trains through predetermined routes
- Control additional trains including late running, changes, freight
- Enter train descriptions
- Answer phone calls from drivers
- Monitor and operate signal crossings
- Handle track possessions
- Control patrolman's protection
- Acknowledge and take action on alarms
- Supervise Automatic Route Setting (ARS) and override when required

The task analyses covered the plans, goals, actions, decisions and information sources necessary to carry out each task. An example is given in figure 2 for the task of controlling a patrolman's protection. Figure 3 shows the analysis for the task of entering train descriptions. All task analyses were constructed after observation of NX power boxes and were then verified with signalmen.

Task analyses of emergency and contingency tasks

Similarly, task analyses of seven emergency or contingency events were also constructed for the operation of the NX panel. These events were chosen after consultation with experienced signalmen. The events are listed below:

- Switch off power
- Operate ground frame release
- Points failure
- Signal passed at danger
- Track circuit shows "occupied" unexpectedly
- Goods on line
- Send emergency alarm

It is vitally important to consider such abnormal events when designing or evaluating a new control system. When emergencies arise the operator will be under considerable stress and the system must be able to support his actions and decisions and provide him with the relevant information quickly.

Comparison of operating modes of NX and VDU based system

A comparison of the operating modes of the existing and the proposed systems was carried out using the following data sources:-

- Questionnaire of users of related system
- Demonstration of prototype system
- Detailed questionning of designers of VDU system

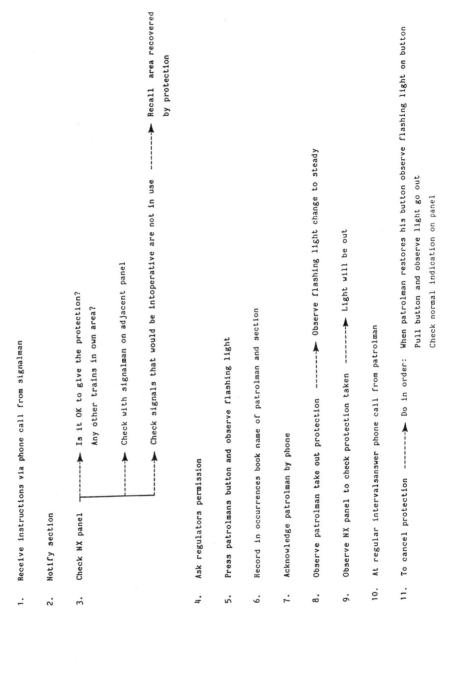

Plan: When instructed do 1 to 4

When received clearance do 5 to 10

When instructed do 11

1. Receive instructions via phone call from signalman

2. Notify section

3. Check NX panel - - - - - - - ▶ Is it OK to give the protection?

Any other trains in own area?

- - - - - - ▶ Check with signalman on adjacent panel

- - - - - - ▶ Check signals that would be intoperative are not in use - - - - - - ▶ Recall area recovered by protection

4. Ask regulators permission

5. Press patrolmans button and observe flashing light

6. Record in occurrences book name of patrolman and section

7. Acknowledge patrolman by phone

8. Observe patrolman take out protection - - - - - - ▶ Observe flashing light change to steady

9. Observe NX panel to check protection taken - - - - - - ▶ Light will be out

10. At regular intervalsanswer phone call from patrolman

11. To cancel protection - - - - - - ▶ Do in order: When patrolman restores his button observe flashing light on button

Pull button and observe light go out

Check normal indication on panel

FIGURE 2

Task analysis of task of controlling patrolman's protection

Plan:

As required do steps 1 to 6.
If necessary do step 7.

1. Check correct T.D. of train --------> Refer to last T.D.
                                          Refer to updates
                                          Refer to latest additions
                                          Refer to clock

2. Select correct T.D. berth --------> If provided use set-up button
                                        If failure occurs, enter berth number via keyboard
                                        Alternatively, enter appropriate signal no. --------> Read signal no. off NX panel
                                        using keyboard

3. Type in code of train (a 4 letter/number code)

4. Observe "scratchpad" to check berth and train no. are correct

5. Press "Int" (interpose) key

6. Watch T.D. appear on NX panel

7. If necessary, cancel or change T.D. --------> Either: Enter SN via keyboard
                                                         Operate "cancel" button
                                                         Watch no. disappear
                                                         Go to step 1

                                                 or   Call berth using set-up buttons
                                                         Operate "cancel" button
                                                         Go to step 1

FIGURE 3
Task analysis of task of entering train descriptions

The nine task analyses of routine tasks together with the analysis of contingencies were used as an essential part of the comparison process. This process allowed potential problems to be identified. This comparison is a vital step in developing what is often referred to as a "use model" for the new system. A use model specifies exactly how the system will be used in terms of what information is displayed to the user, how users enter commands and in what sequence, etc.

Estimates of information workload

One disadvantage of task analysis techniques is that they tend to treat each task as being independent. In everyday situations, of course, a person may be carrying out two or more tasks concurrently. It is therefore important to consider those performance influencing factors which will affect human reliability. These include:

-    the effects of multi-tasking
-    the traffic workload
-    whether information sources and job aids are appropriate for the signalman
-    levels of experience of users

These issues may be considered by conducting an information needs and job aids analysis and by asking signalmen to make self ratings of "information workload". This includes ratings of factors such as:

-    the need to think and concentrate almost continuously,
-    the perceived complexity of the task,
-    the perceived level of environmental distractions,
-    the level of stress/strain felt.

Establishing estimates of such information workload enabled a comparison to be made for the nine routine tasks under both normal and very heavy traffic conditions. Those tasks which were perceived to be particularly stressful and complex were identified. This analysis provides vital information for the design of job aids, training and procedures. It may also be used to assist in determining appropriate manning levels and rest periods for each workstation.

Formal audit of proposed system

A formal audit of the proposed VDU system was also undertaken. Eight areas were reviewed:

- workstation design
- working environment
- visual display requirements
- input/output devices
- task requirements
- training issues
- documentation
- human reliability considerations

This audit made full use of the Health and Safety Executive (HSE) booklet containing guidance on good practice concerning the introduction and use of VDUs. The results of the audit are documented in detail in Lucas (1988) and are not discussed further here.

SUMMARY OF MAIN RESULTS

Omissions encountered in the introduction of the system.

The review showed that the designers of the system had not fully considered the needs of the signalmen. In particular, those tasks and information used during emergency or contingency events had not been thoroughly evaluated. This may have been due to a lack of human factors advice during the design process. For example, one earlier review of the prototype IECC system had concentrated on the ergonomic aspects of the workstation and no formal task analysis or user needs analysis appear to have been performed.

The safety of the train operation is governed by the interlocking equipment although certain tasks performed by signalmen are safety critical. British Railway's approach to the design of the IECC system was to retain established procedures used for NX control panels. However, no formal human reliability analyses were carried out to confirm the validity of this transposition. Hardware and software reliability analyses were performed.

A further omission was the lack of a formal training specification and no continuing user involvement in the design of the system or the documentation.

Potential human reliability problems of the IECC system.

This study identified a number of potential problems with the operation of the prototype IECC system including:

- Manual route setting may be more difficult especially for non-scheduled trains.

- Responses in an emergency could be slower and more subject to error.

- The probability of a mistake when operating signal crossings may be increased.

- The automatic route setting introduces all the standard "ironies of automation" including the need to employ infrequently used skills in non-routine situations where other error inducing tendencies (stress, time pressure, etc.) may exist (see Bainbridge, 1987).

Reasons for major human reliability problems

These human reliability problems were not identified during design and earlier evaluations. This was primarily due to a failure to systematically consider the causes of human errors. No structured framework was used to consider the effects of the following factors:

- turbulent environment (e.g. noise, distractions, etc.)
- peak workload
- inexperience with rarely used instructions
- heavy demands on working memory and long term memory
- high demands on attention
- mental and physical "impossibilities" e.g. monitoring 3 fast moving systems simultaneously.

There was a tendency to over-concentrate on the perceptual and motor aspects of Human Computer Interface (HCI) design and the health and safety issues as evidenced by use of HSE VDU guidelines. There was inadequate consideration of other factors related to HCI and to the organisational issues of introducing new technology.

RECOMMENDATIONS

A selection of the specific recommendations which were made in the project is given below. The intention here is merely to illustrate the benefits which can be gained from conducting such a human reliability appraisal on prototype equipment. It may be difficult for the reader who has not viewed the operation of the prototype system to understand all of these recommendations in detail.

Recommendations made for improving the design of the equipment included:

- The quality of the visual display units is high. However, there are problems with the numbers of colours displayed on the general purpose screen. The displaying of soft keys which have no function should be eliminated.

- The trackerball control is appropriate for the tasks required. However, the design and location of the 5 function keys associated with the trackerball needs immediate attention.

- Overview maps should show regularly used sidings.

- An indication of which areas of the overviews individual detailed maps correspond to should be given.

- The density of information on the overview screens is high. Guidelines should be set for their content. This should be determined using functional criteria.

- The method of removing collars should be reviewed. There may a case to allow such removal only through a keyboard command.

Recommendations for improvements to the operating regime were:

- No arrangements for rest pauses have been specified. It is recommended that 10 minutes break should be taken away from the workstation every 2 hours.

- The use of the automatic route setting introduces additional considerations. It is recommended that a certain percentage of each shift should be spent with this switched off in order to preserve the skills of the signalmen. Manning levels on workstations with CCTVs should be carefully considered.

- A quick reference list of commands should be written and made available to all signalmen using the new system.

Training recommendations included:

- Detailed arrangements for training signalmen in the use of the new system should be drawn up.

- Training should include the use of the standby keyboard operation as well as the trackerball control.

- Training must include how to send emergency alarms through both trackerball and keyboard commands.

Actions taken

It is pleasing to report that the British Railways Board accepted the majority of the recommendations which emerged from this study and had independently initiated a number of improvements consistent with these findings. Further changes to the IECC system were effected before installation. The remaining recommendations are to be evaluated after a period of operational experience.

DISCUSSION

Applicability of methods

The majority of the methods and techniques presented in this paper may be used by designers with minimal formal training in human factors. Task analysis techniques are described in a number of texts and there exist some software packages which assist the analyst who is performing a task analysis. The questionnaire used in this case study may be modified for other applications and therefore has been reproduced in an appendix. Formal human factors audits of prototype systems will probably require expert advice although the emergence of comprehensive human factors standards for VDUs may reduce this need to some extent. The benefits to be gained from the use of such systematic approaches during evaluation of a prototype system should be evident from the case study reported here.

It must be emphasised that the methods described here should ideally also be used during design in order to fully understand the user requirements for the new system. A design philosophy in which users needs are central is referred to as user-centred design. Further details of this approach may be found in the many publications on this topic.

The use of user-centred design

User-centred design concepts are vital for the production of a usable and error tolerant system. However, as is evident from the case study reported here, they are not necessarily widely used by suppliers of systems nor is their use always required by customers. Why is this so?

This organisational issue has been considered by other researchers looking in particular at factory automation systems. One feature that has emerged repeatedly has been referred to as "technical myopia" (Clegg and Wall, 1987). Technical myopia is the tendency to see problems as essentially technical in nature. Blackler and Brown (1987) similarly describe a "technology led" style of "muddling through". They contrast this "task and technology" centred approach to new technology with an "organisational and end-user" centred approach. The two models are closely linked to the assumptions of planners, to alternative styles of planning and to organisational policies. A fundamental change in the planning styles and the organisation may therefore be required before user-centred design is implemented effectively. For such an attitude shift to occur it may even be necessary for the management of a company to experience the failure of a computer system either through user rejection, or as a result of a costly production failure, or through the occurrence of a safety critical situation.

The impact of human factors standards and guidelines

There is currently a great deal of effort being made to issue international human factors standards for VDUs in both office and industrial environments. The impact of such standards remains to be seen. However, case studies, such as the one given here, provide anecdotal evidence of their probable impact. Judging from the present study the standards will increase awareness of the role of human factors. However they may have a limited effect on improving the design of any particular system. For example, in the design of the IECC system the HSE advice on the use of VDUs was formally cited but not always followed, even with respect to simple design features such as the number of colours on a screen. The more widespread use of systematic approaches to establishing user needs for a system, together with the adoption of an organisational and end user approach to design, would appear to be the factors needed to ensure that future computer-based systems are of a satisfactory human reliability and human factors standard.

DISCLAIMER

The results and conclusions given in this paper are solely the opinion of the author and do not necessarily represent the views of the National Union of Railwaymen or the British Railways Board.

ACKNOWLEDGEMENTS

The study reported in this paper was commissioned by the National Union of Railwaymen and we are most grateful for their permission to publish the results of the research. Thanks are also due to the British Railways Board for their cooperation during the study and for their permission to publish.

REFERENCES

Bainbridge, L. (1987) Ironies of automation. In: J. Rasmussen, K. Duncan and J. Leplat (eds.) New technology and human error. London: Wiley.

Blackler, F. and Brown, C. (1987) Management, organisations and the new technologies. In: F. Blackler and D. Oborne (eds.) **Designing for the future: Information technology and people.** Leicester: British Psychological Society.

Clegg, C. and Wall, T.D. (1987) Managing factory automation. In Blackler and Oborne (eds.) op. cit.

Health and Safety Executive (1983) Visual Display Units. HMSO.

Lucas, D.A. (1988) An examination of the use of visual display units for the task of signalling trains. Report prepared for the General Secretary, National Union of Railwaymen.

Rasmussen, J., Duncan, K. and Leplat, J. (eds.) (1987) **New technology and human error.** London: Wiley.

APPENDIX

Questionnaire given to operators of similar VDU system

Your opinion on the "Trackerball" system.

The NUR in conjunction with HRA Ltd. is studying the implications of introducing the new "trackerball" system in power signalboxes. As part of this study we would like to find out your experiences of the trackerball system. Please answer every question in this survey by placing a circle round the number that best represents your opinion. There are no right or wrong answers but please try to be as honest as possible. Try to answer all the questions even if you have to give a best guess for some of them. You do not need to put your name on the form.

These questions ask about your overall impression of the trackerball system".

How satisfying is the trackerball system to use on a daily basis?

    Frustrating   1   2   3   4   5   6   7   Satisfying

How easy do you find the system to use on a regular basis?

    Difficult   1   2   3   4   5   6   7   Easy

How do you rate the overall design of the system for the tasks you use it for?

    Poor design   1   2   3   4   5   6   7   Good design

These questions ask about the operation of the trackerball control

How do you find the use of the trackerball control?

    Awkward to use   1   2   3   4   5   6   7   Easy to use

Have you had any aches and pains in your arms and hands recently?

    Severe   1   2   3   4   5   6   7   None

These questions ask about the design of the display on the VDU

What is your impression of the display on the screen?

    Cluttered   1   2   3   4   5   6   7   Clear

How do you find the size of the text on the screen?

    Too small   1   2   3   4   5   6   7   Ideal

Is the use of colours on the screen helpful?

   Not helpful   1   2   3   4   5   6   7   Helpful

How do you feel about the amount of information on the screen?

   Too detailed   1   2   3   4   5   6   7   Appropriate

How easy is it to find the information you want on the screen?

   Difficult   1   2   3   4   5   6   7   Easy

Have you had any discomfort from your eyes recently e.g. dryness, irritation, difficulty in focussing, headaches?

   Severe   1   2   3   4   5   6   7   None

These questions ask about the design of the workstation

How do you feel when seated at the workstation?

   Uncomfortable   1   2   3   4   5   6   7   Comfortable

How do find your distance from the screen?

   Too close   1   2   3   4   5   6   7   Ideal

Have you had any backache or neck/shoulder aches recently?

   Severe   1   2   3   4   5   6   7   None

These questions ask about learning to use the system

How easy is it to learn to use the system?

   Difficult   1   2   3   4   5   6   7   Easy

When you make a mistake how helpful are the error messages?

   Never helpful   1   2   3   4   5   6   7   Always helpful

Do the terms used in the trackerball system relate to the task?

   Distantly   1   2   3   4   5   6   7   Closely

How do you find the use of computer-related terms?

   Too often used   1   2   3   4   5   6   7   Used appropriately

How do you find the written instructions and documentation?

    Not helpful   1   2   3   4   5   6   7   Always helpful

These questions ask about the use of the system

How do you find the speed of response of the system?

      Too slow   1   2   3   4   5   6   7   Fast enough

Does the trackerball system simplify your tasks?

 Never simplifies   1   2   3   4   5   6   7 Always simplifies

How much concentration do you need to use with the trackerball system?

Lot of concentration 1   2   3   4   5   6   7 Little concentration

How much do you have to remember the information needed to use the system?

 Must be memorized 1   2   3   4   5   6   7 Is visible

Thank you for your help. Please check that you have answered all the questions. If you have any other comments about the trackerball system please add them below or on the back of this survey.

A KNOWLEDGE-BASED ASSISTANT FOR REAL-TIME PLANNING AND RECOVERY IN AUTOMATIC TRAIN PROTECTION SYSTEMS

Evelina Lamma, Paola Mello
DEIS - Universita' di Bologna
Viale Risorgimento, 2
40136 Bologna - ITALY

ABSTRACT

In this paper we present the basic design guidelines of a system able to assist a station-master in real-time planning and recovery of railway signalling systems. The system heavily uses the knowledge-based system technology. Its architecture is based on a blackboard model - implemented in Prolog- and the knowledge of railway signalling is explicitly stated in the system.

INTRODUCTION

The train traffic control problem consists in automatically controlling the safe movement of trains within a railway station by means of a set of logical networks that constitute the Automatic Train Protection system (ATP) of the station.

The capabilities of an ATP system are limited to relatively low-level automatic remote controls of devices such as points, level- crossings and signals.

Route planning, and other high-level decision making are left to the human operator, i.e. the station-master, who often suffers from information overload, particularly when trains delay - and therefore do not respect the railway time-table - or failures occur in the ATP system.

In both cases, the operator must take corrective action to avoid, whenever possible, long waits of trains to enter/leave the station or, in the worst case, station traffic blocks. When a failure occurs, he/she must also detect and diagnose the failure.

The corrective actions have to be planned and performed by the operator quickly and in a continuous state of stress. They may require some exceptional, manual operations which, if incorrect, may generate accidents.

For this reason, a knowledge-based assistant for real-time planning and recovery in ATP systems would be highly suitable for railway station safety and reliability.

The main aim of the paper is to show how such a system can be designed and take advantage of knowledge-based system technology [1]. Knowledge-based systems, in fact, proved to be very flexible, modular, easy to maintain and understand for final users, and they are particularly suitable for knowledge-intensive applications.

The paper is organized as follows.

In the first section a brief overview of the ATP problem will be given. In section 2 the basic functions of the system will be presented. In section 3 explicit knowledge on the ATP constraints will be discussed together with its automatic generation.

In section 4, the monitoring function will be sketched. In section 5, planning and recovery, together with the blackboard architecture supporting them, will be described.

1. ATP SYSTEMS

An Automatic Train Protection system (ATP) is a railway traffic control system - constituted by a set of logic circuits - that regulates the circulation of trains within railway stations by remotely controlling devices such as points, level crossings and signals. Each ATP circuit implements a boolean function by means of relays, and determines the value of its output by "and/or" combining its inputs. Setting -if possible- the state of relays corresponding to signals is the ultimate aim of the ATP system.

But any action performed by the ATP system is the consequence of a command, given by a human operator, i.e. the station-master. When a train has to enter or leave a station, the station-master selects a route R for that train and pushes a button corresponding to R. Each route is identified by an initial and a final position in the station and by a letter (e.g. a, b, etc). For example (see figure 1), route 1-3a starts from position 1 and ends at position 3 on track 1. Route 1-4a starts from the same initial position, covers point 1 in shunting position and ends at position 4 on track 2. Route 1-4b starts from 1, covers point 1 in non-shunting position and point 3 in the shunting one and ends at position 4 on track 2.

After selecting a route (from now on we will refer to this as the command phase) the ATP system automatically controls all the devices related to that route.

In particular, after the command phase, the ATP system checks that no other route interferes in any way with the chosen one, moves points as needed for the chosen route, locks the chosen route to prevent possible interference with other routes and, finally, operates signals correctly. Once the train has covered the selected route, the ATP system unlocks it.

Note that the capabilities of an ATP system are limited to relatively low-level automatic remote controls of devices and that all the high-level decision making (e.g. route planning, diagnosis) are left to the station-master.

In practice an ATP system implements a set of constraints that the National Railway Authority imposes on railway traffic within a station. Traffic constraints are characteristic of the station, since they depend on its topology - i.e. the number of tracks, the relative position of points, signals, etc. These constraints must be considered as the basic requirement for designing the ATP system [3]. In section 3 we outline how these constraints can be used not only to design the system, but also to assist the station-master to perform some forms of planning, diagnosing and recovery on the ATP system.

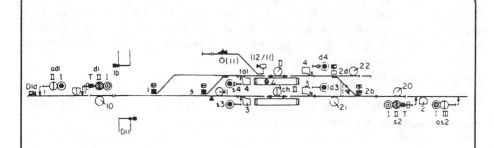

Legend

Numbers within a box represent starting and ending positions of routes (1, 2, 3, 4 in the figure).

ad1, as2 represent first-class signals.

d1, s2, are second-class signals.

They are constituted by two different signals, whose light can be of different colors (i.e. red, green, yellow).

s3, d3, s4, d4 represent departure signals. They can be red or green.

Numbers within a circle represent track segments (ba1, 10, 11, 1, 21, 22, 2, 22 in the figure).

pl1 is the only level-crossing within the station.

Figure 1: A sample station

2. BASIC FUNCTIONS

The basic functions of the ATP assistant are sketched in figure 2, where:

- **CP** is the constraint generator which, given a representation of the station topology, produces the constraint relations. The automatic generation of constraints implies greater generality of the system: the ATP assistant can be applied to different stations without any significant modification;

- **MONITORING** controls the station and permanently produces a consistent representation of the state of ATP station devices.

  MONITORING also detects some forms of device failures, for example if points or signals are out of control;

- **PLANNING** is the planning block. When a train has to enter/leave the station, starting from position X to position Y, the planning block presents the list of routes from X to Y coverable within the station to the station-master. At this stage, the station-master can choose between the following two actions:

  - select and command a particular route from X to Y (represented as <X,Y,L>) on the basis of the information on coverable routes;

- select and simulate the command of a particular route R from X to Y, then obtain from the assistant some information to evaluate whether the choice is optimal before really commanding R. This information consists of:
  - the number of track-segments and points involved in the route;
  - the number of incompatibilities that arise from commanding R, i.e. the routes that become no longer coverable due to R.

Since this kind of simulation can be done for a sequence of commands involving different routes, the station-master can achieve long-term planning that is very useful in anomalous situations. For example, if two or more trains are approaching the station at very short intervals, due to delays with respect to the time-table, the station-master can take advantage of the ATP assistant to simulate different sequences of commands before his/her final decision.

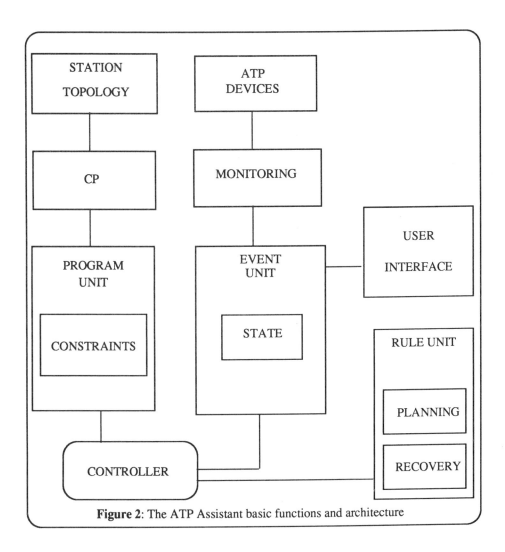

Figure 2: The ATP Assistant basic functions and architecture

• **RECOVERY** is the recovery block. While the detection of device failures is performed by the monitoring block, RECOVERY is able to detect errors occurring when a route is commanded, and to suggest corrective actions. Up to now we have considered three kinds of error, when a track-segment TS, a point P or a signal S is no longer reliable.

If this is the case, in fact, a route R involving TS, P or S is coverable providing exceptional action is taken before the station-master commands R. The effect of this action is to allow the automatic check performed by the ATP system on the freedom of TS, on the position of P or on the efficiency of the signal light to be by-passed. Of course this exceptional action -which could be very dangerous- has to be executed only after the station-master has directly checked that the train can cover the route safely.

3. CONSTRAINTS

3.1 Station topology

Station topology can be considered the static input data of the problem, i.e. it is the only information concerning the specific station for which an ATP assistant has to be designed. In this sense it is very "specific knowledge", qualitatively different from the more general knowledge described later.

Station topology, traditionally represented in graphic form, is described by means of a set of relations (or facts) of the form: *db(<relation_name>(<argument_list>))*, where 'db' is introduced just to indicate that relations represent data and could be collected in a database. Relations in figure 3 describe the topology for the station presented in figure 1.

3.2 ATP Constraints

Constraints specify, for each route in the station, the position of points, the track segments that must be free, the controlled signals and the incompatible routes, i.e. all the conditions that must be verified by the ATP system before a train can cover any route in a station.

In more detail, constraints are used to specify for each route:

• Signals that are met when a train covers the route. For example signals ad1 and d1 along route 1-3a.

• Points that are involved in the route. They are classified as:

•Covered points. These points are covered by a train, when it covers the route. They can be in non-shunting position (*normal*) or in shunting position (*reverse*).

•Lateral points. They lie behind the route, and can be controlled in normal position to prevent converging routes.

•Output points. They lie after the last track segment of the route and are controlled in normal position to obtain greater safety when covering a route.

•Track segments that are covered by a train on a given route or that lie beyond that route. They are classified in:

• Covered track segments. To command the route they must be free.

•Output track segments. They lie after the last track segment of the route. To command the route they must be free.

•Incompatible routes. In particular, different kinds of incompatibility are considered:

Tracks inside the station.
db(track(1)).
db(track(2)).
Track_segments in the station. In a track_segment relation, the first argument is the name as the track on which the track_segment 'T' lies; the second argument is 'T' name; the third and fourth arguments represent the two track_segments besides 'T' ('nil' for no track segment).
db(track_segment(2,22,2,nil)).
db(track_segment(2,2,nil,22)).
db(track_segment(1,ba2,20,nil)).
db(track_segment(1,20,21,ba2)).
db(track_segment(1,21,1,20)).
db(track_segment(1,1,11,21)).
db(track_segment(1,11,10,1)).
db(track_segment(1,10,ba1,11)).
db(track_segment(1,ba1,nil,10)).
Positions from and to which a route can be covered. In a 'place' relation, the first argument is the name of a place, 'P', while the second argument is the track_segment on which 'P' lies.
db(place(4,2)).
db(place(3,1)).
db(place(2,ba2)).
db(place(1,ba1)).
Signals in the station. In a 'signal' relation, the first argument is the name of signal 'S'; the second argument is the name of the track_segment on which 'S' stands; the third argument represents the direction of route 'R', controlled by 'S'. The fourth argument specifies the type of 'R' (arrival or departure route).
db(signal(d4,n2,right,departure)).
db(signal(s4,n2,left,departure)).
db(signal(s3,n1,left,departure)).
. . .
Points in the station. In a 'point' relation the first argument specifies the type of a point 'P' (single or double); the second argument is 'P' name; the third argument represents 'P' direction (positive or negative); the third and fourth arguments represent track_segments that are joined by 'P'.
db(point(double,2,negative,21,22)).
db(point(single,1,positive,11,2)).
db(point(single,101,negative,2,t1)).

Figure 3: Station Topology Relations

- Inverse route, i.e. the route that covers the same track segments as a given one, but with different direction. For example, route 3-1a is the inverse of route 1-3a.
- Opposite routes. Routes that cover different track segments but stop in the same final position of the given one. For example route 2-3a is the opposite of route 1-3a.
- Inhibition of non-stop routes. A non-stop route is always composed of two routes in the station (i.e. the coming route and the departure route). The non-stop route can take place only on the first track, and must be forbidden on other tracks. For example routes 2-4a and 4-1a cannot take place simultaneously.

The set of routes R within the station match the topology and features of the railway line on which the station lies. For example, in a one-way line with direction 'd', only the routes in direction 'd' will be considered. Dynamically, the set of possible routes is generally smaller than R due to the incompatibilities introduced by the constraints.

The knowledge on constraints is represented by means of relations, following the same syntax used to represent the station topology. The relations in figure 4 represent some of the constraints for the station of figure 1.

Routes in the station. In 'arrival' and 'departure' relations the first argument is the origin of the route, the second its destination, the third is a letter identifying the route.
db(arrival(1,3,a)).
db(arrival(1,4,a)).
db(arrival(1,4,b)).
db(arrival(2,3,a)).
. . .
Controlled signals for route 'R'. In a 'controlled_signal' relation, the first three arguments identify 'R'. The fourth argument is the signal name.
db(controlled_signal(1,3,a,ad1)).
db(controlled_signal(1,3,a,d1)).
db(controlled_signal(1,4,a,d1)).
db(controlled_signal(1,4,a,ad1)).
. . .
Incompatible routes. In the following relations the first three arguments identify a route 'R'. The others represent a route incompatible with 'R'.
db(inverse(1,3,a,3,1,a)).
db(inverse(1,4,a,4,1,a)).
db(inverse(1,4,a,4,1,b)).
db(opposite(1,3,a,2,3,a)).
db(opposite(2,3,a,1,3,a)).
db(inib_ns_route(2,4,a,4,1,a)).
db(inib_ns_route(2,4,a,4,1,b)).
db(order_ns_route(1,3,a,3,2,a)).
. . .
For each route a set of controlled track-segments and a set of controlled points are specified. The first three arguments identify a route 'R'. The fourth argument represents the name of a track_segment or the name of a point to be controlled.
db(normal_covered_point(1,3,a,1)).
db(normal_covered_point(1,3,a,3)).
db(normal_covered_point(1,4,a,101)).
db(normal_covered_point(1,4,b,1)).
db(normal_covered_point(3,1,a,1)).
db(output_point(1,4,a,2)).
db(output_point(1,4,b,2)).
db(covered_track_segment(1,3,a,1)).
db(covered_track_segment(1,3,a,11)).
. . .

Figure 4: Constraint Relations

In each relation, the first three arguments identify a route by respectively specifying its origin and destination and the letter that identifies it univocally.

For example, in figure 4, the fact: ***db(inverse(1,3,a,3,1,a))*** states that route 1-3a has an inverse route, called 3-1a.

Constraints are automatically produced by the CP block when a representation of the station topology is given. The first step performed by CP is to identify all the possible routes within the station. Then, for each route R, the CP module produces a set of relations stating the conditions to be verified to cover R.

3.3 The CP module

The CP module automatically produces the train traffic constraints starting from representation of the railway station topology, which can be considered the static input data of the assistant.

The knowledge required to produce constraints has been represented by means of rules that are applied in backward chaining, using a depth-first strategy with backtracking. Since the Prolog interpreter implements this control policy precisely, the CP module has been easily and naturally implemented in `Prolog. Rules for constraint generation are expressed as Prolog clauses. For example, the following rules (reported in a simplified form):

```
left_right_route(X,Y,L):-db(place(X,TS1)),db(place(Y,TS2)),
                         path(TS1,TS2,right,[TS1],Track_list),
                         assert_route(X,Y,L,left_right),
                         assert_track(X,Y,L,Track_list).
path(TS,TS,_,Track_list,Track_list) :-!.
path(TS1,TS2,right,TLold,[TS2|TLold]):- db(track_segment(_,TS1,_,TS2)),!.
path(TS1,TS2,right,TLold,TLnew):-   db(point(_,P1,_,TS1,TS3)),
                         path(TS3,TS2,right,TLold,TLnew),!.
path(TS1,TS2,right,TLold,TLnew):-
                         db(track_segment(_,TS3,TS1,_)),
                         path(TS3,TS2,right,[TS3|TLold],TLnew).
```

generate the routes with direction from left to right, while the rule:

```
opposite(X,Y,L):-  db(route(X,Y,L,left_right)),
                   db(route(Y,W,K,right_left)),
                   assert_opposite(X,Y,L,Y,W,K).
```

determines the opposite routes of a given one.

A uniform and well-integrated system has been obtained with no interface problems between the CP module and the the others since all modules are implemented by using Prolog.

4. MONITORING

In designing the ATP assistant and, in particular, its monitoring block, we consider a dynamic model of the station given by the state of a limited set of devices, i.e. signals, points, and track segments. Such devices are assumed to be monitored continuously since they are subject to failures. In the following we will not take into account how such monitoring is performed, but for the sake of simplicity suppose that a consistent representation of their state is made explicit within the system.

The state of the station devices is represented by relations that follow the syntax of Prolog structures. In more in detail: **<relation_name>(<name>, <state>, <reliability>)** describes station devices. In the structure above:

• <relation_name> identifies the kind of device: *ts* for track segments, *pn* for points and *sg* for signals.

•<name> is a Prolog constant representing a single identifier for the particular device.

•<state> represents the physical current state of the device. In particular <state> is:

> • *free/notfree* for track segments. A track segment is free if no train is covering it. In more detail, the state *free* denotes that nothing caused a short circuit between the two rails of the track segment.

> •*normal/reverse* for points. The state *normal* corresponds to a point in non-shunting position, the state *reverse* to a point in shunting position.

> •*green/red* for signals. A signal with state *green* allows a train to go on its way, while a *red* signal forces the train to stop.

• <reliability> can be *yes/no* to show whether the device is working correctly or not.

5. PLANNING AND RECOVERING

Planning and recovery functions have been implemented by using a blackboard architecture [4]. A parallel blackboard system has been implemented in Prolog [2] and used to determine, in parallel, the set of coverable routes (i.e. routes that, if commanded, will be used since no incompatibility exists). The planning and recovery functions performed by the ATP assistant are better explained in the flow-chart of figure 5.

5.1 The Blackboard System

The overall organization of the blackboard system is reported in figure 2, together with the ATP assistant basic functions. The basic building blocks are:

• Rule unit, where knowledge on planning and recovering is specified in order to determine the set of coverable routes when a modification occurs in the blackboard;

• Event unit, where the global, time-dependent state of the ATP system is represented. In the event unit both the ATP dynamic state, inserted by MONITORING, and the information on coverable routes -determined by using the knowledge in the rule unit- are represented. Moreover, the station-master himself can modify the content of the event unit, thus simulating some state changes in the ATP system. For example, he can require the system to determine the different routes from a position X to a position Y that can take place (coverable) or could take place if some exceptional actions were executed (conditioned coverable);

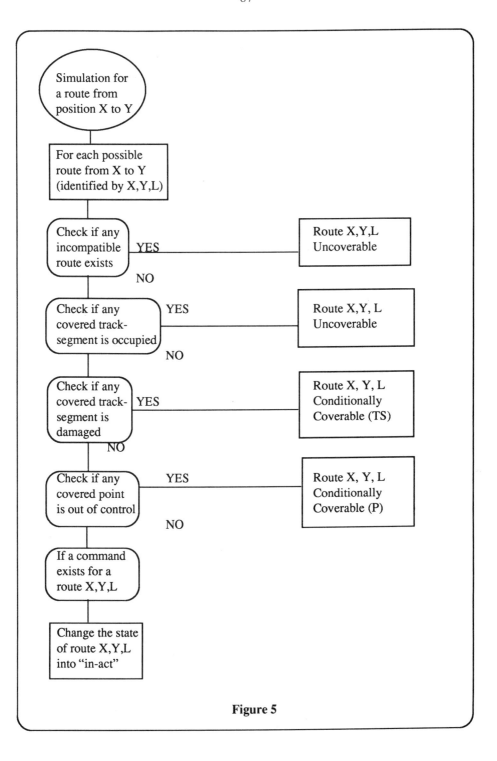

Figure 5

• Control unit (or Controller) that selects a set of actions to be executed in parallel on the basis of the rule and event units;

• Program unit, where additional knowledge on the problem domain is stored. In particular, constraints are inserted in the program unit.

Rules in the rule unit have the following syntax (identifiers starting with an uppercase character represent variables):

[<name>:] <condition> / <action>

where:

- <name> represents a unique identifier for the rule;
- <condition> is a conjunction of positive Prolog literals;
- <action> is the conjunction/disjunction of positive Prolog literals.

In particular, each literal in the <condition> part can be:

- an element matching one item of the event unit;
- a goal 'G' to be demonstrated by using the content of the program unit. This condition can be expressed as follows: ask(G), where 'G' follows the syntax of Prolog goals;
- the built-in operator: ?(<event>). This can appear only in the <condition> part of a rule R and it is successfully evaluated if <event> unifies with an item E in the event unit. The matching event is said to be consumable. Only if the rule instance that consumes event E is activated, E will be dropped from the event unit as a permanent side-effect.

The <action> part of a rule is constituted by an ordered collection of single actions that will be executed sequentially. When implementing the ATP assistant two different actions can be specified:

- an action toward the user, e.g. a print action;
- an action involving the built-in operator !(<event>). This operator can appear only in the <action> part of a rule and its effect is to change the content of the event unit with a new one constituted by the previous set of events plus the new <event>. This operator is used to dynamically change the event unit.

Starting from the state corresponding to the initial content of the event unit, at each step of execution a set of "non-interfering" rules is selected by the Controller, and some *processes* are activated within the system.

A process corresponds to the execution of the action part of a rule. At any time, not only many rules have conditions that match the content of the event unit, but also a single rule can have multiple possible instances (referred to as rule instances, from now on).

The maximum degree of parallelism is exploited by the Controller by activating the maximum number of rule instances.

In particular, at each cycle, the Controller finds all the rules that are satisfied by the current content of the event unit on the basis of their condition parts, i.e. all the possible rule instances. Then it selects the instances to be executed in parallel, adopting the following criteria:

1. All the rule instances activated in previous cycles are eliminated to prevent an infinite number of subsequent activations of processes performing the same actions;

2. Since each consumable event has to be consumed by at most one rule instance, a conflict set [8] is built and only one set of rule instances is selected from it.

The selection strategy used in the ATP assistant chooses the set of rule instances with greater rule cardinality (i.e. the greater number of conditions). In this way the most constrained rule instances have priority, since their probabilty of being satisfied in the following, is lower. Finally, the controller activates the action part of each selected rule instance after evaluation of the condition part.

Depending on the rule instances that are selected by the Controller (i.e. the action parts that are executed by processes), the content of the event unit may vary.

In particular, the content of the event unit varies when:

- Some literals of the ?(<event>) kind occur in the <condition> part of a rule instance selected for execution. If this is the case some events will be dropped from Event unit;
- Some operators of the !/1 kind are executed in the <action> part of a rule. If this is the case, some events will be added to the event unit;
- External events (i.e. changes in the state of station devices) coming from the environment. When a state modification occurs, some computations might be carried on in response to the changes in the event unit in order to modify the set of coverable routes.

5.2 Implementing planning and recovery

In order to implement planning and recovering, the following kinds of knowledge are stated and represented:

•The initial content of the event unit. We assume that the ATP assistant is activated when no route is in operation within the station, all the track-segments are free, signal lights are red, points are in normal position and no failure exists. The content of the event unit changes if the state of some devices changes or if the station-master requires execution of the planning and recovering functions for a route from a position X to Y;

• Knowledge to perform planning and recovery is given by rules, represented as condition/action pairs. In particular, a rule specifies a set of actions to be performed when its condition part matches the content of the event unit and/or some conditions are proved true. The set of rules -represented in the rule unit - determines the set of transformations that could take place on the event unit, i.e. the real or simulated trasformations that can take place in the ATP system;

• Constraints are additional knowledge on the problem domain, automatically produced by CP, and explicitly represented in the program unit.

Usually the initial content of the event unit and the content of the program unit change if station topology changes, while rules to perform planning and recovering do not.

Some rules to perform planning and recovery are reported in a simplified form in the appendix.

Note that for a given route <X,Y,L>, rules to determine whether it is coverable are activated sequentially. The parallelism of the blackboard model is, instead, exploited when the station-master requires the list of possible routes from position X to Y, or when it is necessary to determine the set of possible routes within the station, after any modification of the state of the ATP system.

CONCLUSIONS

This paper shows how the knowledge-based approach can be most suitable to build systems that improve railway station safety and reliability.
The application discussed is an assistant for real-time planning and recovery in ATP systems which, thanks to knowledge-based technology and the blackboard model, proved to be very flexible, modular and easy to maintain.
The main feature of the ATP assistant, from an architectural point of view, are:

1. *Uniformity* of the different parts of the system, since they are all built on top of Prolog [2];
2. *Generality*, since the ATP model is kept separate from the general knowledge on planning and recovery that holds for each ATP system;
3. *High integration* of the overall system, since all the parts of the system operate on the same ATP representation.

The system described in the paper is part of a broader project that aims to intensively apply Artificial Intelligence techniques to railway signalling. In particular, two different expert systems have already been successfully developed. The first, ADES [5], produces the ATP design, starting from a railway station topology. The second [6] is a simulator of the designed ATP system to test its correctness.
Up to now the new features introduced, i.e. planning and recovery, have been implemented in a prototypical way but we intend to integrate them within the two systems mentioned above. In more detail, the blackboard system that supports the ATP assistant has only been simulated on a mono-processor system, i.e. a SUN/3 workstation. It has been implemented by using an extended Prolog, called Communicating Prolog Units (CPU), supporting modularity and concurrency (see [7]).
Of course, we are aware that the ATP assistant here presented is only a starting point. In the near future we intend to refine and improve the ATP model as well as the rules for planning and recovery and to implement it in a real, parallel system.

Acknowledgements
The work here presented has been partially supported by SASIB S.p.a. and MPI 60%.

REFERENCES

[1] Hayes-Roth F., Waterman D. A., Lenat D. B., "Building Expert Systems", Addison Wesley, 1983.

[2] Clocksin W.F., Mellish C.S., "Programming in Prolog" Springer-Verlag, New-York, 1981.

[3] Cremonini R., Lamma E., Mello P., "ADES: An Exper t System for ATP Design", to be published in AIEDAM, Elsevier Science Pub.

[4] Nii H.P., "Blackboard Systems", AI Magazine, Vol. 7, No. 2, pp.38-53, No. 3, pp. 82-106, 1986.

[5] Cremonini R., Lamma E., Mello P., "Optimization Techniques in Building Expert Systems", in "Microprocessing and Microprogramming", Vol. 21, 531-538, North-Holland, 1987.

[6] Cremonini R., Lamma E., Mello P., "A Simulator for an Automatic Train Protection System", in "Proc. 1988 Eastern Simulation Conferences", Orlando, Florida, April 1988.

[7] Mello P., Natali A., "Programs as Collections of Communicating Prolog Units", in "Proc. European Symposium on Programming ESOP86", Saarbrucken, March 1986, and in LNCS, n. 213, Springer-Verlag.

[8] Brownston L., Farrell R., Kant E., Martin N., "Programming Expert Systems in OPS5", Addison-Wesley, 1985.

APPENDIX

Rule r0 applies if an <X,Y,L> route is in operation that is incompatible with a route <W,Z,K> defined as coverable. If this is the case, it is necessary to re-check the incompatibilities for <W,Z,K>. Let us note that rule r0 is in conflict with rule r10. The the selection strategy adopted ensures that for a given route <W,Z,K> r0 is selected.

```
r0:    route(X,Y,L,in-act),
          ?(route(W,Z,K,coverable)),
          ask(incompatible(X,Y,L,W,Z,K)) /
                    !(check-incompatibilities(W,Z,K))
```

Rule r1 applies if there exists a route <X,Y,L> not in operation that is incompatible with a route <W,Z,K> defined as not coverable. If this is the case, it is necessary to re-check the incompatibilities for <W,Z,K>, since might now be coverable.

```
r1:    route(X,Y,L,not-in-act),
          ?(route(W,Z,K,not-coverable)),
          ask(incompatible(X,Y,L,W,Z,K)) /
                    !(check-incompatibilities(W,Z,K))
```

To check incompatibilities for a given route, consider rules r2-r9.
Rule r2 tests if some incompatible route is in operation.
If this is not the case, r2 will not be activated and the less specific rule r3 will be selected.

```
r2:    ?(check-incompatibilities(X,Y,L)),
          ask(incompatible(X,Y,L,W,Z,K)),
          route(W,Z,K,in-act) /
                    !(route(X,Y,L,not-coverable))
```

Rule r3 simply starts the check of the freedom of covered track-segments.

```
r3:    ?(check-incompatibilities(X,Y,L)) /  !(check-freedom-tracks(X,Y,L))
```

Rule r4 tests the existence of some occupied track-segment covered by the route. If this is the case, the route is considered not coverable. Otherwise, the less specific rule r5 is selected.

```
r4:    ?(check-freedom-tracks(X,Y,L)),
          ask(db(covered_track_segment(X,Y,L,C))),
          ts(C,notfree,_) /
                    !(route(X,Y,L,not-coverable))
```

If no covered track-segment is occupied, the reliability of the station devices (track-segments and points) is checked (rule r5 and r7).

```
r5:    ?(check-freedom-tracks(X,Y,L)) /
                    !(check-reliability-tracks(X,Y,L))
```

Rule r6 tests the existence of some damaged track-segment, TS, covered by the route. If this is the case, the route is considered not coverable due to track-segment TS. Otherwise, the less specific rule r7 is selected.

r6:   ?(check-reliability-tracks(X,Y,L)),
         ask(db(covered_track_segment(X,Y,L,TS))),
         ts(TS,_,no) /
                  !(route(X,Y,L,not-coverable-Ts(TS)))

r7:   ?(check-reliability-tracks(X,Y,L)),
                  !(check-reliability-points(X,Y,L))

Rule r8 tests the existence of some damaged point, P, covered by the route. If this is the case, the route is considered not coverable due to point P. Otherwise, the less specific rule r9 is selected.

r8:   ?(check-reliability-points(X,Y,L)),
         ask(db(normal_covered_point(X,Y,L,P))),
         pn(P,_,no) /
                  !(route(X,Y,L,not-coverable-Pn(P)))

If all the previous tests succeeded, the route is defined coverable (rule r9).

r9:   ?(check-reliability-points(X,Y,L)) /
                  !(route(X,Y,L,coverable)),

A coverable route can be commanded by the station-master, becoming a route in operation (rule r10). To this end, the station-master explicitly inserts in the event unit one of the command/3 kind.

r10:   ?(route(X,Y,L,coverable)),
         ?(command(X,Y,L)) /
                  !(route(X,Y,L,in-act))

A coverable route can change into non-coverable if some covered track-segments or points are damaged (rule r11 and r12).

r11:   ?(route(X,Y,L,coverable)),
         ask(db(covered_track_segment(X,Y,L,TS))),
         ts(TS,_,no) /
                  !(route(X,Y,L,not-coverable-Ts(TS)))

r12:   ?(route(X,Y,L,coverable)),
         ask(db(normal_covered_point(X,Y,L,P))),
         pn(P,_,no) /
                  !(route(X,Y,L,not-coverable-Pn(P)))

A route defined not coverable due to some track segment TS (rule r13) or some point P (rule r14), can be commanded only if an exceptional action related to TS or P has been executed. Forthis purpose, the station-master explicitly inserts in the event unit one of the command/3 kind , and an event of the exceptional-action-Ts/1 or exceptional-action-P/1 kind.

```
r13:  ?(route(X,Y,L,not-coverable-Ts(TS))),
         ?(exceptional-action-Ts(TS)),
         ?(command(X,Y,L)) /
                        !(route(X,Y,L,in-act))
```

```
r14:  ?(route(X,Y,L,not-coverable-Pn(P))),
         ?(exceptional-action-Pn(P)),
         ?(command(X,Y,L)) /
                        !(route(X,Y,L,in-act))
```

If the state of a covered track-segment for a route <X,Y,L> changes free, then it is necessary to re-test the incompatibility conditions for the route.

```
r15:  ?(route(X,Y,L,not-coverable)),
         ask(db(covered_track_segment(X,Y,L,C))),
         ts(C,free,_) /
                    !(check-incompatibilities(X,Y,L))
```

To modify the state of a route in operation, after the train has completely covered it, the station-master explicitly inserts an event of the release/3 kind in the event unit (rule 16). For the released route, the incompatibility check is required (rule r17).

```
r16:  ?(route(X,Y,L,in-act)),
         ?(release(X,Y,L)) /
                        !(route(X,Y,L,not-in-act))
```

```
r17:  ?(route(X,Y,L,not-in-act)) /
                    !(check-incompatibilities(X,Y,L))
```

At each cycle, the list of all the coverable routes is printed (rule 18), together with the list of routes that could be commanded by executing exceptional actions (rule 19 and 20).

```
r18:  route(X,Y,L,coverable) /
             print(X,Y,L,coverable)
```

```
r19:  route(X,Y,L,not-coverable-Ts(TS)) /
             print(X,Y,L,not-coverable-Ts(TS))
```

```
r20:  route(X,Y,L,not-coverable-P(P)) /
             print(X,Y,L,not-coverable-P(P))
```

SAFETY AND RELIABILITY ANALYSIS OF THE HERMES CREW ESCAPE MODULE

Ian Jenkins, BSc.
MBB GmbH Space Communications and Propulsion Division,
Munich, Federal Republic of Germany

SYNOPSIS

The HERMES Spaceplane is a manned Space Transportation System with very high safety risks for the crew during certain missions phase. The need for a crew escape and rescue capability has become a firm requirement in the HERMES System Requirements Document.

MBB is contracted to investigate the feasability of a Crew Escape Module. In this contract, the technical feasability of the system is studied, and is supported by detailed Safety and Reliability Analysis.

In this paper, the author summarizes the specifications and design of the Crew Escape Module (CEM). The spaceplane Safety and Reliability requirements and their deriviation for CEM will be described. The use and experience of the Prime Contractor developed computerization tool "SARA-H" Safety and Reliability Analysis-Hermes will be discussed.

Historical Perspective

The requirement for a crew escape and rescue system was implemented into the HERMES system requirement after extensive review by the European Space Agency following the Space Shuttle Challenger accident.

The idea for a rescue system is not new. Ships are routinely provided with life boats and life rafts. According to a recent article in MBBs "New Tech News" (1) patents for aircraft rescue facilities were applied for as early as 1913 (Figure 1).

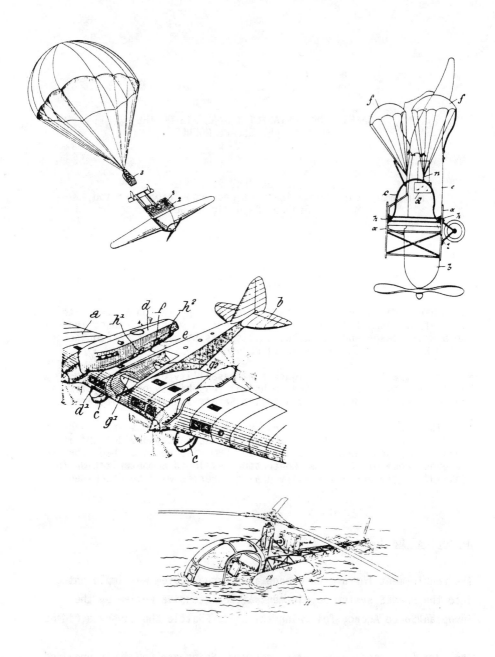

FIGURE 1: Historical Escape and Rescue Concepts (Ref. 1)

Some very interesting ideas are evident in this picture: A separable cabin, descent parachutes and floatation devices are to be seen. Apparently flying was seen as a risky business then!

In order to present this paper at SARSS89, the author had to board a plane in Munich and fly to the UK. The aircraft is provided with emergency exits, and life jackets etc. to ensure survival in case the aircraft lands on water. There is however, no facility for passengers or crew to escape the aircraft in air. It is normally assumed that sufficient time is available in an emergency situation for the pilot to take corrective action. Whether such an escape system would be desirable from a passenger acceptance point of view can be questioned, however commercial aviation can be regarded as adequately safe and the need cannot be justified.

If a comparison is made to military aircraft (Table 1), it can be seen that the safety risk is significantly higher. Ejection systems are therefore provided for many military aircraft to reduce the risk of fatality. Typically, ejection seats have been used, and in some instances an escape module (for example F111,an aircraft escape module for which considerable flight experience has been accumulated).

A review of Janes Manned Spaceflight Log (Ref 2) shows, that for 128 manned space flights up to 1986, 5 mishaps involving fatality have occured (all flights, worldwide). Thus, manned spaceflights can be seen as a high risk venture. The Challenger accident demonstrates that statistically, space transportation systems have the same order of risk magnitude as previous space missions. Early American space missions, up to the Space Shuttle prototypes, and all Soviet missions have had crew escape systems, at least for the launch phase. The Soviet Union has demonstrated 2 successful escape during launch phases.

For the HERMES a Safety risk of 10^{-3}/mission for fatality has been specified. This extremely optimistic goal is only achievable with a crew escape and rescue system. The contract with MBB, which was placed in 1988, was to study the feasability of a minimum Crew Escape Module (CEM Type B) which is a capsule ejected from the topside of the HERMES Space Plane.

TABLE 1 Comparative Risk Levels and   Accident Consequences

TRANSPORT SYSTEM	FATALITY RATE	ACCIDENT CONSEQUENCE		
		FATALITY	FINANCIAL	PUBLIC CONCERN
JET AIRLINE	2/1 000 000 departures	VERY HIGH	VERY HIGH	HIGH-VERY HIGH
MILITARY AIRCRAFT	5/ 100000hrs	LOW (2/3)	HIGH	LOW-MEDIUM
MANNED SPACE FLIGHT	4/ 100 FLIGHTS	MEDIUM -LOW (3-7)	EXTREMELY HIGH	EXTREMELY HIGH

(References: 2,5,6,7)

TABLE 2 : CEM Key Performance Data

Operating Domain

Launch:
Time   t   seconds =   (Launch Ho - 10s)   to (Ho + 120s)
Altitude h   meters =   < 55 000 m
Velocity V   Mach   =   < 6.5

Reentry:
Time   t   seconds =   (Touch Down Ti - 720s) to (Ti - 165s)
Altitude h   meters =   45 000 to 550 m
Velocity V   mach   =   < 3

Escape and Rescue

Escape from launcher   =   200 m in 3 s

Pressure wave   =   200 hPa at 200m

Thermal Flux   =   1.5W/cm^2 for 20 s at 1000m

Landing distance   =   > 1000m from launcher
                            in defined direction

Landing velocity   =   10m/s on ground or water

Waiting time for rescue =   24 hours

In March 89, a major change was introduced to investigate the type A module which is described later. The basic reason for this change was to reduce the overall HERMES mass. An alternative escape system, the encapsulated ejection seat, is not part of MBBs contract.

System Description

The HERMES spaceplane, with Crew Escape Module is shown in Figure 2. The CEM is required to provide the safeguard functions during Ariane 5 and spaceplane launch, and for reentry. Typical scenarios which require CEM use are explosion or fire at or shortly after launch, non ignition of boosters and degradation of performance.

Within its operational field, the CEM must, within physiological limits for crew survival:-
- rapidly separate from the spaceplane
- stabilize in near vacuum and aerodynamically
- descend, and land on water or ground in a controlled manner
- provide life support for the crew and localisation of the module while waiting for rescue.

Key Performance Data is shown in Table 2.

The CEM consists of:
Rescue Assembly (CEMRA), with following subassemblies:

- Electrical Assembly (CEMES), consisting of
    o   Lithium Batteries
    o   Computer
    o   Sensors
    o   Actuators for Pyrotechnics and Boosters, etc
    o   Transmission and Localisation Devices

    The CEMES provides all the ectrical and electronic control functions for CEM operations.

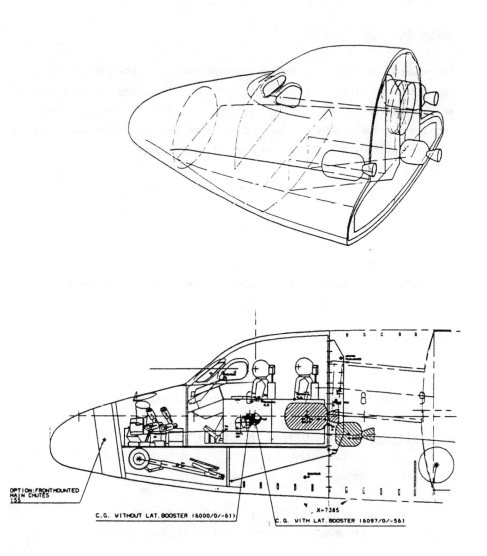

FIGURE 2:   The HERMES Crew Escape Module

- <u>Cabin Extraction Assembly (CEA) with</u>
    2 lateral solid rocket boosters for the launch phase

    escape.These boosters must be ejected from the spaceplane after
    the launch vehicle Ariane 5 solid boosters are depleted.
    1 solid booster for the reentry phase escape.

- <u>Control Assembly (CONA)</u>:
    o   Thrust Control Actuators (Bipropellant Thrusters)
    o   Aerodynamic Control Surfaces
- <u>Descent, Impact, Floatation Assembly (DIFA)</u>
    o   Drogue, and Main Parachutes
    o   Impact Damping assembly,consisting of:
            Retro rockets, with earth proximity sensing devices
            or Crushable structure, or airbags
    o   Floatation and bouyancy devices

<u>Structure</u>, with thermal protection (as part of the spaceplane fuselage)
<u>Pyrotechnical</u> cabin separation (external to CEM)

<u>Reliability and Safety Analysis</u>

Obviously, it is hoped that the CEM may never be used, and if it is
used, then it can be used only once.This use must be both reliable and
safe. There is no valid statistical test verification of reliability
possible in the cost and schedule constraints, therefore emphasis must
be placed on analytical verification. Requirements are derived from
system requirements defined by the European Space agency (ESA) and the
French National Space Centre (CNES) (References 3, 4). These requirements are both qualitative and quantitative in nature.

The requirements differentiate between:-
- Reliability (e.g. mission interrupt) and
- Safety (the potential for death, disabling injury, or loss of
    spaceplane/facilities).

The qualitative requirement provides (Table 3):
- classification of failure condition into 4 categories

TABLE 3 FAILURE TOLERANCE CRITERIA

CRITERION	SPACEPLANE REQUIREMENT	IMPLICATIONS FOR CEM
FAIL OPERATIONAL	NO SINGLE FAILURE SHALL CAUSE MAJOR CONSEQUENCE	o APPLIES DIRECTLY FOR CEM o INDEPENDANCE FOR SP FUNCTIONS o IN FLIGHT CHECK OUT REQUIREMENT?
FAIL SAFE	o NO SINGLE FAILURE SHALL CAUSE HAZARDOUS OR CATASTROPHIC CONSEQUENCES o FAIL SAFE CRITERION SHALL APPLY AFTER FAIL OPERATION o EXCEPTIONS ARE "DESIGN FOR MINIMUM RISK AREAS" (PRESSURE VEŞSEL; STRUCTURE etc.) FOR WHICH SPECIFIC DESIGN RULEŞ APPLY	o INHIBITS FOR INADVERTANT OPERATION, BOTH WITHIN AND OUTSIDE OF OPERATING DOMAIN o CEM PROVIDES SAFEGUARD FUNCTION FOR HERMES. THERE-FORE A NON REDUNDANT SYSTEM MEETS REQUIREMENTS o REDUNDANCY TO BE CONSIDERED ONLY IF PROBALISTIC TARGETS NOT ACHIEVED

SEE TABLE 4 FOR DEFINITION OF MAJOR, HAZARDOUS AND CATASTROPHIC CONSEQUENCES

TABLE 4 DERIVIATION OF SAFETY AND RELIABILITY QUANTITATIVE OBJECTIVES

CATEGORY	CONSEQUENCE	CLASSIFICATION	OBJECTIVE / MISSION FAILURE PROBABILITY			
			AS + HERMES COMPOSITE	SPACE-PLANE	FAILURE CONDITION	CEM
RELIABILITY	MISSION INTERRUPT	MAJOR	2.10^{-2}	10^{-2}	10^{-4}	----
SAFETY	DESTRUCTION OF - SPACEPLANE - GROUND FACILITIES DISABLING INJURY	HAZARDOUS	10^{-3}	10^{-3}	10^{-5}	5.10^{-2}
	FATALITY	CATASTROPHIC	5.10^{-4}	10^{-4}	10^{-6}	

EACH CEM FAILURE PROBABILITY, FOR OPERATION WHEN REQUIRED

- development of failure tolerance criteria. Failure tolerance
  requirement apply independently of any probability considerations.

The CEM provides the crew safeguard function for the HERMES System in
the case of catastrophic events during launch and reentry. During other
mission phases,it has been determined that the spaceplane can sustain
failures and still provide crew safety. The Spaceplane Fail Safe
requirements state that no single failure in the spaceplane shall have
the potential for death.Thus, for the CEM, the implications of this
are, that a simplex (non redundant) system is adequate. (for the safety
specialist this means trying to convince engineers to reduce the amount
of redundancy!).

Inadvertant CEM operation is classified " hazardous " (i.e. loss of
spaceplane), if it occured inside its intended operational domain and
"catastrophic" (i.e. loss of life) outside of this field. No single
failure is allowed to cause this event. Indepentant inhibits must
preventinadvertant operation. This has design implications to cover
human error possiblities; to cover the possibility of inhibit removal
during in orbit testing and to ensure that the computer does not
control all inhibits.

In the normal spaceplane operations, the lateral booster must be
ejected. If this does not occur,then the mission is interrupted, and
a safe return to earth may be precluded.Thus redundancy must be
provided to meet the Fail Operational/Fail Safe criteria.

Derivation of quantitative reliability and safety goals is shown in
Table 4. The HERMES can only achieve it safety target when the CEM is
apportioned a reliability target of .95/rescue mission, as is
illustrated by Figure 3.

In an intial step of analysis, this reliability (failure probability)
was apportioned to the different assemblies, as shown in Table 5. Each
subcontractor has to perform analyses on his design in accordance with
ESA standards to verify whether this goal is achievable. At time of
writing, results are not available. The best available data indicates

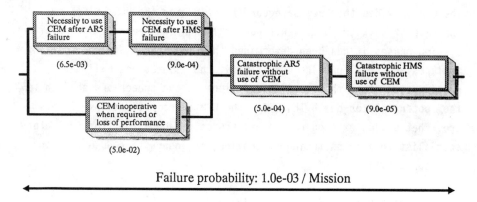

Spaceplanc with Ariane 5

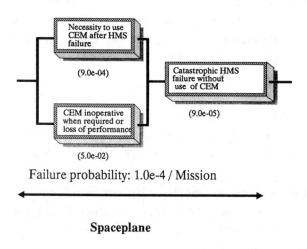

Spaceplane

Fig. 3: CEM Reliability Diagram

TABLE 5: CEM Failure Probability apportionments

Subsystem	Failure Probability / Apportionment	Rescue Mission Current Best Estimate	Notes Source
Total CEM	5.10^{-2}	5.10^{-2}	
Cabin Extraction Assembly (CEA)	1.10^{-2}	2.10^{-2}	Subcontractor Data
Electrical Assembly (CEMES), incl. SW	2.10^{-2}	1.10^{-2}	Subcontractor Data Phase B3, Part Redundant Configuration
Control Assembly (CONA)	1.10^{-2}	1.10^{-2}	Trade-Off
Descent, impact floatation Assembly (DIFA)	5.10^{-3}	$< 1.10^{-2}$	Estimate For a passive impact system
Structure, Aerodynamic, Thermal	Negligable	--	
External Functions (Commands , Pyro etc.)		--	Provided by Prime

TABLE 6: Typical Safety Risk introduced by CEM

Assembly	Equipment	Hazards	Remarks
Cabin Extraction Assembly(CEA)	Solid Boosters	Explosion,burst fire,corrosion,toxicity Inadvertent operation	Challenger !
Eletrical System (CEMES)	Lithium Battery	Explosion,burst fire,corrosion,toxicity chemical reactions	To be qualified at Spaceplane level
Control Assembly (CONA)	Pressurized system	Explosion,burst	Similarity to devices in Propulsion system
	Bipropellent	Explosion,burst fire,corrosion,toxicity	Similarity to devices in Propulsion system
	Pyrotechnics	Explosion,burst fire,corrosion,toxicity Inadvertent operation	Spaceplane qualification
Descent,Impact, Floation Assembly (DIFA)	Pressure system	Explosion,burst	
	Pyrotechnics	Explosion,burst fire,corrosion,toxicity Inadvertent operation	

that the Cabin Extraction Assembly and the Descent,Impact, Floatation
Assembly are critical for achieving this goal.Much better mission
profile and failure rate data base is needed to verify the data. Update
of this data can be expected in Autumn 1989.

Safety and Reliability trade offs have been performed in 3 areas in
support of design engineering:
- Studies of simplex, fully and partially redundant CEMES show that a
  non redundant design fulfill the mission success criteria, but
  separate arming and firing units are required to prevent inadverant
  operation.

- Comparison of 4 x 400 Newton or 18 x 20 Newton bipropellant
  thrusters. The trade off was performed 2 times using different data
  sets for mission profile and failure rate data. It was determined
  that the theoretical reliability results are dependant on the
  assumptions made, and it was concluded that for the purposes of
  study no significant difference was evident. Either version can be
  implemented within the allocated Reliability/Safety goal.

- Comparison of the Impact Damping alternatives (Retro-Rocket Airbag,
  Crushable Structure). Results of this analysis show that the
  crushable structure is preferable, since it represents the least
  complex design regarding active functions, and therefore the highest
  reliability is achieved.

The CEM, due to the fact that it has active systems, adds hazard risk
to the spaceplane. A summary of some of these hazards is shown in
Table 6.

One of the areas of technological importance is the aerodynamic
response of the cabin in the rescue mode. A software tool adapted from
supersonic aircraft simulations, is used to develop the hull shape.
This is then verified by wind tunnel tests. In some instances it is not
possible to simulate all the responses by test, especially the higher
mach numbers. In order to reduce the safety risk due to non test
verified software, MBB requires a full Software Product Assurance
program on this simulation tool in order to reduce risk. This includes

verification, validation and configuration control of the software. Currently these are no requirements for quantification of risk in this area.

Analysis Methodology

The methodology for Safety and Reliability Analysis was reported by Heckmann in Straβbourg, 1988 (Ref. 5). The basic methodology which is derived from that used on the Airbus, has been computerized for HERMES on software called SARA-H (Safety and Reliability Analysis-HERMES).The methodology is a considerable change from that normally required by the European Space Agency (ESA).

The prime contractor requires the use of this software for the HERMES/CEM project, and preliminary software was installed at MBB in December 1988. In order to ensure that subcontractors perform Safety and reliability analysis in an adequate manner, they have been requested to perform these in accordance with ESA standards. Conversion to the prime contractor formats is to be performed by MBB. An initial evaluation of the SARA-H software tool has been made and comments provided to the customer. Final software is planned to be installed in 1989.

The program currently requires manual entry of data, and has a large number of input screens and pages. This means that the capability of the program cannot be fully exploited during the current project phase. It has to be established how the results of the standard ESA analysis methodologies, as performed by subcontractors, can be efficiently translated to this new programme.

Conclusions

An acceptable risk level for HERMES spaceplane crew is only possible with the use of a crew escape system. Quantification of risk is only possible analytically. Verification of the CEM Probability of success has to be performed. The analytical computerization tools for safety and reliability analysis are under evaluation during this phase.

Acknowledgements

Extract from MBB New Tech News used with permission.
The author would like to thank both MBB and Aerospatiale for permission
to present the data in this paper. The opinions addressed are those of
the author only.

References

(1)   New Tech News, 1989, MBB Munich

(2)   Janes Manned Spaceflight Log 1986

(3)   HERMES System Requirements Document (ESA-RQ-HERMES-1, Draft,
       25 March 88)

(4)   Specification System HERMES (H-ST-0-10-CNE) Iss. 2, Oct. 87

(5)   Heckmann
       Objective Methods and Computerization Tools to handle Safety
       and Reliability Risks in the HERMES program.
       6th International Conference on Reliability and Maintainabili-
       ty, Strasbourg 1988.

(6)   Aviation Week and Space Technology/ May 29,1989

(7)   Macidull, Safety Awareness Continuity in Transportation and
       Space Systems,Brighton 87, IAA-87-568

A Study of Severe Air Crash Environments with Particular Reference to the Carriage of Radioactive Materials by Air

by

H L Wilkinson, PhD, GRSC
Safety and Reliability Directorate, UKAEA, Culcheth

SYNOPSIS

The regulations governing the transport of nuclear materials are based on the IAEA Regulations for the Safe Transport of Radioactive Material. A major feature of these regulations is that the principal protection against the hazards of the radioactive material should be provided by the packaging. To ensure this the IAEA have specified a series of tests for the certification of packages. The most severe tests are designed to demonstrate the ability of a package to withstand, essentially intact, severe accident conditions. Recent assessments suggest that the IAEA regulations give protection in a very high percentage (over 99% for example) of expected road accidents. However, during air transport, package impact speeds could be an order of magnitude greater than during other transport modes. Hence, current IAEA accident condition tests may not provide such a high level of confidence in the package surviving an air crash. It has therefore been suggested that additional tests should be specified for packages intended to transport significant quantities of activity by air.

This paper reports a piece of work undertaken recently by SRD to provide material for discussions on the transport of radioactive materials by air and in particular on the formulation of fireball and sequential impact and fire tests. It comprises a search of aircraft accident reports for data relating to the occurrence, temperature and duration of fireballs, and the duration and temperature of fires following a severe impact. A qualitative analysis of the data obtained is also presented.

The study concentrated on a small sample of aircraft accidents during the years 1975 and 1985 inclusive, that fulfilled the following criteria:

Aircraft accident reports for the incident were readily available.

The aircraft involved had a maximum take-off weight of about 20 tonnes or greater.

At least one fatality among passengers or crew and/or destruction of the aircraft had occurred.

Only crashes fulfilling these latter criteria were believed to have the potential to damage a robust package significantly.

No attempt was made to quantify the impact parameters such as impact forces, fire temperature and fire intensity. Instead, the incidents were classified qualitatively into broad categories by examining the type and extent of damage done to the aircraft and persons involved in the crash.

Out of a total of 31 accidents, 12 involving a fireball, flash-fire or explosion were identified. Ten accidents were identified in which the crash environment was considered to be of such severity that the possibility of a package being breached must be considered. Six of these involved high impact forces, four involved large ripping or tearing forces in conjunction with a considerable fire. One extremely severe and prolonged fire (36 hours) was reported; the impact forces associated with it were negligible. The majority of the accidents occurred on, or close to, an airfield; however, fire fighting forces did not always find extinguishing fires straightforward.

From this limited study the following tentative conclusions were drawn.

A proposed fireball test is not supported; in general a fireball is followed by a ground fire with potential to cause much greater damage.

Very high impact forces are not reported in association with fires of greater than 30 minutes' duration. However, two incidents were identified in which considerable ripping or tearing forces were experienced followed by long fires (9 hours and 49 minutes). This type of scenario deserves more detailed consideration.

The possibility that an undamaged package may be subjected to a very prolonged engulfing fire does exist; however, the probability of this occurring will be very small.

Introduction

New tests for packages designed for the transportation of significant quantities of radioactive materials by air have been recently proposed. The USA[1] have implemented tests specifically for the transport of plutonium which are particularly severe, being intended to ensure survival of a package in 100% of all possible air crashes. In view of the difficulty in defining exactly the conditions a package may experience in an air crash and of the very low probability of a package being involved in an air crash, a basis for a series of tests that lie somewhere between the American regulations and the current IAEA regulations has been proposed. This makes the assumption that a very severe impact, in which considerable forces are transferred to the package, will not be followed by a prolonged fire. This follows from the hypothesis that such an impact will lead to a rapid dispersion of fuel over a large area. The impact velocity has been chosen such that it yields the same level of confidence in a package surviving an air crash impact as the current tests provide for road transport. The possibility that a fireball may occur is recognised and a fireball test included in the proposals.

The following fire tests are suggested:

An 800 °C fire for one hour on an undamaged package.

A high temperature, short duration "fireball" test.

An impact velocity of 90 m/s is suggested for a drop test.

These tests are in addition to the current IAEA tests which specify a fire test of a 30 minute, fully engulfing, 800 °C hydrocarbon fire following a 13 m/s impact on to a rigid target (or a dynamic crush test for packages less than 500 kg) and a 1 m drop on to a punch[2].

This scheme does not consider scenarios in which the package undergoes either:

i) some form of considerable tearing or puncturing impact, more severe than the IAEA test, and is then engulfed by fire, or

ii) a high velocity impact followed by a fire.

This paper presents the results of a search of aircraft accident reports for data relating to the type of severe environments a package may encounter in a crash.

Impacts that may Threaten the Integrity of a Transport Package
_____

Only accidents that lead to the destruction of an aircraft and generally at least one fatality have the potential to breach a robust radioactive materials' transport package carried in the hold of the aircraft. Only aircraft of about 20 tonne take-off weight or greater will carry these packages.

In order to obtain details on the type of impact forces and fire environments that a package in a serious accident might experience, the Aircraft Accident (AA) Summaries published by the Civil Aviation Authority were examined for accidents occurring over an 11 year period (1975-1985 inclusive) that fulfilled the criteria given above and for which Accident Investigation branch (AIB) AA reports or National Transportation Safety Board AA reports were available. The AIB reports are published by HMSO and the NTSB AA reports are published by the Accidents Investigation Bureau of the United States Government. Crashes involving planes with only a few personnel on board who managed to escape before the planes were destroyed by fire were included although there were no associated fatalities.

In total 31 incidents were identified, 24 in NTSB reports and 7 in AIB reports (table 1). Details relevant to the impact and fire environments experienced in each accident have been recorded on a standard data sheet, an example of which is given in figure 1.

The reports record all data pertinent to the cause of the crash in detail; however, the consequences are generally recorded in much less detail. Even where quantitative data, such as the velocity of the aircraft immediately prior to impact, is available from flight recorder information, it is difficult to obtain from this the magnidude of the impact forces on the package because of uncertainty about the nature of the impact surface, the exact impact angle and the energy absorbing effect of the aircraft fuselage. A certain amount of judgement is therefore required to extract data from the information given.

Preliminary Analysis

The reports were examined for data relating to the following:

The duration and temperature of any fireball, flash-fire or explosion.

The duration, temperature and intensity of any post crash fire.

Table 1

Serious Aircraft Crashes Identified from the Aircraft Accident
Summaries

Report no	Date	Aircraft	Data Base no
NTSB-AAR-86-01	21:01:85	L188	20
85-03	11:10:83	HS748	1
85-04	30:05:84	L188	9
85-06	23:01:82	DC10-30	23
84-09	02:06:83	DC9	10
83-02	09:07:82	B727	8
83-05	03:01:83	CL-600	6
83-07	11:01:83	DC8	2
81-07	21:11:80	B727	7
81-12	17:02:81	B737	17
81-13	11:02:81	JETSTAR	21
80-09	14:09:79	DC7	19
80-11	18:11:79	L188	16
80-14	22:06:80	L-1049H	14
79-07	28:12:78	DC8	5
79-17	25:05:79	DC10-10	22
78-03	04:04:77	DC9	15
78-08	18:12:77	DC8	18
77-01	27:04:76	B727	24
76-01	30:08:75	F-27	11
76-08	24:06:73	B727	13
76-17	08:02:76	DC6	4
76-19	12:11:75	DC10-30	3
76-20	05:04:76	B727	12
AIB-AAR-2/86	19:08:84	Vickers Varsity	30
1/81	31:07:79	HS 748	25
3/81	16:02:80	Bristol Britannia	27
8/81	25:04:80	B727	28
8/80	02:09:77	CL44-D4	29
9/78	14:05:77	B707-321C	31
6/78	17:03:77	B707-436	26

Figure 1

Example sheet from the Serious Aircraft Accident Database

REPORT NO. - NTSB-AAR-76-8

AIRCRAFT -   B 727-225   DATE - 24 June, 1975

PHASE OF FLIGHT - A (*approach*)

AIRCRAFT WEIGHT - 63 t   C o G - within limits

DESCRIPTION OF INCIDENT - The aircraft crashed into the approach lights
of the runway as it came in to land, it caught fire and came to rest on
a road.

FLIGHT-RECORDER INFORMATION

      AIRSPEED -   125 knots   VERTICAL ACC -

      ALTITUDE -   AT - first impact

IMPACT VELOCITY - 125 knots first impact with approach lights

IMPACT SURFACE - steel non-frangible light towers, earth, large boulders

IMPACT ANGLE - 4.5 deg to ground from   ROLL - over 90 deg left
               first tower   wing down

DISTRIBUTION OF WRECKAGE/FUEL - Wreckage was spread from the first tower
struck to the road. Fuel was first spilt when the aircraft first struck
the ground seriously damaging the left wing.

FIRE ? - YES   FIRE DURATION - 7 minutes

DESCRIPTION OF FIRE - Fire erupted after the left wing failed and
released fuel as the aircraft skidded through the approach towers.
Destruction of the fuselage caused more fuel to be released and the fire
continued to burn after the aircraft came to rest. Firemen reached the
scene in about 2 minutes, brought the fire under control in 2 minutes
and extinguished it 3 minutes later. Small fires were extinguished with
portable fire extinguishers. The prompt response of the firemen saved
the people who survived in the aft section from receiving fatal burns.

DESCRIPTION OF DAMAGE TO FUSELAGE - The fuselage collapsed and
disintegrated due to the effects of the approach towers and large
boulders. Seats were torn from there supporting structures, mangled and
twisted. One engine was severely damaged by the impact. The rear part of
the passenger cabin and the empennage remained relatively intact. Both
flight recorders were recovered intact.

COMMENTS -

The severity of direct impact force and any ripping or tearing forces particularly at the aft of the aircraft where radioactive materials' containers will usually be carried.

The following preliminary observations were made:

The aft fuselage generally experiences much less damage due to impact than the forward fuselage; in the majority of cases studied it was the forward fuselage that impacted the ground, trees or other structure first and hence this area absorbed much of the impact damage. In many cases the aft pressure bulkhead and the tail assembly survived intact.

Two incidents in which the aircraft broke up in mid air were recorded; in this type of incident much of the impact energy may be experienced by the package.

The majority of the accidents occurred on or close to an airfield; however, fire fighting forces did not always find extinguishing the fire or access to the aircraft straightforward.

In many of the fires reported, material other than the aviation fuel was also involved, ie. construction materials such as aluminium and cargo. Burning of such materials can cause local temperatures to vary considerably from those predicted from hydrocarbon burning, for instance, aluminium can burn with a flame temperature of 2815 °C.

One incident involved an aircraft carrying radioactive materials; the cargo included a consignment of Americium-241. About 1 hour after the impact, by which time the initial large fire had been knocked down and the search for survivors had been completed, the officer in charge was informed of the cargo. He immediately pulled out his men until material and dose rate information became available. Fire fighting resumed 20 minutes later.

Fireballs and Explosions

Fireballs, flash fires or explosions were reported on 11 occasions; on only one of these was the duration indicated, an eyewitness observation setting this at 3 - 4 seconds. On 9 out of the 11 occasions the fireball was followed by a ground fire; hence, it was virtually impossible to assess what damage was caused by the fireball alone. The 3 - 4 second fireball was not followed by a ground fire; the only damage recorded was scorching of paper and card. The second fireball with which no subsequent ground fire was associated, was observed inflight just before the aircraft plunged into the ocean. The only other information available was from a stewardess, who reported seeing a flash-fire moving along the ceiling of the passenger cabin and setting passengers alight.

Fire and Impact Analysis

A preliminary, highly qualitative analysis of the data collected so far has been carried out. The severity of fire, direct impact forces and ripping/tearing forces has been assessed on the basis of damage caused to personnel and to the aircraft and classified as **Severe**, **Significant**, **Minor** or **Negligible** (table 2). In particular, damage to the aft fuselage was assessed, where possible, as this is where large packages of radioactive materials would generally be carried. The basic criteria employed in the classification are listed in table 3; where there was insufficient information in the report to assign definitely an incident using these criteria, judgement based on the available information was used. Hence, the classifications are highly subjective and extreme caution should be used in any attempt to quantify them.

Two diagrams were developed (figure 2) in which fire severity was plotted against the severity of direct impact forces and ripping/tearing forces. The significance of the hatched areas is described below;

   CE-I - indicates a relatively mild crash environment in which (in the judgement of the author) the integrity of a robust package stored in the aft of the aircraft would not be compromised by the relevant forces (ie. figure 2a direct impact forces, figure 2b ripping and tearing forces).

   CE-II - indicates a severe crash environment, with respect to the relevant forces, which a robust package will probably survive but in which there exists an element of doubt.

   CE-III - indicates a very severe crash environment in which the possibility of a package being breached should be considered.

Hence, the diagrams allow the severity of the **total crash environment (CE)**, to be determined (in terms of the 3 broad categories defined above) and, therefore, the rapid identification of aircraft accidents that warrant further investigation.

The diagrams indicate that the majority of **Severe** fires were associated with **Minor** or **Significant** impacts; none were associated with **Severe** impacts. Ten incidents were identified as having particularly severe CE-III crash environments.

Six of the CE-III incidents involved large direct impact forces. Two were caused by the aircraft breaking up in flight, with wreckage consequently falling from a considerable height and impacting at high velocity. Under these conditions it is believed that ground fire generally need not be considered; however, one impact was followed by a

Table 2

Classification of Aircraft Accidents

No of Report	Phase a	Impact Angle	Impact b Surface	Direct Impact	Ripping/ Tearing	Fire	Fireball noted ?	Fire length
85-03	L	shallow	medium	minor	significant	negligible	no	–
83-07	T	steep	soft	significant	minor	significant	yes	7 mn
76-19	–	–	–	negligible	negligible	severe	no	36 hr
76-17	L	shallow	medium	minor	significant	minor	no	?
79-07	L	shallow	medium	minor	significant	negligible	no	–
83-05	A	medium	hard	significant	minor	negligible	no	–
81-07	L	shallow	medium	minor	minor	severe	no	8 hr
83-02	C	shallow	medium	significant	significant	severe	yes	?
85-04	E	steep	soft	severe	minor	negligible	no	–
84-09	–	–	–	negligible	negligible	significant	yes	56 mn
76-01	A	steep	medium	minor	minor	minor	no	long
76-20	L	shallow	hard	minor	minor	severe	no	2 hr 40
76-08	L	shallow	hard	significant	severe	significant	no	7 mn
80-14	T	shallow	soft	minor	minor	severe	no	2 hr 50
78-03	L	shallow	medium	minor	significant	severe	yes	30 mn
80-11	E	steep	medium	severe	minor	significant	yes	?
81-12	L	shallow	medium	minor	minor	minor	no	?
78-08	A	steep	hard	severe	significant	negligible	yes	–
80-09	C	shallow	medium	significant	significant	severe	yes	9 hr
86-01	A	shallow	medium	minor	minor	severe	yes	25 mn
81-13	A	medium	medium	significant	significant	minor	yes	?
79-17	T	steep	soft	severe	minor	significant	yes	?
85-05	L	shallow	soft	negligible	negligible	negligible	no	–
77-01	L	shallow	medium	minor	significant	significant	no	?
1/81	T	shallow	soft	negligible	negligible	negligible	no	–
6/78	T	shallow	medium	minor	minor	significant	no	?
3/81	C	shallow	medium	significant	significant	severe	no	45 mn
8/81	A	medium	hard	severe	minor	minor	no	?
1/80	A	steep	soft	significant	minor	negligible	yes	–
2/86	A	medium	soft	significant	minor	severe	yes	?
9/78	A	steep	soft	severe	minor	significant	no	23 mn

a Phase   T=Take-off, C=Climb, E=Enroute, A=Approach and L=Landing plus
          emergency landing

b Surface Soft = Earth etc.,   Medium = Trees, buildings, concrete etc.   and
          Hard = Rocks

118

Table 3

Classification Criteria

	NEGLIGIBLE	MINOR	SIGNIFICANT	SEVERE
DIRECT IMPACT FORCES	people not injured, or minor injury only	people injured, but no people killed	people killed, extensive structural damage	people killed, aircraft broken up
RIPPING TEARING FORCES	minor or no structural disruption	considerable structural damage	impact with large trees or concrete structures or buildings	impact with large rocks or steel structures
FIRE	no fire	fuselage remains largely intact	fuselage or Al melted	fuselage or Al consumed

Figure 2

Fire Severity versus a) Direct Impact, b) Ripping/Tearing Forces

76-19 etc. = NTSB-AAR report numbers
3/81 etc. = AIB-AAR report numbers

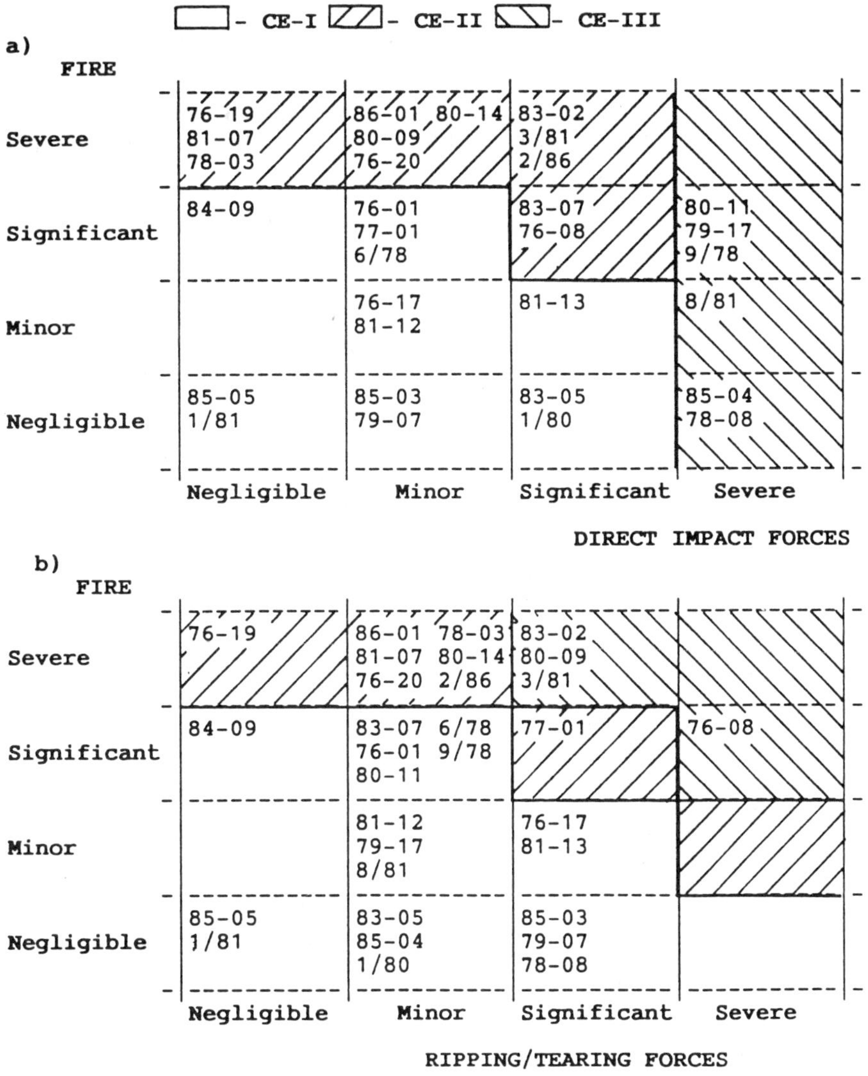

☐ - CE-I ▨ - CE-II ◪ - CE-III

a)

FIRE

	Negligible	Minor	Significant	Severe
Severe	76-19 81-07 78-03	86-01 80-14 80-09 76-20	83-02 3/81 2/86	
Significant	84-09	76-01 77-01 6/78	83-07 76-08	80-11 79-17 9/78
Minor		76-17 81-12	81-13	8/81
Negligible	85-05 1/81	85-03 79-07	83-05 1/80	85-04 78-08

DIRECT IMPACT FORCES

b)

FIRE

	Negligible	Minor	Significant	Severe
Severe	76-19	86-01 78-03 81-07 80-14 76-20 2/86	83-02 80-09 3/81	
Significant	84-09	83-07 6/78 76-01 9/78 80-11	77-01	76-08
Minor		81-12 79-17 8/81	76-17 81-13	
Negligible	1/81 85-05	83-05 85-04 1/80	85-03 79-07 78-08	

RIPPING/TEARING FORCES

ground fire. Unfortunately very few details are given concerning damage caused by the fire and the duration of the fire, but melted aluminium was found near the centre (aluminium melts at 620 °C). Two incidents involved the aircraft power diving into the ground; the cockpit and forward fuselage contacted the ground first, nevertheless the aft fuselage was still extensively broken up. Both cases involved a ground fire, but the aft fuselage was in each case thrown further along the wreckage trail than the main fire region. The remaining two incidents involved aircraft flying at cruising speeds (ie. about 250 knots) into the sides of mountains. Again the main impact forces were absorbed by the forward fuselage; however, the aft fuselage and heavy items of cargo were thrown forward, and in both cases wreckage was discovered scattered down the opposite side of the mountain.

The four remaining CE-III incidents combined large ripping or tearing forces with **Significant** or **Severe** fires. These are considered very severe CE-III crash environments because of the possibility of the outer layer of a container being damaged exposing the shock absorber to the fire. The crashes involved impact of the aircraft with obstacles such as trees, large boulders, service poles and steel pylons. Again most of the impact force was absorbed by the forward part of the fuselage and the wings, however the aft part of the aircraft still received substantial damage. Three of the impacts were followed by intense and prolonged ground fires. The last involved a particularly severe impact as the aircraft crashed into the non-frangible steel towers supporting the approach lights of the runway; the fire that erupted was extinguished within 5 minutes and the aft fuselage remained relatively intact.

Fire Duration versus Impact Severity

Fire duration information is often not given in great detail in the reports; usually only the time at which the fire brigade extinguished the fire or sometimes the time at which they brought it under control is given. It is not always clear how long the aircraft fuselage itself was engulfed in the flames or whether much of the time the fire fighters were just mopping up odd isolated fires or extinguishing fires in the surroundings. For this reason the fire severity as defined by the damage caused to the aft fuselage is probably a better indication of the type of fire environment a package might experience. However, in order to define tests for radioactive materials' packages, fire duration information is required.

In the following analysis, the time when the fire was brought under control was employed if possible. Where this was not available, the time to 'fire extinguished' has been used. Where no fire duration was indicated the incident has been left out of the analysis. All the figures used are likely to be an over-estimation of the time the fuselage was engulfed by the fire. A fire test duration of 30 minutes

121

Figure 3

Fire Duration versus a) Impact Forces and b) Crash Environment

a)

            x direct impact   o ripping/tearing

FIRE
DURATION -|-------------|-------------|-------------|-------------|-

            o x   o x   o x   o x
>30 min.   o x   o x   o x   o x
                    o x

          -|-------------|-------------|-------------|-------------|-
>10 min.
<30 min.   o x
                    o x   o   x

          -|-------------|-------------|-------------|-------------|-

<10min.   o   x x   o

          -|-------------|-------------|-------------|-------------|-
            o   o x   x
no fire   o x   o x   o o   x x
            o x   o x

          -|-------------|-------------|-------------|-------------|-
           Negligible   Minor   Significant   Severe

                                           IMPACT FORCES

b)

*' direct impact only   *" ripping/tearing only   * both forces

FIRE
DURATION -|-------------|-------------|-------------|-
                              * *
>30 min.   * * *   * *   *" *"

          -|-------------|-------------|-------------|-
>10 min.
<30 min.   * *   *'

          -|-------------|-------------|-------------|-

<10 min.   *'   *"

          -|-------------|-------------|-------------|-
             * * *
no fire   * * *   *' *'

          -|-------------|-------------|-------------|-
             CE-I   CE-II   CE-III

              TOTAL CRASH ENVIRONMENT

sequential to drop and puncture tests is specified in the IAEA regulations. Figure 3a gives a plot of fire duration versus impact and rip/tear severity. Nine fires of a duration greater than 30 minutes were identified; none of these was associated with impact or rip/tear forces defined as **Severe**, the majority being associated with **Minor** forces. However, a plot of total crash environment versus fire duration (figure 3b) shows that 2 of the 9 incidents has a crash environment defined as **CE-III**.

One of the incidents occurred only 7 minutes after take-off and therefore the aircraft could have been carrying a substantial amount of fuel; the actual amount was not specified in the report. The crash caused the surrounding forest to set alight and therefore the fire duration (9 hours) may not relate to the time the fuselage of the aircraft was engulfed. However, the fuselage was so extensively damaged by impact and fire that the investigators were obliged to examine a similar aircraft to identify the parts.

The second incident involved the aircraft crashing into a wooded area, again shortly after take-off. Initially the fire was concentrated at the aft of the fuselage and then spread gradually forward. The fuselage structures were nearly consumed. The aft fuselage received less impact damage than the forward fuselage; people there survived the impact but were unable to escape the fire. The aircraft was carrying 27 t of fuel at take-off, but was dumping when it crashed. The fire duration was 49 minutes.

Four of the remaining incidents had crash environments described as **CE-II**. One of these involved a particularly severe and prolonged fire (36 hours). The aircraft aborted take-off, but could not be stopped by the end of the runway, the right landing gear collapsed and the right wing was damaged causing fuel to be released from the wing tank. The aircraft came to a halt over a storm drain that filled up with burning fuel which continued to feed the fire. All the passengers escaped, but the combination of a flammable cargo and the presence of the storm drain hampered fire fighters who applied large amounts of foam and water without success. The fire was finally extinguished 36 hours later using dry chemical extinguisher.

Discussion and Conclusions

This study has concentrated on a small sample of aircraft accidents (ie. 31 incidents) during the years 1975 and 1985 inclusive that fulfilled the following criteria:

The aircraft involved had a maximum take-off weight of about 20 tonnes or greater.

At least one fatality among passengers or crew and/or destruction of the aircraft occurred.

NTSB or AIB aircraft accident reports for the incident were available.

No attempt was made to quantify the impact parameters such as impact forces, fire temperature and fire intensity. Instead the incidents were classified qualitatively into broad categories by examining the type and extent of damage done to the aircraft and persons involved in the crash. Where possible the damage sustained by the aft fuselage in particular was used as the basis for the classification.

Twelve incidents involving a fireball, flash-fire or explosion were identified. In only two incidents was the fireball not followed by a ground fire; in one of these the aircraft subsequently fell into the sea. The only damage reported, associated with the second fireball, was scorching of paper and card. The duration of this fireball was 3 - 4 seconds.

Ten incidents were identified in which the crash environment was considered to be of such severity that the possibility of a package being breached must be considered. Six of these involved high impact forces (two due to aircraft break up in mid flight, two due to powered dives into the ground and two due to a crash into a mountain at cruising speeds with subsequent ejection of heavy items of cargo out of the aircraft and down the opposite side of the mountain). Four involved large ripping or tearing forces in conjunction with a considerable fire; in one of these the impact forces were particularly severe being due to an aircraft crashing in to non-frangible steel towers, that supported the approach lights to the runway, as it came into land.

Only two of the above were associated with a fire known to be longer than 30 minutes; in these incidents the ripping and tearing forces were considerable but the direct impact forces were not.

In many of the fires reported, material other than the aviation fuel was also involved, ie. construction materials such as aluminium and cargo. Burning of such materials can cause local temperatures to vary considerably from those predicted from hydrocarbon burning, for instance, aluminium can burn with a flame temperature of 2815 °C.

One of the inflight breakup incidents was associated with a ground fire. Unfortunately, very little information was given about the fire; however, it was sufficiently intense in places to melt aluminium.

One extremely severe and prolonged fire (36 hours) was reported but the impact forces associated with it were negligible. It resulted from a combination of circumstances,

ie. the flammable cargo aboard the aircraft and the proximity
of a storm drain, which made it virtually impossible to
control the fire.

The majority of the accidents occurred on, or close to, an
airfield; however, fire fighting forces did not always find
extinguishing the fire or access to the aircraft
straightforward. The following general observations can be
made concerning fire fighters' priorities:

The initial priority is the protection of possible
survivors.

When all the survivors have been removed or are
receiving adequate attention effort is concentrated on
the flight recorder region and the cockpit, if the fire
is very large, in order to preserve any data regarding
the cause of the incident.

If the fire fighters are informed of any hazardous cargo
aboard the aircraft, effort will be concentrated on the
cargo holds. However, one incident involving a
radioactive shipment was reported; in this case, the
fire fighters withdrew when they had rescued all the
survivors until material and dose rate information was
obtained.

From this limited study the following tentative conclusions
may be drawn.

A fireball test is not supported; in general a fireball
is followed by a ground fire with potential to cause
much greater damage.

The possibility that a package may be exposed to
temperatures in excess of the temperatures proposed for
tests other than the fireball test does exist.

Very high impact forces are not reported in association
with fires of greater than 30 minutes' duration.
However, two incidents were identified in which
considerable ripping or tearing forces were experienced
followed by long fires (9 hours and 49 minutes). This
type of scenario deserves more detailed consideration.

The possibility that an undamaged package may be
subjected to a very prolonged engulfing fire does exist;
however, the probability of this occurring must be very
small.

In conclusion, this study supports the proposal that some alterations may be required to the regulatory design criteria for packages used in transporting significant quantities of radioactive materials by air. Areas that deserve particular consideration are listed above.

REFERENCES

1. Qualification Criteria to Certify a Package for the Air Transport of Plutonium, NUREG-0360, January 1978.

2. Regulations for the Safe Transport of Radioactive Material, Safety Series No. 6, IAEA, Vienna, 1985.

THE USE OF RISK ANALYSIS IN THE FORMULATION OF POLICY FOR THE TRANSPORT OF DANGEROUS GOODS THROUGH TUNNELS

M. McD. Grant BSc. PhD

W.S. Atkins Engineering Sciences
Woodcote Grove, Ashley Road, Epsom, Surrey KT18 5BW

ABSTRACT

The means for assessing the risk of dangerous goods transportation through tunnels are reviewed. Probability and consequence are treated separately. Emphasis is given to the use of techniques which can be readily applied in practice but which yield credible answers. The manner in which risk levels thus obtained can be used to determine policy for dangerous goods transportation is also discussed.

INTRODUCTION

Industry relies heavily upon the road and rail network for transportation of its raw materials, intermediates and output. For some industries the products being transported may be such that they pose a toxic, explosive or other risk. Should the hazard be sufficiently large then the regulatory authorities will classify the material as 'hazardous' or 'dangerous' and various regulations will apply to its transport concerning packaging, vehicle construction, labelling, segregation etc.

The risks associated with the transport of dangerous goods are particularly worthy of study as they inevitably involve hazard to the general public. The management of these risks is problematic as concern for public safety must be tempered with the unarguable need to maintain an efficient transportation network. To date the authorities have succeeded in this role : the UK in particular has an excellent safety record despite the movement of large quantities of dangerous goods each year.

However complacency is not appropriate. Change requires that risk levels be reviewed and the transportation of dangerous goods is changing for a number of reasons. Traffic densities are increasing and new routes are opening in response to this pressure. The commodities being transported vary continuously and our knowledge of the hazards associated with particular commodities is increasing. Additionally the public demands higher safety levels, particularly from the transportation industry. The use of risk analysis has a vital role to play in the management of this change. This paper outlines how risk analysis may be used to aid decision making in the particular case of dangerous goods transportation through tunnels. Both road and rail tunnels are considered.

In the Risk Identification section, the risks associated with dangerous goods transportation are identified. In the sections on Estimation of Probability and Consequence Analysis, the estimation of probability and consequence are respectively addressed. The product of these two parameters, risk, is discussed in Utilisation of Calculated Risk Levels section with particular attention being given to its use in policy formulation.

RISK IDENTIFICATION

Types of hazard

Clearly the hazard will initially depend on the type of product being transported. A commonly used European classification of goods considered dangerous for transport is shown in Table 1. It is seen that materials are grouped according to their hazard. It is necessary to be aware however that a material is assigned to a particular class according to its largest hazard. Thus a liquid defined as toxic for example may also be flammable.

TABLE 1

Dangerous goods classification scheme

Class	Description
1a	Explosive substances and articles
1b	Articles filled with explosive substances
1c	Igniters fireworks and similar goods
2	Gases : compressed, liquefied or dissolved under pressure
3	Flammable liquids
4.1	Flammable solids
4.2	Substances liable to spontaneous combustion
4.3	Substances which give off flammable gases in contact with water
5.1	Oxidising substances
5.2	organic peroxides
6.1	Toxic substances
6.2	Infectious and repugnant substances
7	Radioactive substances
8	Corrosive substances

Types of incident

In order to determine how transport of such materials might give rise to a hazard it is useful to consult records of transportation incidents which have involved dangerous goods. The rail networks have tended historically, to maintain excellent incident reporting procedures therefore they have extremely rich sources of data. These are not however, necessarily in the public domain.

As a result of not being controlled by a single nationwide organisation the road networks do not present such a straightforward situation. However in certain countries (e.g. France [1], Belgium [2] and W. Germany [3]) the relevant government departments do collate and publish yearly statistics of road based dangerous goods statistics. Unfortunately this is not the case in the UK although an attempt was made to redress the situation in 1980 [4].

It can be noted that extensive recording of both road and rail accidents takes place in the United States. The difficulty is that differing standards and conditions render the application of such data to European situations a dubious practice.

From reference to applicable data sources it is possible to identify two principal causes of an incident involving dangerous goods:

- vehicle accident
- packaging failure

The types of vehicle accident that can lead to a dangerous goods incident are collision and derailment for rail. For road transport the important types of accident are collision (with another vehicle or a stationary object), overturning and skidding.

Packaging failure describes an event when, through no untoward external influence (such as vehicle accident), a leak of the contents occurs. Typically this will be a leaking valve or loose hatch on a tanker. Much less likely but more severe would be a catastrophic rupture of a gas tanker.

In general the largest leaks will occur as a result of accident as opposed to package failure. An exception to this would be a situation where a small leak of flammable liquid ignited and caused further package failure. Another might be the situation where drums fall off the back of a lorry due to poor loading.

ESTIMATION OF PROBABILITY

Leakage due to vehicle accident

The probability of this event is the product of the probability of an accident and the conditional probability of package failure. The probability of an accident can be obtained by using an accident rate obtained from one of the data sources discussed in the previous section. However care must be taken as to the applicability of the data. The traffic conditions for both road and rail are sufficiently different in tunnels from overland networks to give very different accident rates.

For example many tunnels are twin bore thereby the risk of head on collision does not usually arise. There are no junctions or level crossings in tunnels. Particular speed limits may apply in the tunnel. Thus accident statistics from overland networks should be interpreted with care. The ease with which this can be done depends on the quality of the database; that is to say the extent to which accident causes are classified. Thus the detail with which accident records for rail are kept is of distinct advantage.

The conditional probability of package failure is somewhat more problematic. The issue can be tackled by reference to the data banks. However the difference between overland and tunnel transport is particularly critical here. For example a derailed train or skidding lorry may tend to fall down an embankment with a high probability of leakage. In a tunnel however the trajectory of the vehicle will tend to be contained. A further problem is lack of data: this is a particular problem for gas tankers as their in service record is very good.

Rigorous qualitative assessment is therefore not possible. The application of engineering judgement is therefore perhaps the most sensible recourse. Given that overland conditional probabilities of failure are likely to be lower than those for tunnels the former could be used as a conservative assumption. Typical values might range between 0.3 and 0.05 for a liquid tanker. The greater strength of gas tankers suggests much lower figures are appropriate.

CONSEQUENCE ANALYSIS

General approach

In most risk analyses it is to be expected that the analyst will have full details of the materials from which the hazard arises. In transportation this is not necessarily the case as the range of materials that might be transported runs to many hundreds if not thousands of commodities. As was noted before, these commodities are conveniently classified with regard to their particular hazard(s). Thus it is usual, in transportation risk analyses, to choose a small number of commodities from each class for detailed study. The choice must be made with regard to the range of hazard property within each class. For example if a commodity is the least or most toxic within a class this must be borne in mind when interpreting the results. Often the choice is influenced by the availability of data on particular materials. Thus one would probably choose to analyse Chlorine rather than another toxic gas such as Fluorine. This approach is, however, quite appropriate as the commodities for which data are available will tend to be those that are transported in the largest quantities.

Having considered how the choice of commodities to be studied is made, it is now appropriate to consider how consequence is analysed. This is done in the following sections with the constraint that only the more commercially significant classes are considered. It is estimated that the classes considered below (2,3,6.1 and 8 - see Table 1) make up at least 90% of the dangerous goods transportation market.

The commodities not considered here can be subjected to risk analysis; see for example [5] which deals with the transport of Class 7 Radioactive materials through tunnels. On the other hand it may be decided that a more pragmatic and/or judgemental approach is the most appropriate for those materials moved in lesser quantities.

Gases

There are three main groups which can be considered as follows:

FLAMMABLE   eg LPG or Hydrogen
TOXIC   eg Chlorine or Ammonia
ASPHYXIANT   eg Nitrogen or Helium

The state of the commodity must also be considered; compressed gas, liquefied vapour, cryogenic liquid etc.

Before considering the individual hazards of these groups some general points can be made about leakage and dispersion. As discussed previously two main scenarios may arise : leakage from static vehicle and leakage from moving vehicle (that is to say whether leakage is due to accident damage or 'spontaneous' package failure).
For each type of scenario it is necessary to postulate a breach configuration (size, loss coefficient, above or below vapour line etc); accident records can be useful in this respect. However the paucity of accidents involving this type of commodity, at least in the UK, may render the application of judgement necessary. A range of breach diameters should be considered. Typically the range will include a diameter of about 50mm, this being assumed to occur below the liquid level [6].

Having specified the breach configuration, the release rate can readily be calculated by application of well known procedures [7]. Again using fairly well understood approximations it is possible to deal with the evaporation of vapour from a pool of liquefied vapour on the tunnel floor.

The calculation of resulting concentrations of gas in the tunnel environment is however more problematic. At the simplest level it can be assumed that even mixing occurs across the tunnel cross section. This might be a valid assumption for the case of a release from a moving vehicle in a small diameter tunnel. For more complex scenarios a different approach must be taken. Clearly the application of classic dispersion formulae, as might be used for a release from a chemical plant, is inappropriate in the closed environs of a tunnel. An alternative is to use Computational Fluid Dynamics techniques to model dispersion of the gas in 2 or preferably 3 dimensions. The relevant software must however be able to take account of the fact that the gas is likely to be heavier than air [8]. As an alternative [9] proposes an analytical approach developed for the analysis of methane layers in mines.

In general the concentrations arising from a moving vehicle will be much less as the gas will be diluted into a much larger volume and also the breach sizes will be smaller. However should a moving vehicle generate a hazardous concentration this may be spread along a long length of tunnel with a concomitant increase in risk to life.

FLAMMABLE GASES can produce a large hazard by reason of their ability to generate an explosion. Thus the dispersion analysis will be looking for concentrations of gas between the upper and lower explosive limits. The calculation of overpressures along the tunnel following ignition of such a mixture is much more difficult than the corresponding situation for a release outdoors. This is because the walls of the tunnel will provide a degree of confinement. This can be analysed using computer codes although such computation is highly complex and it may be deemed more sensible to simply postulate an initial overpressure at the value for a fully confined explosion (typically about 8 Bar). Because a large explosion can only propagate in one dimension it may be that little decay from this value will be seen along the tunnel. Experience gained from research into explosions in mines may be of relevance here.

TOXIC GASES have the potential for generating large scale loss of life in tunnels. Having calculated the relevant concentrations it is necessary to determine the residence times of people in the toxic cloud. This allows calculation of the toxic load given the availability of a relationship in the form of :

$$C_x^n \times t = K \tag{1}$$

where C_x is the concentration which will kill x percent of the population following an exposure for time t and n and K are constants specific to a particular gas. See for example [10] for the form of this relationship for Chlorine.

If people are in vehicles it is necessary to consider how this will alter the concentration profile with time. In general this will reduce the hazard : see [11] for further guidance.

ASPHYXIANT GASES present a hazard due to displacement of oxygen. The quantity of leakage required to threaten life in this manner is much greater than that for toxic gases. For this reason the transport of asphyxiant gas is seen as acceptable in some tunnels where toxic gases are banned. One difficulty in considering asphyxiant gases is that they are often transported in cryogenic form. This requires particular consideration in predicting their rate of evaporation following spillage.

Flammable liquids

The spillage of a flammable liquid can give rise to a number of hazardous phenomena as follows:

    pool fire
    smoke production (especially toxic gases)
    explosion

The latter is particularly undesirable and may arise from a number of causes:

liquid spray from moving tanker
vapour cloud from pool of low flashpoint liquid
sudden oxygen injection to fuel rich fire
tanker overpressure due to heat input from fire

Each of these aspects must be considered. It is suggested that an analytical approach based on well understood principles (as opposed to computational modelling) is the most appropriate approach here.

The problem of fires in tunnels is an important subject in its own right and has received much consideration in the literature [12]. It is not possible within the confines of this paper, to do the subject justice.

Toxic substances

Note that this class considers solids and liquids: toxic gases are considered under class 2. Materials tend to be defined as toxic for transport by reason of their acute toxicity. It is this aspect that will be considered here although this should not be taken as an implication that chronic effects can be ignored.

Three pathways can be identified:
dermal
oral
inhalation

Within the tunnel itself the most likely pathway will be via inhalation. Calculation of the concentration of the vapour in the tunnel will require an assessment of the evaporation rate. For liquids this can be done using the type of technique outlined in [7].

Having calculated the concentration it appears, on first view, that the toxic hazard could be readily assessed by use of the LC_{50} (lethal concentration for 50% of the population) values associated with the relevant substances. However various problems require consideration before this can be done. One is that 50 % fatality is unlikely to be viewed as an acceptable criteria; 1% is a more commonly used value in risk analyses (whereas 0% is the real aim such a figure is not available from toxicity data given its stochastic nature; 1% is seen as a reasonable compromise). Additionally the LC value quoted in the literature will have been obtained by sacrificing rabbits, rats or some such; human responses are not always available. Finally, the time of exposure for the experimentally derived value may be in the order of hours whereas exposure in the tunnel may be much shorter.

For a very well studied material these problems may be overcome with some degree of confidence. This will be achieved by use of Probit equations for interpolating between different times of exposure and percentages of fatality (see, for example [10]) . However for the majority of toxic substances extrapolation from the laboratory to real life is a very uncertain business indeed due to the paucity of data. The application of generous factors of safety (spanning orders of magnitude) may be necessary.

Corrosive substances

The spillage of a corrosive substance can generate a threat to life by generation of fumes or direct contact. Without suggesting that this aspect can be ignored we concentrate on the other important aspect which is damage to the fabric of the tunnel itself. This has the potential for causing protracted tunnel down time.

The problem is essentially one of potential reactions between the spilt substance and the tunnel construction materials. Given that all the substances in this class have been defined as being corrosive it is to be expected that many of them will react with many of the construction materials. For certain combinations, sulphuric acid at a given concentration on concrete for example, it may be possible to estimate an erosion rate. This estimation will be based on available laboratory data. However for the majority of cases no such data will be available. We are therefore at the mercy of the judgement of an expert in the field of corrosion.

The consideration of corrosive effects must take into account both short and long term effects. The latter may be the most difficult to assess and may also be the most problematic due to their insidious nature. It is considered that there will always be a degree of uncertainty regarding the assessment of the extent of tunnel damage due to corrosive substance spillage. On a more positive note this may not be seen as a major problem as it does not necessarily concern risk to life.

UTILISATION OF CALCULATED RISK LEVELS

Having considered probability and consequence it is now possible to calculate the overall risk level. This may be expressed simply as fatalities per tonne transported for each class of dangerous goods. Alternatively a sophisticated analysis may justify expression of the results in the form of an F-N curve.

Assessment of the risk level will be achieved by comparison with some measure of acceptable risk. The type of risk which is deemed acceptable will depend on individual circumstances; the following are possible approaches:

- risk level must be below N fatalities per annum
- risk level must be lower than alternative transportation routes
- no acceptance of incidents which can generate more than a given number of fatalities
- tunnel down time must not exceed N days per annum
- no acceptance of incidents which can generate a tunnel down time of more than a given number of days

If the risk is deemed acceptable then, in theory, the exercise can be concluded. That is to say the tunnel operator need not restrict the flow of dangerous goods. In practice the operator will always be interested in risk reduction strategies as long as they have no major deleterious effects on commercial and operational aspirations. However, if the risk is deemed unacceptable then the operator has no choice but to consider how it might be reduced.

It is possible to reduce the risk level by adapting certain features of the tunnel design. For example an efficient drainage system may go a long way to preventing the build up of vapours from spilt liquids. However the critical factor here is one of cost. It is the authors belief that only a few design features installed specifically for dangerous goods are likely to be cost effective. The choice of these features is therefore critical and can only be sensibly made against a solid background of risk analysis.

It is considered unrealistic to attempt to change the design of the dangerous goods package itself (e.g. a tanker). This is because such design is already very heavily regulated and hence costly for the operator. The imposition of further constraints would likely lead to operators seeking other routes. Additionally such an increase would be extremely difficult to enforce.

A more realistic means for reducing risk is the enforcement of operating procedures. The following are some examples:

- speed limits for DG vehicles
- DG vehicles to travel in convoys, overtaking of convoys is prevented
- DG vehicles can only travel during quiet hours such as at night
- clear tunnel during the passage of DG vehicles

If the risk level cannot be reduced to a value which is acceptable by design or operational factors then consideration must be given to restricting the types or quantities of materials which can pass through the tunnel. The risk analysis will indicate which materials generate the most risk. For tunnels these are likely to be toxic and flammable gases by reason of their high hazard potential. Additionally the risk from flammable liquids will be significant by reason of their hazard potential and also the high traffic in this type of commodity. Having identified the most problematic materials a number of strategies are possible:

- complete ban
- restriction on package size per shipment
- restriction on quantity transported per annum

Again the risk analysis will allow assessment of the most effective strategy.

CONCLUSIONS

The means by which the risk levels associated with the transport of dangerous goods through tunnels can be calculated have been considered.

The data sources and computational techniques which are available are of sufficient quality to suggest that a degree of confidence can be placed in the calculated risk levels. Thus it is proposed that the use of risk analysis in this area is a vital aid to decision making.

REFERENCES

1. Statistiques 1987 des accidents et incidents concernant le transport par voie routière et ferroviaire des matières dangereuses, Ministère de l'équipement du logement de l'aménagement du territoire et des transports (Paris).

2. Transport Routier des Marchandises Dangereuses en Belgique. Bilan des enquetes relatives aux accidents, Institut du Transport Routier, 1985.

3. Unfalle mit Gefahrguten auf Schiene und Strasse, Antwort des Bundesregierung, Drucksache 11/1095, 1987.

4. MacLean, A.D., 1980 Chemical Incidents Survey : statistical Analysis, Home Office Pub. 17/83, 1983.

5. Fixation d'une limite d'activité pour le transit des produits radiopharmaceutiques à travers le tunnel du Mont Blanc : éléments d'appréciation, Centre d'Etude sur l'Evaluation de la Protection dans le Domaine Nucléaire, Rapport No. 90, 1985.

6. Purdy, G., Campbell, H.S., Grint, G.C. and Smith L.M. An Analysis of the Risk Arising from the Transport of Liquefied Gases in Great Britain, Int. Symp. on the Transport and Storage of Pressure Liquefied Gases, Univ. of New Brunswick, 1987.

7. Methods for the Calculation of the Physical Effects of the Escape of Dangerous Materials (liquids and gases), report of the Committee for the Prevention of Disasters, published by the Directorate-General of Labour, Netherlands, 1979.

8. Deaves, D. M. 3-Dimensional Model Predictions for the Upwind Building Trial of Thorney Island Phase II. Proc. Symp on Heavy Gas Dispersion Trials at Thorney Island, ed. McQuaid, Sheffield, 1984.

9. Considine, M. Risk assessment of the Transportation of Hazardous Substances through Road Tunnels. Conf. on Recent Advances in Hazardous Materials Transportation Research, Florida, 1985.

10. Toxicity of Chlorine, I. Chem. E, Monograph, 1987.

11. Davies, P. C and Purdy, G. Toxic gas Risk Assessment - The Effects of Being Indoors. I. Chem. E. Conf. on the Refinement of Estimates of the Consequences of Heavy Toxic Vapour Release, 1986.

12. Gossard, W. H. Fire Protection in Underground Systems - Some Lessons Learned. 6th Int. Fire Protection Seminar, Karlsruhe, 1982.

MODES AND CONSEQUENCES OF THE FAILURE OF ROAD AND RAIL TANKERS CARRYING LIQUEFIED GASES AND OTHER HAZARDOUS LIQUIDS

V.C. MARSHALL
Disaster Research Unit,
Department of Industrial Technology,
University of Bradford, UK.

ABSTRACT

The differing circumstances of the transport of hazardous liquids by road and rail tankers are described. The mechanical design considerations involved in the design of these vehicles is outlined. Causes of failure are listed as are the consequences of failure which are related to the geometry of the escape and the nature of the contents. Appendices provide a scenario which could lead to hydraulic rupture, a discussion of the behaviour of flashing liquids and a note on the acronym BLEVE.

INTRODUCTION

This paper is intended to survey the bulk transport of hazardous liquids by road or rail in custom built vehicles in relation to the modes and the consequences of failure of such vehicles.

The liquids surveyed may be carried at, below, or above, the ambient temperature and at atmospheric pressure or above it. These conditions, with examples of each, are set out in Table 1.

TABLE 1
Summary of conditions of use.

	Pressure at atmospheric	Pressure above atmospheric
Temperature below atmospheric	Liquid oxygen	Not applicable
Temperature at atmospheric	Petroleum spirit	LPG, Chlorine, Ammonia
Temperature above atmospheric	Sulphur, Molten Metals	Not applicable

THE DESIGN OF TANKS AND PRESSURE VESSELS

Nomenclature

There is a problem of nomenclature in this area in that the transport industry uses the term "thin walled" to describe tankers designed to carry liquids at atmospheric pressure and "thick walled" to describe tankers designed to carry liquids with appreciable vapour pressures as, for example, 10 bars absolute. On the other hand designers of pressure vessels for static use use the term "thin walled" for all situations in which there is no significant difference in stress between the inside wall and the outside wall, and "thick walled" for situations in which the difference in stress is significant.

However the pressure region which required cylinders to be "thick walled" in the meaning ascribed by designers of static installations lies well outside of the pressures which are feasible for mobile vessels. In the paper the terms "thin" and "thick" will have the meanings ascribed to them by the transport industry.

The Transport of Liquids at Atmospheric Pressure and Atmospheric Temperature

The theoretical minimum wall thickness for such tanks would be that which resist the hydraulic forces which arise from the liquid contents. For a tank at rest these forces would be at a maximum at the bottom of the tank and would be governed by the depth and the density of the liquid.

For a mobile tank the theoretical hydraulic forces would be greater than these because of the need to take account of kinetic effects consequent upon accelerations and decelerations especially those arising from sudden change of course, emergency braking, or collision. The magnitude of the forces would be proportional to the length of the compartments and the rate of acceleration or deceleration. The more internal baffles are provided, the less will be the forces on the ends of the vessel.

Even so, and speaking generally, the design of transport vessels, though it takes hydraulic and kinetic forces into account, has to pay more attention to rigidity. This is because a tank whose design was based upon hydraulic and kinetic considerations alone would be too fragile for transport use; such tanks would not withstand slight blows or bear the weight of a person standing on them. Moreover corrosion might result in them having a very short life. All in all, these practical design considerations are likely to lead to wall thicknesses ten or more times as great as those which would be dictated by hydraulic forces alone.

The vessels may also be reinforced by fenders and roll-over rings to protect them in the event of a collision.

However vessels designed to take account of the factors discussed above are not capable of withstanding the external pressure of the atmosphere if they are subjected to evacuation. This could happen, for example, to a tank whose liquid contents are pumped out without the tank being vented to atmosphere. Such collapses are perhaps the commonest mode of major tank failure in static installations. In transport vessels they are much more likely to occur in a depot than en route.

Transport of Liquids at Atmospheric Pressure and at Temperatures below Atmospheric

Some substances such as oxygen and nitrogen are carried as liquids at low temperatures (ca −183 to −196 C). They are carried in tanks made from stainless steel or aluminium which retain their impact strength at these cryogenic temperatures. These tanks require thermal insulation. The tanks are sometimes giant Dewar flasks; in other cases they may be double walled with a low temperature insulant such as slag wool between the walls.

Tankers carrying liquefied gases may be subject to contact with cold product (eg at about −25 C). Where such tankers are made from carbon steels these must satisfy the requirements of adequate impact strength at these low temperatures such as are defined in Appendix D of BS 5500.

Transport of Liquids at Atmospheric Pressure and at Temperatures above Atmospheric

Such cargoes are now fairly common as, for example, molten sulphur. Such tanks will be designed to the conditions outlined above. They will have to be resistant to corrosion by the hot liquid being conveyed and they will be thermally insulated against loss of heat.

Transport of Liquids above Atmospheric Pressure and at Atmospheric Temperature

These are the liquefied gases (strictly liquefied vapours) such as LPG, chlorine and ammonia. It may be assumed that a pressure of 10 to 20 bars will be the pressure usually designed for. Such vessels will differ significantly from those designed for operation at atmospheric pressure, in that their design and construction will be governed by a pressure vessel code such as BS 5500.

CAUSES OF FAILURE

Introduction

The discussion below sets out a number of possible circumstances of failure. Though it includes the most important, it should not be taken as constituting an exhaustive list of all possible modes.

Location of Areas of Failure

(a) Shell

(b) Branches, including instrument connections

(c) Valves

(d) Pumps

(e) Connections to a container

(f) Inspection covers

It may be noted that, at the time of writing, no example exists of the catastrophic failure of a thick walled transport vessel in the UK. The consequences of such failures when described below are entirely drawn from incidents which have occurred abroad. [2]

Class of Failure Mode

Due to Excess Internal pressure. This may be caused by:-

(a) Abnormal meteorological conditions

(b) Contents having higher vapour pressure than designed for

(c) Hydraulic rupture consequent upon over-filling

(d) Internal chemical reaction such as decomposition or polymerisation

(e) Flame impingement

Notes. General. Vessels fitted with pressure relief are much less likely to fail from internal overpressure than vessels not so fitted. However the question of whether to provide pressure relief is a complex one. In static installations hazardous substances vented off can be discharged to flare stacks or scrubbers in a way which is not possible in the mobile situation. In some past incidents abroad pressure relief has been provided but has proved inadequate to prevent catastrophic failure.

(a) Exposure to direct rays of the summer sun, especially when stationary, may produce unanticipated levels of internal pressure. However adherence to BS5355 which defines temperatures to be encountered under different conditions of insulation should avoid this problem.

(b) Design needs to take account of possible variations in composition. LPG is not a single substance but is a mixture of hydrocarbons of differing volatility. Also the vapour pressure may be higher than designed for if the contents should be fed in at a higher temperature than in the design specification.

(c) Hydraulic rupture, in which the vessel bursts through being heated up after over-filling, has been blamed for a number of serious accidents abroad which involved tank cars. The important of allowing sufficient ullage cannot be overstressed. Appendix 1 shows sequences which can involve hydraulic rupture.

(d) Chemical reaction, in which heat is generated, could, in principle, produce rapid temperature rise even beyond the capacity of relief valves. Any monomer which can produce a polymer is a candidate though some are much less dangerous than others. Admission of undesired material, which may react with the contents or catalyse polymerisation or decomposition, could lead to overpressurisation en route.

(e) There have been a number of examples, none of them in the UK, of thick walled transport vessels bursting after flame impingement. These circumstances are sometimes called "BLEVEs" but the use of this imprecise term may lead to difficulties (see Appendix 3). A description of a so-called "BLEVE" is provided in [1].

Due to mechanical causes other than overpressure.

(a) Implosion due to the creation of partial vacuum

(b) Collision with a fixed object such as a bridge

(c) Collision with another vehicle

(d) Collapse of a structure onto it

(e) Moving away when connected to a loading/unloading facility

(f) Damage by an external explosion

(g) General wear and tear

(h) Modifications in violation of original specification

Notes. (a) and (e) are likely to occur only in a depot. (a) is much less likely to occur to a thick walled vessel.

Metallurgical failure.

(a) Vessel designed and/or constructed to an inadequate specification

(b) Failure to meet specified construction codes

(c) Use of wrong or inadequate materials of construction

(d) Modifications which substitute materials of construction not in original specification.

(e) Vessel used for purpose not covered by specification

(f) Corrosion, whether internal or external

(g) Erosion

(h) Fatigue

(i) Embrittlement by chemical action

(j) Embrittlement by low temperature

Notes.

(a) For example by underestimating internal pressure.

(b) There could be many possible faults. One would be failure to avoid sharp edges which act as stress raisers. Methods of fabrication such as welding may not conform to specification. Inspection may be inadequate.

(c) Materials may have to be specified in great detail; small variations in chemical composition of alloys may be highly significant. Metals of the same chemical analysis may vary in mechanical properties according to the thermal and chemical regimes involved in their fabrication.

(e) Though some materials of construction have a fairly wide range of application moving outside this range may lead to failure.

(f) Corrosion may occur even when the materials of construction are correctly specified. Air or moisture may contribute as may impurities in the substances handled.

(g) Erosion may occur during filling or emptying.

(h) Any mobile structure may suffer fatigue because of rapidly changing stress levels.

(i) Pressure vessels need to be tough. Embrittlement which can lead to brittle fracture is very dangerous. Some steels for example are embrittled by anhydrous ammonia.

(j) As has been previously referred to, some low carbon steels can exhibit brittleness at temperatures below 0 C. These effects can be controlled by the use of appropriate grain refining alloying elements and/or heat treatment. Appendix D of BS 5500 defines the procedures that ensure safe operation.

CONSEQUENCES OF LOSS OF CONTAINMENT

Introduction

There are five principal, interdependent, factors to be considered which influence the nature of the consequences.

(1) The physical state of the contents

(2)   The location and size of any leak which develops

(3)   The mechanism of dispersion

(4)   The chemical nature of the contents

(5)   The surroundings

Physical State of Contents

The four main conditions have been set out previously in Table 1.   They are:-

Case (1).   Liquids at atmospheric pressure and at a temperature below atmospheric which is the boiling point of the substance.

Case (2).   Liquids conveyed at atmospheric temperature and pressure. The atmospheric temperature will be, in general, appreciably below their atmospheric pressure boiling point.

Case (3).   Liquids conveyed at atmospheric pressure and at a temperature above atmospheric.

Case (4).   Liquefied gases which are stored at, or near to, atmospheric temperature but under a pressure equal to their vapour pressure.

Location and Size of Leak

Case (a). Leak is above the Liquid Line.   Case (1) above will discharge some of the substance as vapour as it will be slowly boiling off at a rate which is proportional to the rate at which heat passes in from the surroundings.   In Case (2) the rate of discharge of vapour will depend upon the volatility of the substance.   It may present a danger of fire for substances such as petrol.   Case (3) may discharge vapour.   Case (4) will give rise to the discharge of vapour which will continue until the leakage is stopped or until all the contents have been vaporised.   The rate of flashing will depend upon the size of the leak but could be very violent for large ruptures even when these are entirely above the liquid line. Initially this process is adiabatic, i.e. it does not require the input of heat from the surrounds. [See Appendix 2 The Behaviour of Flashing Liquids].

Case (b). Leak is below the Liquid Line.   All cases will discharge liquid to form a stream or a pool.   The behaviour of the liquid will depend upon its temperature and other physical properties.

Case (1) is that of a liquid at its boiling point which is much below atmospheric temperature.   Boiling will occur because of the input of heat by contact with the surroundings.   The rate of boiling is likely to be governed by the phenomenon of film boiling in which the boiling liquid is levitated on top of a blanket of its vapour. (The same phenomenon can be observed if water is poured into a hot frying pan). Eventually the surroundings cool and may become frozen hard and the rate of vaporisation becomes governed by the rate of inleakage of heat from the main body of the surroundings into the frozen core. Frost bite or cold burn injuries may be caused.

Case (2). When a substance such as petrol is spilled, though it is below its boiling point, it still has a vapour pressure sufficiently high as to create a flammable cloud above its surface which wind may carry for an appreciable distance.

Case (3). When a hot molten substance is spilled it will cool and eventually solidify in contact with the ground. If sufficiently hot, as for example a molten metal, it may start fires.

Case (4). Liquefied gases will flash and give rise to a vapour cloud. The process may be very violent and give rise to dangerous clouds; it is further discussed below and in Appendix 2. Low temperature effects may give rise to frost bite or cold burns.

The Mechanism of Dispersion

As recently as the early seventies, practically nothing was known about the formation and dispersion of vapour clouds. Since that time intensive theoretical investigation, together with field trials such as those at Thorney Island, have greatly increased understanding of the phenomen.[2]

The behaviour of vapour clouds is determined by four main factors. The first is the "source term" which depends upon the chemical nature and physical state of the contents and the nature of the leak. The second depends upon the meteorological conditions. These include the wind direction and speed and also the stability of the atmosphere which is related to the "lapse rate" which is the rate at which the air temperature falls off with height. On a hot summer's day the lapse rate is at a maximum and on a cloudless winter's night it may be negative, i.e. temperature increases with height. Thus a breezy, hot summer's day will promote dispersion and a calm, cold winter's night will slow it down. However, though dispersion may be rapid in the summer conditions referred to, the time available to warn people will be less. The third factor is surface roughness which is analogous to the influence which the roughness of the interior of pipes has upon the regime of flow and the pressure drop produced. These three factors are now sufficiently well understood that they can be modelled in computer programmes some of which are commercially available.

The fourth factor is concerned with topography which includes the surface contours and the presence of physical obstructions such as trees or buildings. The influence of this factor is not, as yet, understood as well as that of the other three but work is proceeding on it. Recent research suggests that the presence of obstructions and of semi-confinement may enhance the probability that a flammable vapour cloud, if ignited, may give rise to a vapour cloud explosion.

The significance of dispersion is at its maximum in case (4), the liquefied gases, which can give rise to vapour clouds within seconds without the need for heat input from the surroundings. Case (1) liquids come next where the rate of vaporisation depends upon the rate of heat input from the surroundings. Case (2) liquids, depending upon their chemical composition and volatility, may give rise to flammable or toxic clouds but these are not likely to extend to anything like the distance of clouds arising from case (4) or case (1) liquids. Case (3) liquids do not seem likely to be important in this context.

Flammable clouds, depending upon the nature of the flammable substance, cease to be dangerous when diluted to about 2% by volume whereas toxic clouds may be dangerous at much lower concentrations. Other things being equal it is apparent that toxic clouds may be dangerous at much greater distances than flammable clouds.

Chemical Composition

Four main kinds of substance which may give rise to vapour clouds may be distinguished. They are (a) flammables, (b) toxics, (c) combustion enhancers and (d) inerts.

Flammable clouds may give rise to flash fires, fire balls or vapour cloud explosions.

Toxic substances are each unique in their properties and may vary greatly in their intensity. They may affect the respiratory system, the blood, the central nervous system, the eyes or the skin. Each must therefore be studied in its own right.

The most obvious, if not the sole, example of a combustion enhancing agent which is transported in bulk, is liquid oxygen. Enhancement of combustion becomes significant at about 25% oxygen and is likely to be of the greatest danger to people in the immediate vicinity as clothing will burn readily. There are no case histories of widespread effects from oxygen spillages.

The effects of inert substances are likely to be highly localised and to take the form of asphyxiation.

The Nature of the Surroundings

It is evident that the consequences which follow loss of containment are much dependent upon the nature of the surroundings as, for example, the population density.

CONCLUSIONS

Road and rail tankers today carry a variety of hazardous materials. In some cases these cargoes are carried at above atmospheric pressure and in some cases above, or substantially below, atmospheric temperature.

There are many possible causes of failure. Some are due to external impact and others to internal causes. They may give rise to a series of consequences.

The record in the United Kingdom has been very good; unlike abroad where there have been a number of serious accidents involving, in some cases, heavy loss of life. This good record largely arises through careful attention to design and to the conditions of operation, with especial attention to the avoidance of overfilling.

REFERENCES

1. Marshall, V.C., Major Chemical Hazards, Ellis Horwood, Chichester, UK, 1987, p 179.

2. McQuaid, J. [Editor]. Heavy gas dispersion trials in Journal of Hazardous Materials. Vol II, June 1985, Elsevier Science Publishers, Amsterdam.

3. Nomenclature for Hazard and Risk Assessment in the Process Industries, Institution of Chemical Engineers, Rugby, UK, 1985.

APPENDIX 1

THE SEQUENCE OF EVENTS CONSEQUENT UPON HEATING A LIQUID STORED IN A TANK WITHOUT PRESSURE RELIEF

Stage	Description	Pressure Regime
1	The tank is loaded with liquid.	Vapour pressure of the liquid, increasing with temperature. Failure may occur due to vapour pressure alone.
2	The contents expand on heating but the expanded volume is less than the internal volume of the tank.	
3	The expanded contents have a volume exactly equal to the internal volume of the tank.	
4	Further expansion of the liquid occurs which is accommodated by stretching of the tank walls within their elastic limit. The compressibility of the liquid is a factor.	Hydraulic pressure of liquid is added to vapour pressure.
5	Further expansion is accommodated by stretching of the tank walls beyond the elastic limit.	
6	A crack develops and rapidly propagates.	Rapid fall in pressure but during these phases the total pressure is higher than the vapour pressure of the liquid.
7	The strain energy in the liquid and tank walls is dissipated; this may be accompanied by missile projection.	
8	The internal energy in the liquid is dissipated. In the case of a liquefied gas this will be a function of the energy which would be required to liquefy the gas. This dissipation will occur through the medium of flashing.	Pressure falling from vapour pressure of liquid towards atmospheric pressure.
9	Where flashing occurs reactive forces may operate, tending to propel the whole or the parts of the tank.	
10	The flashing will produce a vapour cloud with a degree of admixture with air.	Atmospheric pressure.

NOTES: The table is intended to cover the general case of a tank loaded with a liquid which therefore may, or may not, be a liquefied gas. Obviously in the vast majority of cases the sequence stops at stage 2. In some cases of malpractice the sequence may start at stage 3, i.e. where the tank is completely filled with cold liquid at loading. For non-volatile liquids the sequence stops at stage 7.

APPENDIX 2.

THE BEHAVIOUR OF FLASHING LIQUIDS

Some substances which are in the gaseous phase at ordinary temperatures are capable of being liquefied by pressure alone. The physical state of such substances is described scientifically as "vapour". Examples are propane, butane, chlorine and ammonia which are handled in bulk as "liquefied gases". Substances which cannot be so liquefied, and which require cooling as well as pressure to turn them into liquids, are called "permanent gases". Examples are oxygen, nitrogen and methane.

When the pressure is released from a liquefied gas "flashing" occurs. This takes the form of a fraction of the liquid immediately boiling off and the residual liquid cooling to the atmospheric pressure boiling point of the substance. The process is "adiabatic" in that it occurs without the need for heat to enter the system to provide the heat of vaporisation (latent heat). This heat is obtained at the expense of the sensible heat of the liquid. The fraction which will vaporise may be calculated from tables of thermodynamic properties to give a "theoretical adiabatic flashing fraction" or "TAFF".

In practice the quantity of liquid left may be much less than would be calculated above as the boiling in some circumstances is so violent that a substantial fraction of the liquid is projected as spray or froth. This may be demonstrated by removing the cap from a car radiator when the contents are boiling under pressure and when the water is these circumstances is a liquefied gas.

The value of the TAFF varies according to the volatility of the substance, its temperature at the time of release and the ratio between the specific heat capacity of the liquid phase of the substance and its specific latent heat of vaporisation. Indicative figures are 0.35 for propane and 0.15 for chlorine and ammonia.

The volume of vapour released may be very large. A vessel containing air compressed to 8 bars, if it burst, would allow the air to expand to 8 times its initial volume. A vessel full of propane at ordinary temperatures, if it burst, could yield a volume of propane vapour about 80 times its initial volume. The large reactive forces arising from the volumes released by flashing liquids in such circumstances help to account for the great distances over which parts of tankers have been propelled in incidents which have occurred abroad.

Such disintegrations are, therefore, accompanied by localised blast effects which have nothing to do with combustion but arise from the rapid expansion of the vapour released. They are, in fact, no different in nature from those produced by the explosion of steam boilers which have long been noted for their destructive effects.

After flashing is completed the residual pool, which is at a temperature below atmospheric, will continue to evaporate. The rate of this evaporation will be governed by the rate of heat input from the surroundings.

For further discussion see Ref [1].

APPENDIX 3.

A NOTE ON THE EXPRESSION "BLEVE".

This is discussed in "Nomenclature for Hazard and Risk Assessment in the Process Industries". [3].

"The term BLEVE (Boiling Liquid Expanding Vapour Explosion) is similar, to the extent that the limited blast involved arises only from physical energy. The acronym BLEVE is now used widely and is abused. It was introduced originally in the USA to describe a specific sequence of events commencing with the sudden rupture due to fire impingement, of a vessel/system under pressure containing liquefied flammable gas. The release of energy from the pressure bursts and the flashing of the liquid to vapour (flash fraction) creates a localised blast wave, this being in no way due to the flammability of the material. However, if immediate ignition of the expanding fuel-air mixture occurs, this leads to intense combustion creating a fireball which rises away from the ground due to buoyancy. This is the principal hazard, together with the missile effects of the ruptured containment system. In recent times, attempts have been made to widen the usage of the term BLEVE to include any sudden failure of a system containing any liquefied gas under pressure. It is felt that to avoid confusion, the name BLEVE should be avoided wherever possible and terms such as pressure burst, flashing and fireball should be used to describe the particular scenario. If the term BLEVE is to be used then it is recommended that it should only be used in its original sense as described above."

The flame impingement referred to above is more specifically related to flame impingement where this occurs on a part of the wall above the liquid/vapour interface. Below that level the boiling mechanism prevents the wall temperature rising much above the boiling point of the liquid. Above it there is no such mechanism operating. If the wall temperature exceeds about 600°C, structural steel becomes weak. Taken in combination with an internal pressure probably above design blow off pressure, a petal fracture may ensue.

The circumstance has occurred many times in the past with Lancashire type boilers or with steam locomotives when the boiler attendant had allowed the water level to fall so that the fire tubes or fire box were no longer fully immersed in liquid.

SHOULD DANGEROUS GOODS BE MOVED BY RAIL RATHER THAN BY ROAD?

DAVID BEATTIE M.A.

Transport Engineering Section Manager
ICI Engineering

ABSTRACT

The paper examines the transport of dangerous goods by road and rail. The methods used for assessing the frequency of incidents are discussed, and the results are considered qualitatively against the factors relevent to each mode.

INTRODUCTION

The number of fatalities caused by the transport of dangerous goods is low, and other activities with significantly higher risks are accepted by the general public. Nevertheless unease about such transport remains, and this is coupled with a widely held belief that rail transport for such commodities is safer. This paper examines the comparative risks of road and rail transport.

SIGNIFICANT INCIDENTS

The public concern about an activity is heightened if the number of potential fatalities is high even if the frequency is very low. The number of fatalities that could result from an incident involving the flammable or corrosive liquids normally carried in bulk is unlikely to rise into double figures. With flammable or toxic gases the effects could spread over a much wider area, and so the study will concentrate on incidents involving gases.

SEQUENCE OF EVENTS

The necessary factors to be considered here are

1.   The frequency of a transport accident.
2.   Given an accident occurs, the likelihood of that leading to
     puncture.
3.   Given a puncture, how many people are there likely to be in the
     affected area.
4.   What proportion of these are likely to succumb.

In the case of gases, spontaneous failure of the vessel is (for modern
technology) assessed as vanishingly small. (This is discussed in Appendix
1). Similarly leaks from fittings are not likely to be of such a magnitude
as to affect a large area. And fire engulfment is a lower order happening
than puncture (Appendix 2). The significant happening is therefore a
puncture as a result of an accident.

DETERMINATION OF PUNCTURE FREQUENCY

In the event of puncture frequency in the UK, a fundamental difficulty
exists. Despite the long history of transport (eg toxic gases such as
chlorine have been transported by rail for more than seventy years) there
have been few incidents. On rail there have been no punctures of gas
tankers, and on road only one puncture. This was a tanker carrying vinyl
chloride in 1947, which rolled over and was punctured by a sharp
holding-down bracket. (The gas evaporated without incident). Subsequent
designs were altered to delete any such self-puncturing tools. In
addition such small leaks that have occurred from inadequately closed
valves have been minor, of a nuisance nature rather than a significant
hazard, and speedily dealt with.

With this inadequate data base one could use statistical methods to
project forward. Or alternatively one can examine areas of similar
operations. This latter approach was adopted by the author in work done
by industry in conjunction with a recent joint study carried out with the
Health and Safety Executive.

RAIL FREQUENCY

The initial attempts to proceed along the path of taking frequency of
accidents and then postulating a secondary puncture rate was abandoned as
impractical. To determine the likely frequency one needs to know the
circumstances of each accident – the speed, circumstances, type of
impingement etc. In most cases this is not available. A wider data base
was examined.

USA DATA

The traffic in hazardous materials in the USA is extensive, exceeding by a large margin in tonnage and even more in ton mileage that of Europe. The reporting of incidents is well documented and thus a large data base exists.

However the US and UK rail systems differ in several important particulars. The US network is fragmented, generally in a poor standard of maintenance, speed restrictions abound and derailment frequencies are high compared with European experience. The rail tankers themselves are larger and heavier and generally more vulnerable than their UK counterparts. US trains are very long, unbraked and often of mixed riding characteristics. In the UK by contrast through braking is the norm, and to travel on BR's Speedfreight system tankers have to be suitable for 60mph traffic without instability. BR goods traffic lines have over the recent years been upgraded closer to passenger standards.

It was held therefore that the US data was unrepresentative of UK conditions.

UK DATA

Instead of looking at a larger system, the net was widened by extending the area of examination to all punctures in the UK to rail tankers rather than just to thicker walled gas tankers.

Examining all the punctures of liquid tankers for the period 1979-1985, each accident was considered in turn. It was considered that a thick walled gas tanker had been involved in the crash rather than the thinner liquid tanker that actually ruptured. By considering the relevant factors such as speed and type of puncturing tool and then applying engineering judgement, probability was assessed of a gas tanker rupturing in the particular accident. To get a true frequency for the product, this figure is multiplied by the probability of a chlorine tanker being in the crash position. This is taken as the ratio of tanker miles for the product to total tanker miles. This produces a frequency of puncture of 0.4 per 10^9 loaded tanker Kms.

The details are shown in Appendix 3.

ROAD FREQUENCY

For road, detailed data of punctures in the UK to all road tankers does not exist; certainly not in the form that would enable a similar exercise to be carried out by considering each accident.

The conditions of USA and UK road networks are sufficiently similar in accident frequency, road construction and average speeds for direct comparison to be viable. The accident reports are available in the USA in sufficient detail for analysis to be carried out. The type of accident selected were those to LPG tankers where the ton mileage was also known. For the period 1971-1977 there were 12 punctures equating to a puncture rate of 5 per 10^9 loaded tanker Kms.

However although the road conditions in the two countries are similar, the tanker designs are not. In the USA extensive use is made of quenched and tempered steel which has a much poorer resistance to impact damage than the low carbon steels almost universally used in the UK. The use of these steels with their elevated mechanical properties also results in thinner tanks. The individual accidents were therefore analysed and a factor allocated to it in a similar manner to the rail exercise, to obtain a figure for a probability that a UK gas tanker would have punctured had it been involved. After applying these correcting factors, the resultant puncture frequency for chlorine road tankers in the UK was 0.1 per 10^9 loaded Kms.

RESULTANT FATALITIES

To determine the resultant fatalities the density and magnitude of the population at risk needs to be determined. This will vary from route to route.

The consequences for chlorine traffic on a particular route in the North of England were assessed in a recent paper. Densities of population were calculated for the two routes, and using gas dispersion models isopleths were determined for the various release scenarios. The number of people likely to be affected were determined using the population densities. Coupling these figures with the puncture frequencies previously determined, produced the Societal Risk figures given in Appendix 4.

DISCUSSION

Although the figures indicate quite convincingly that there is no general case for preferring one mode to another for the transport of dangerous goods it is interesting to examine in qualitative terms whether this conclusion is realistic.

The factor most frequently quoted by the protagonists of rail is the lower frequency of accidents. For example in 1987 the relative rates (in the case of rail averaged over the 4 previous years) for fatalities were

road   10
rail   2 per thousand million passenger kilometers.

It is also claimed that in the rail mode track circuiting (which automatically alters signals to prevent other trains entering a block with a derailed train) and absence of pedestrians limits the number of people affected.

However although the frequency of accidents per se is lower in the rail mode, the likelihood of an accident leading to a puncture is that much greater. The factors that cause this are the greater energy available (trains weigh around 1,000 tons, and have negligible braking capabilities compared to road) and the much high availability of puncturing tools. The rail mode has tight clearances and an abundance of solid objects (points, buffers, hooks, wagon corners) of sufficient rigidity to puncture a thick vessel. In the road mode, on the other hand, vehicles and street furniture are designed to crumple, and the rigid tools necessary to puncture a thick walled vessel are not that readily available.

The number of people affected is likely to be similar. Although the road mode is closer to individuals, the motorway network (where the higher speeds necessary for puncture are more likely) is generally away from areas of high population density. Railways on the other hand tend to go through the centres of towns. And rail accidents occur predominantly in areas of points and crossings which are generally in urban areas rather than on stretches of plain track.

The travelling population is also unlikely to be significantly different. An accident on a road could result in a long tail back of vehicles; but the interaction of a laden passenger train could also bring a large number of people into the danger area. The recent accident in USSR underlines this point.

The economics of rail transport are such that banks of tankers carrying the same product are frequently marshalled together, whereas road tankers travel individually. The scope for knock-on effects due to the larger volumes involved in a single accident is thus higher on rail.

An examination of the above factors clearly indicates that the figures obtained are credible.

CONCLUSION

The analysis of the comparative risks of the transport ofdangerous goods by rail and road needs to take into account many factors; the type of overall system, the design of tankers, the disposition of population, and type of dangerous goods for example. The cost of switching traffic from road to rail would in many cases require considerable expenditure as many sites are not rail connected. There is no case for a general change from road to rail as far as dangerous goods are concerned.

APPENDIX 1

In the early days of welded vessels weld quality was variable, and control of all the parameters was uncertain. There were some failures of transport tanks which with more recent knowledge would be attributed to brittle fracture.

The only documented "spontaneous" failures of transport tanks occured in the USA. On 24 February 1978 a derailed tank car carrying LPG ruptured at Waverly, Tennesee 40 hours after the accident. A similar rupture happened to an ammonia tanker near Cumming, Iowa in 1969 two days after the derailment. In both cases the tanks had suffered denting and gouging across a weld (in the case of the Waverly tanker a gouge some 16 feet (5m) long). These effectively formed a significant defect leading to a failure at below design pressure.

In the UK gas tankers are made from ductile low carbon steel with guaranteed low temperature notch ductibility and are fully radiographed and stress relieved. Their ability to resist damage is superior, and hence failure of the pressure vessel per se can be considered a low order probability.

APPENDIX 2

Fire engulfement.

The following is a coarse scale calculation, based on UK data.

1. BR figures report only 5 major fires over a period of 18 years.

2. On average, 0.5 in 100 of freight train incidents per year results in a collision with a passing train.

3. Probability of a single train containing a gas tanker is ratio of their mileage.

    Gas tanker train mileage $= 10\%$ of 4.5×10^6
    Total   "   " $= 275 \times 10^6$
    Therefore ratio $= \dfrac{0.10 \times 4.5}{275} = 0.0016$

Therefore probability of a gas tanker being involved in a fire per year is

$$\frac{5}{18} \times \frac{0.5}{100} \times 0.0016 = 2.2 \times 10^{-6}$$

With a total of 4.5×10^6 loaded wagon miles, the chances of a gas tanker being involved in a fire is

$$\frac{2.2}{4.5} \times \frac{10^{-6}}{10^6} = 0.5 \text{ per } 10^{12} \text{ loaded wagon miles}$$

- clearly insignificant compared with puncture.

APPENDIX 3.   TANKER PUNCTURES.   B.R.   1970-1985.

DATE	LOCATION	BRIEF DESCRIPTION	CHANCE OF CHLORINE TANKER BEING PUNCTURED
17 MAR 70	Worksop	Crude oil tankers in major derailment.	0.1
21 MAY 73	Heaton Norris	Phosphoric acid train ran away, crashed into another freight train. 3 punctures.	0.02
26 MAR 76	Chester	Phosphoric Acid tanker overturned at low speed after axle failure.	NIL
03 APR 79	Ellesmere Port	Empty oil tankers (two axle) derailed on poor track. One holed.	0.01
01 MAY 80	Whitmoor March	ICI Methanol tanker punctured by hook in hump shunting.	NIL
21 JAN 81	Thames Haven	45T Gas oil tankers derailed on trap points. One tanker holed.	NIL
17 JUL 81	Dringhouses	ICI Methanol tank punctured in shunting incident. Fire.	NIL
16 DEC 81	Sighthill	45T Diesel oil tankers derailed due to excessive speed. Two tanks ruptured.	0.03
30 JUL 82	Lindsey	Head on train collision at crossover resulted in puncture of 100T petrol tanker by buffer of barrier wagon.	NIL
24 AUG 82	Shanden	Petrol tankers derailed down embankment. One split.	0.02
03 MAR 83	Moore	Train of gas oil tankers derailed down embankment, spillage ignited by arcing.	0.02

APPENDIX 3. (Cont'd)   TANKER PUNCTURES.   B.R.   1970-1985.

DATE	LOCATION	BRIEF DESCRIPTION	CHANCE OF CHLORINE TANKER BEING PUNCTURED
04 DEC 84	Salford	Train crashed into rear of stationary petrol tankers, 3 punctured.	0.2
20 DEC 84	Summit Tunnel	Seized axle box caused petrol tankers to crash in tunnel. No puncture shells, although major fire developed from spillage.	NIL
TOTAL			**0.40**

(The accident at Weaver Valley 6 August 1975 has been discounted because the cause – a mixture of vacuum and air brakes – no longer applies on BR). The average yearly loaded tanker mileage is taken as 4.5×10^6 per year.

APPENDIX 4

Societal Risk results expressed in frequencies ($*10^6$) of N or more fatalities per year:

Number of Fatalities (N)	1	10	30	100	300	1000
Rail Route						
Nearby populations	98	50	26	25	6	4
Passenger train casualties	29	25	23	11	5	0
TOTAL	101	61	33	27	7	4
Road Route						
Nearby populations	15	4	1	.7	.5	0
Motorists	20	11	9	5	4	0
TOTAL	20	13	10	6	2	0

From "The Transport of Chlorine by Road and Rail in Britain –
a Consideration of the Risks". By I C Canadine ICI and G Purdy HSE, 6th
International Symposium, – Loss Prevention and Safety Promotion in the
Process Industries. Oslo June 1989.

TREMEX : TRANSPORT EMERGENCY EXPERT SYSTEM

*J.E. LYCETT, *D. MAUDSLEY and +D.L. MILNER

*Division of Instrumentation and Control Engineering, School of Information Engineering, Teesside Polytechnic, Middlesbrough, Cleveland TS1 3BA (0642 218121).

+ICI Chemicals and Polymers
Wilton, Cleveland

ABSTRACT

Expert system techniques offer many advantages in transport emergency situations. When an emergency involves a hazardous chemical, such as ethylene oxide (UN 1040), a chemical expert is required at the incident as soon as possible. Arising out of an idea from ICI, Teesside Polytechnic developed an expert system (TREMEX) which offers advice to the officer in charge of an incident, before the arrival of the expert. The paper describes key areas of design including structuring, knowledge formalisation, advice presentation, user interfacing and graphical representation. TREMEX captures expertise from ICI Chemicals and Polymers and Cleveland County Fire Brigade. The system was implemented in SAVOIR (an expert system programming environment) at Teesside Polytechnic and funded by the Health and Safety Executive.

INTRODUCTION

Throughout the UK and Europe large quantities of chemicals are transported by road tanker. Some of these chemicals are classified as dangerous goods and can present a risk to other road users, local population, the environment, and emergency services. Recently a 'top ten' list of chemicals has been identified as the more hazardous chemicals transported by road. An incident involving any one of these chemicals requires special consideration. Should a road tanker carrying such a dangerous chemical break down or be involved in a traffic incident, such as a collision, then fast appropriate action must be taken to avoid a dangerous situation developing, or to deal with the incident in the appropriate way to ensure minimum risk to life, ecology and property.

Emergency action codes and procedures, such as HAZCHEM, TREM cards and CHEMDATA, already exist for dealing with incidents. However in incidents involving certain classes of chemicals a specialist is summoned to the incident to give additional advice and support to the officer in charge. Depending on the location it may take two to four hours for the specialist to arrive at the incident. During this time the emergency services attempt to contain the incident until the expert arrives. When the expert arrives he uses his senses and specialist knowledge to assess the situation, and gives advice to the emergency personnel. Can an Expert System fill the gap before the expert arrives to:

a) contain the hazardous situation

b) prevent a non-hazardous situation developing into a hazardous one

c) deal successfully with the incident ?

For this to be done an expert system must firstly contain the expert's knowledge and secondly be able to obtain information which allows this knowledge to be used. In the human expert the latter is done using his 'sensors' ie, eyes, ears, nose. Thus an important element of the expert system is the interface of the system to the emergency personnel who must provide the 'sensors'. This is done by a series of questions posed by the computer, with responses input through the keyboard. A key consideration in the expert system is the design of this interface, the nature of the questions and the prompts for response.

The paper considers the design and development of a prototype expert system to deal with Ethylene Oxide. Details of the knowledge base and its development, the question/answer dialogue with the user and the validation of the system via a 'table top' exercise are presented.

EXPERT SYSTEMS

An expert system may be considered as a computer system which contains expert knowledge in a knowledge base, an inference engine which sorts out the questions which need to be asked to enable conclusions to be reached, an explanation (or output) module for displaying advice, comments, etc, and a user input module for capturing data. A knowledge-based system (expert system) which encapsulates specialist (expert) knowledge would be useful and may reduce the potential hazard by offering decision support to the senior officer in charge of the incident, at an early stage prior to the arrival of the expert. The most significant part of the expert system as far as we are concerned is the creation of a knowledge base for ethylene oxide incidents.

Nature of Expert Knowledge

The expert's knowledge [1] is not just factual information, but includes how and why to use the knowledge. Factual knowledge contained in a book or on a TREMCARD or in a background help facility within an expert system, may give for example, the boiling point of ethylene oxide. The expert not only knows the facts but also the implications. As he begins to assess the situation his line of questioning may change. For example, a certain situation is identified which precludes certain other situations arising or reduces their priority. The expert system must similarly be able to adapt its line of reasoning (inference) as knowledge of the situation increases. As a simple example consider the first question in TREMEX. Figure 1 refers:

Is the tanker on fire

or

is there a fire in close proximity ?

Answer Y for any kind of fire

N for no fire.

Enter A for further information

Figure 1. 'Simplistic' type of question in TREMEX

Clearly this line of questioning provides a routing, one route into a 'fire' incident, the other route into 'no-fire at the moment' incident. If the fire route is considered, further questions are necessary to ascertain the type of fire, or what is burning. Likewise if the no-fire route is considered, different sets of questions concerning the integrity of the tank and vehicle are generated. This leads to an avenue of questions and advice which are dynamic in nature.

A further feature of the 'human expert' is his ability to give interim advice as his understanding of the situation develops. This can be of vital importance to prevent the situation becoming more hazardous. Take for example the situation when the system has established that there is 'no fire,' and 'no obvious leak' of ethylene oxide, part of the advice given is 'go and look closer.' However, there may be a small leak, so that the advice offered may place the fireman in a hazardous, possibly fatal situation. The human expert would advise what precautions need to be taken before attempting a closer look. The expert system must similarly give warning and interim advice, even though the situation has not been fully assessed. Refer to figure 2.

DO not approach the tanker until proper safety precautions have been taken. You must wear breathing apparatus and full protective clothing.

Do not approach the vehicle until water has been sprayed over it. Ethylene Oxide is very explosive and needs to be diluted with water to stop it from igniting. Continue spraying with water while working near the tanker. Do not let this spray get on to the skin.

more......

Figure 2. Typical interim advice

The following items are contained inside the valve chest shown below :

Temperature gauge
Pressure gauge
Pressure gauge
Discharge valves :
A. Large valve for liquid (left)
B. Small valve for gas (right)

Figure 3. Graphical representation of the valve chest components.

Another feature of the human expert is his ability to explain his line of reasoning, and the reason for asking certain questions. It is important that the expert system should have the same ability – it will increase the confidence of the non-expert user if the system can justify why certain questions are being asked. One way TREMEX handles this is by using an AMPLIFY facility which allows the user to access further information when the system asks a question by simply pressing a key on the key board as indicated in figure 1. The system designer can include appropriate text and/or directions which appear following this prompt, the user is able to return to the question by pressing a further key. In a further example in TREMEX the user is asked to investigate whether there is a leak from the valve chest on the tanker. By pressing a key (in this case the letter A key) an annotated diagram of the valve chest appears on the screen, this identifies the location and relative size of important components **(figure 3)**.

Structure
Knowledge obtained from the expert requires structuring so that correct and consistent inferences may be made by the expert system. If the purpose of a particular line of questioning is to give useful advice, say in the case of a major fire incident, then a framework is necessary to represent the expert's knowledge. Consider the above case of a major fire incident, a typical inference network, **figure 4** consists of a goal (potential evacuation), several sub-goals (fire, time, environment, resources), questions and advice. The inter-relationship of this goal, the other goals and sub-goals to separate knowledge components very quickly produces an intricate web through which the user is steered by the system's questions.

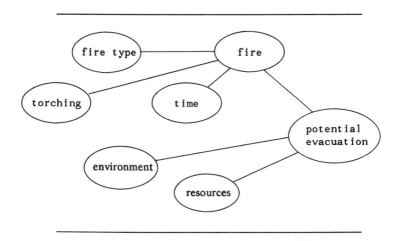

Figure 4. Typical inference network.

DESIGN CONSIDERATIONS of the HUMAN INTERFACE

The human being automatically uses all senses when assessing a situation or problem. Senses such as sight, sound, smell, (the three remote senses) are used in assessing the majority of road incidents concerning possible chemical spillages. Within our questioning framework, provision must be made firstly to alert the user and secondly to ask the user to use the multi-sensoring capabilities of the human body. Our particular system only takes an input from the keyboard, which means that all information must be reduced to a combination of keyboard characters. Given this task several alternatives appear. The obvious method is to ask the user directly,eg, 'can you smell anything unusual' and expect to receive a yes/no reply. An alternative way is 'suggestive' eg, 'Does the leak smell like hospitals?' Finally where all remote senses are required to be used, ie, sight, sound, smell a question can be framed which logically 'ORs' the senses thus simply requiring a yes/no response.

Questioning
Carefully worded questions [2] are essential to lead the user into giving accurate and precise replies. Any uncertainty or doubt in the user's mind, about the meaning of a particular question, must be covered by background explanation (question amplification) so that false or erroneous information is avoided. Questions must first and foremost be lucid. Where necessary, informative text by way of explanation, metaphoric description, or why the question is being asked, should be easily accessible and have a place within the system. The wording on the computer screen should be brief, unambiguous, and in plain simple (non-technical) language. Consider again the opening question screen in TREMEX, illustrated in figure 1. Here we have a plain simple question. All extraneous information has been stripped away and hidden behind the question in the form of an amplification. The user is required to reply either (Y)es or (N)o, but if the user does not understand the question, or why it is being asked, or requires qualification an amplification to the question is provided. This is accessed by entering A instead of Y or N. After reading the amplification the user would be returned to the consultation.

Simplistic type of Questioning
Perhaps the simplest type of question is the straight Yes or No (Condition) type of question. Here the user is given a limited choice. After a brief description the user is required to respond with a yes/no, know/don't know type of answer. To help the user to give the most appropriate reply, informative text may be included in the body of the question. Figure 5 shows a further question from TREMEX (called for convenience [obvious-leak]):

Both liquid and Gas may leak from an
Ethylene Oxide Tanker.

If you can see liquid dripping or running off the
tanker, then you probably have a leak that needs
attention.

Gas leaks may be detected by a hissing noise as it
leaves the tank, however small leaks may be difficult
to hear.

STAND away from the vehicle and look around for liquid
leaks or pools forming on the ground.
LISTEN for hissing noises.

Can you SEE, HEAR or SMELL a leak from the tanker?

Enter   'A' for further information

Figure 5.   Informative type of question.

Complex type of Questioning
Both quantitative and qualitative information is needed to be drawn into the system for any useful inferences to be made. To assist the user, menu-type questions are found to

be the most efficient and least ambiguous way of soliciting information. For example, consider the question shown in figure 6 (called for convenience [fire-type]):

You have indicated that the tanker is involved
in a fire incident.
What best describes the incident?

1: Large product leak on fire
2: Small product leak on fire
3: External fire heating the tank
4: Product leak heating the tank
5: Tanker at scene of fire
   but not directly involved
6: None of the above

Select the number which best describes the incident

for further information enter A

Figure 6.   Menu option type of question.

If the user is uncertain how to reply, additional information is available by entering **A** instead of a number.   The final type of question considered for TREMEX, but later discarded was the NUMERIC type. A numeric question requires a number as a reply. Consider the development of a question called [time]. How best can this be represented? The numeric type may seek a value in minutes and may look like the following:

How long has the fire been burning?

When the reason is examined as to why the time is required, it is found that the precise value is ranged into one of three ranges.   Thus the question could be re-phrased and structured as shown in figure 7:

**Time is important in dealing with
ethylene oxide fires**

Estimate how long the fire has been burning

1: Less than 20minutes
2: Between 20 to 40 minutes
3: More than 40 minutes

Figure 7.   Example of a re-structured numeric type question.

This way the user is not asked to provide too specific or precise information.   This simplification is obviously important when one considers the pressure emergency personnel may be under in dealing with a hazardous situation.

The above examples lead into consideration of what information, if any, should be flagged up in say the fire situation, such as any immediate warnings which may be applicable.

Advice and Information

The 'human expert' is able to give interim advice as his understanding of the situation develops. He is also a source of advice and information which may be accessed by the emergency personnel by questioning. TREMEX replicates these types of advice and information. As knowledge of the situation is accumulated, advice can be automatically and immediately offered, such as, 'set out unmanned fire monitors and keep the tank cool by spraying with water.' This advice should result in some immediate action being taken by the emergency personnel. As indicated earlier question amplification can be added to support the user's understanding of a question and to assist him in giving an appropriate response. Further advice which may help with the incident, but has not the immediate urgency of the former, is available both by request and as part of a report. Such advice and information, is contained in the form of an embedded multi-level 'help system'. This advice, may be considered as a book and should be accessible for reference at any time during the consultation.

In TREMEX the help system is accessed by pressing the 'h' key on the keyboard. A window appears displaying a menu of options shown in figure 8:

```
1: Tremcard           2: Chemdata
3: Tankers            4: Ethylene Oxide
5: Fire Fighting      6: Resources
7: Tanker fires       8: Contents Reactions
         9: Evacuation procedures
```

Figure 8. Help system menu.

By pressing the appropriate numeric key the advice is displayed on the screen.

SCOPE OF TREMEX

Figure 9 shows the overall scope of TREMEX. The first question in TREMEX asks 'is there a fire'. If the answer is yes the fire sub-system is entered. Questions are asked which gather information on the nature and location of the fire. Five possibilies are presented to generate a realistic scenario, these are: large product leak on fire, small product leak on fire, external fire heating the tank, product fire heating the tank, tanker at incident but not directly involved. Advice is offered as the situation is assessed. Other considerations assessed are concerned with the possibility of explosion, BLEVE, and torching. If there is no fire the leak sub-system is entered where such items as obvious leak, what is leaking, temperature rise, pressure venting, etc are assessed and appropriate advice displayed.

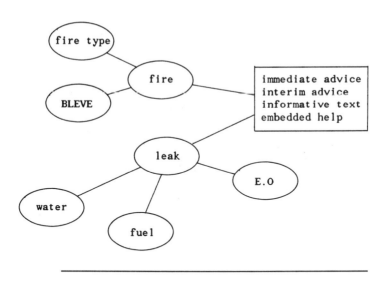

Figure 9.   Scope of TREMEX

IMPLEMENTATION AND OPERATIONAL CONSIDERATIONS

An important consideration is the location of the expert system.   This could be in the control room at the fire brigade head quarters under the control of a senior fire officer, with question/answer communication to the fire officer at scene of the incident via a radio link.   Alternatively a suitable ruggedised portable computer could be taken to the actual scene of the incident. Whilst the system has been designed for the former, subsequent technical development in hardware now makes the latter feasible.   The system is equally valid in this situation with little or no changes.

The system (TREMEX) designed to run on an IBM pc is implemented in SAVOIR a Pascal based expert system programming environment.   The system was constructed in strict accordance with the inference networks produced during knowledge elicitation (KE) sessions.   Advice/display information was given priorities in the KE sessions together with when it should be triggered.

TESTING AND VALIDATION

The system was factually checked as it was developed by the chemical expert and senior fire brigade personnel.   This enabled the inferencing to be developed gradually and the style and language of questioning to be checked.   A fully developed system for ethylene oxide has been evaluated by a 'table top exercise.'   Two rooms were used for this exercise,

1) Incident room − here the incident was simulated by the human expert using an overhead projector. He also acted as the driver of the tanker.   Front line fire brigade personnel were present in the room and had to 'deal' with the incident. They had telephone commumication with the second room − the control room.

2) Control room – this contained the computer running the expert system. The expert system was 'driven' by further fire brigade personnel.

None of the fire brigade personnel had any previous knowledge of the incident. The exercise was observed by personnel from the HSE, ICI, Cleveland County Fire Brigade and Teesside Polytechnic.

FUTURE TRENDS

Funding from the HSE has made possible the development of a 'mother' and ethylene oxide 'daughter' system. The mother system acts as a front–end to many daughter systems. Further chemicals, identified as belonging to the 'top ten' hazardous chemicals are currently being examined with a view to establishing commonality in daughter system design. To enable this work to proceed formalised methods for knowledge representation are being developed at Teesside Polytechnic, together with the development of multi–expert knowledge gathering techniques. New programming environments are being considered to implement this approach. EGERIA, developed by ISI (now EXPERTECH), the SAVOIR developers, offers 'frames' and 'inheritance' which will permit some of the commonality we seek in the daughter systems structures. This allied with the ease of screen graphics makes EGERIA an obvious choice for this kind of application. Parallel to the development of software is the development of computer hardware. Although the original TREMEX system was designed for IBMpc use in a control room, heavy duty portable pc's are becomming available. A portable pc may be carried by the senior officer to the incident or mounted permanently in an emergency tender. A practical alternative to the portable pc is the dedicated computer board which may also be built into an emergency tender. This has many advantages over the portable pc for applications in emergency situations, though the main disadvantages, at the present time, include model size limitations (size of the expert system) and inflexibility with respect to updating.

It is foreseen that systems such as TREMEX will play a vital role not only in actual transport emergencies but also in the training of personnel from the hauliers, users and manufactures of dangerous chemicals, and the emergency services.

REFERENCES

1. Harmon, P. and King, D., Expert Systems – Artificial Intelligence in Business, Wiley and Sons, 1985.

2. Shneiderman, B., Designing the user interface: Strategies for effective Human–Computer interaction, Addison–Wesley, 1987.

HUMAN RELIABILITY AND RISK MANAGEMENT IN THE TRANSPORTATION OF SPENT NUCLEAR FUEL

S. Tuler, R. E. Kasperson, and S. Ratick
Center for Technology, Environment, and Development,
Clark University, 950 Main Street, Worcester, MA   01610   U.S.A.

ABSTRACT

This paper summarizes work completed on human factors contributions to risks from spent nuclear fuel transportation.   Human participation may have significant effects on the levels and types of risks from transportation of spent nuclear fuel by enabling or initiating incidents and exacerbating adverse consequences.   Human errors are defined to be the result of mismatches between perceived system state and actual system state.   In complex transportation systems such mismatches may be distributed in time (e.g., during different stages of design, implementation, operation, maintenance) and location (e.g., human error, its identification, and its recovery may be geographically and institutionally separate).   Risk management programs may decrease the probability of undesirable events or attenuate the consequences of mismatches.   This paper presents a methodology to identify the scope and types of human-task mismatches and to identify potential management options for their prevention, mitigation, or recovery.   A review of transportation accident databases, in conjunction with human error models, is used to develop a taxonomy of human errors during design for the pre-identification of potential mismatches or after incidents have occurred to evaluate their causes.   Risk management options to improve human reliability are identified by a matrix that relates the multiple stages of a spent nuclear fuel transportation system to management options (e.g., training, data analysis, regulation).   The paper concludes with illustrative examples of how the methodology may be applied.

INTRODUCTION

Despite the evident importance of reliable human performance in spent nuclear fuel transportation, no comprehensive analysis of human factors has to date been undertaken in the United States. In general, U.S. federal agency and industry activities reflect the belief that human actions are not significant contributors to risk in the transportation system. However, the two prior risk assessments on which this conclusion is based (i.e., 1, 2) have been evaluated and shown to contain both methodological errors and faulty data (3, 4).

The systematic evaluation of human reliability has become an important need as planning begins for a federal high level radioactive waste repository. The opening of such a site will greatly affect the magnitude of activities associated with spent fuel transportation and the potential for adverse events arising out of human actions. We believe that careful consideration of human reliability is likely to lead to much higher estimated transportation risks than those estimated in prior risk assessments.

"Human reliability" in this paper refers to two different but related aspects of human interaction with technological systems. The first involves those aspects of human interventions in the system that may lead to an incident or exacerbate its adverse consequences, which we have called "human errors." They can affect risks by: 1) initiating risk events, 2) contributing to risk events, 3) altering the frequency of risk event sequences, 4) altering the structure of risk event trees by changing intervention strategies and reliability, and 5) altering couplings and interactions between subsystems and components.

The second type of interactions are those purposeful human interventions that prevent an incident or mitigate its adverse consequences. Two methods may be used to eliminate unwanted effects of human actions and improve human performance in technological systems: 1) programs may be instituted during the design of a transportation system to reduce the probability of human errors, or 2) the effects of human errors may be eliminated, mitigated, or reversed by effective management programs. We call these methods "transportation risk management programs." They should be designed to reduce risks, reduce uncertainties, allow adaptable and flexible responses to events, and reduce the social impacts of unforeseen events.

In this paper, we summarize some of our on-going research related to the transportation of spent nuclear fuel to a national repository in the U.S. Our concern is for incidents and accidents arising from human errors during all phases of the spent fuel transportation system and the identification of risk management programs to reduce their probability and impact. The intent of the paper is to:

1) identify the characteristics of the spent fuel transportation system that suggest human reliability should be an important area of concern and research;

2) provide a broad theoretical framework incorporating characteristics of individual, group, and organizational behavior on system performance and reliability;

3) describe a framework for identifying and evaluating the scope and types of human error sources in a spent nuclear fuel transportation system. In particular, a "human reliability matrix" is used to provide a framework for 1) the identification of previous and potential future human errors in the transportation system, and 2) the identification of risk management options that can be implemented to prevent, mitigate, or recover from human errors and their consequences.

THE IMPORTANCE OF HUMAN RELIABILITY

The results of our work suggest that until recently there was a marked lack of concern over human error as a cause of accidents or incidents in the transportation system within the industry and the relevant regulatory agencies and national research laboratories in the U.S (4). To some extent the lack of regulatory agency and industry concern results because to date there have been no severe incidents or accidents resulting in releases of radioactivity during spent fuel shipments. Indeed, several successful shipment campaigns for spent nuclear fuel have been completed (5, 6, 7). On the other hand, the shipment campaigns were 1) small compared with the expected numbers after a repository opens, and 2) heavily regulated and closely observed to assure operational safety and system reliability. We have identified four characteristics of spent fuel and other high-level radioactive waste transport that suggest why human actions may indeed contribute significantly to both actual and perceived risk of the transportation system.

First, the transportation of spent fuel involves a number of activities (Table 1), all of which depend on effective, safe, and reliable human performance. Improper or inadequate human actions may occur during transportation system design, implementation, operations, maintenance, and accident recovery. In particular, those entities that must respond to events caused by "upstream" human actions, are often separated temporally, spatially, and sectorally (i.e., institutionally) from the sources of the errors. Small failures in human-task systems at any point in the system have the potential for creating vulnerabilities at later times and in distant places in addition to immediate "on-site" effects.

TABLE 1
Spent fuel transportation system phases and activities

Design
- regulations
- institutional structure
- planning criteria (e.g., routing, modes)
- hazard communication
- cask and equipment design

Implementation
- organizational
- technical
- personnel

Operation
- oversight
- pre-shipment activities
- packaging, loading, securing casks
- transportation and transshipment
- receipt and post-shipment activities

Maintenance
- technical
- personnel
- data collection and analysis

Accident response and recovery
- notification
- immediate response
- long-term activities

Second, the magnitude of transportation activities for a national repository will be larger, more complex , and potentially more hazardous than any previous transportation program attempted. Although extensive regulatory oversight of spent fuel transportation activities is intended to reduce the frequency of risk events, the size of the reduction will depend directly on the effectiveness of transportation risk management programs. Numerous risk management strategies are available to affect the reduction of risks from human error. They may be focussed on activities and risks in all phases of the development and operation of the transportation system. Historical evidence, however, suggest that such programs have previously not been completely effective in eliminating human errors during the transportation of spent nuclear fuel (see below).

Third, even minor risk events in the transportation system for spent fuel have the potential for contributing to the social amplification of risk (8). Prior experiences in both hazardous material transportation and nuclear power industries suggest that the public is very sensitive to such risks. Human actions have the potential for exacerbating such concerns by initiating minor risk events in the system as well as increasing the probability of severe accidents. There has been little emphasis, however, on the avoidance of minor events and their effects on risk perceptions related to the assumption--the implications of small events are considered unimportant from a risk perspective.

Fourth, even under the best circumstances the transportation system for spent fuel will remain sensitive to the possibility of human error. Human factors research suggests that it is not possible to eliminate completely human errors in complex technological systems. For example, human actions have been shown to be major causes of system failures in many complex technological systems, including the operation and maintenance of nuclear power plants (9, 10, 11). Human errors have also been estimated to account for at least 62% of hazardous material transportation accidents in the U.S. (12). However, these data are limited and based on incomplete databases. As stated above, the real situation is not adequately known (4).

Within the regulatory agencies, government laboratories, and industry there are strong beliefs that technological features (e.g., cask integrity under severe accident conditions) and the reliability and thoroughness of regulatory requirements (e.g., route selection, equipment maintenance, quality assurance programs) will ensure system safety and reliability. However, these beliefs are based on highly suspect data and assumptions. They may lead to the underestimation of risk probabilities and to a much safer view of the system than is warranted.

Such beliefs are also reflected in technical analyses and assumptions. For example, there is evident reluctance to assess the probabilities of multiple simultaneous events in addition to isolated failings in risk assessments. Similarly, it is assumed that:

1) cask designs are adequate to withstand even the most severe accident conditions,
2) casks are fabricated perfectly according to design standards, and
3) casks are used and maintained properly with respect to design standards.

However, a lack of systematic data collection and analysis limits the ability to perceive patterns of problems. While previous transportation has been safe in that few accidents and incidents have resulted (and none have resulted in radiological releases exposing the public), a more thorough review of relevant data suggest that human error may be extensive within the spent fuel transportation system and an important contributor to total risk (4). The data call into question the validity of these optimistic beliefs. Table 2 illustrates the range of human errors that have occurred during different activities of spent fuel transportation system development and operation.

A SOCIO-TECHNICAL SYSTEMS PERSPECTIVE

Our approach to the identification and mitigation of risks allows us to identify the types of human actions that may affect system safety and reliability and how they may be eliminated or their effects mitigated. The perspective is one of a "system" in which individual components are not only analyzed individually, but as interacting dynamic components that must be examined in their totality. If interactions of different subsystems are not taken into account in transportation risk management activities the result may well be the failure to effectively implement many proposed risk management programs.

TABLE 2

Human errors in the transportation of spent nuclear fuel

- Design errors:
    - designs not tested for maintainability or ease of inspection
    - documentation errors related to cask designs and fabrication
    - cask trailer designs inadequate to support loads

- Implementation errors:
    - defective installation of shielding and valves
    - installation of defective valves and rupture disks
    - continued use of casks after breakdown of manufacturer quality assurance

- Operational errors:
    - improper placarding, labeling, reporting, and pre-departure inspections
    - improper cask loading and securing
    - failure to adhere to preplanned routes

- Maintenance errors:
    - improper repairs using improper materials or faulty parts
    - required repairs not performed on vehicles

- Accident response and recovery errors:
    - inaccurate or false reports of accident consequences
    - lack of familiarity and confusion in novel situations

The confluence of research resulting from both theoretical and applied work on human error suggests that they derive from interactions within the total human-task system. In particular, the organizational and institutional infrastructure and socio-economic context of a system may also affect error causation, definition, identification, and control. For example, interindividual interaction (e.g., group decision making) is an important feature of activity in the transportation system. Problems associated with group processes, however, may lead to failures in decision making and planning. Similarly, organizational and socio-economic factors form the context in which the system operates and may therefore have significant influence on the selection and implementation of system safety and reliability features.

To incorporate these issues into our analysis, we view the transportation system broadly as a socio-technical system. In the context of this work, socio-technical system refers to interacting components of system hardware (e.g., spent fuel casks, trucks, cranes), system personnel (e.g., drivers, crane operators, managers), organizational and institutional infrastructure (e.g., operations, maintenance, management, administration), and social-economic factors (e.g., regulations, legislation, economics, culture) (Figure 1).

FIGURE 1

A SOCIO-TECHNICAL VIEW OF THE HIGH LEVEL RADIOACTIVE WASTE TRANSPORTATION SYSTEM

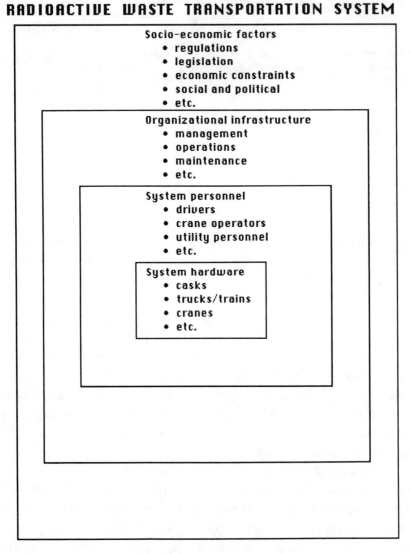

Socio-economic factors
- regulations
- legislation
- economic constraints
- social and political
- etc.

Organizational infrastructure
- management
- operations
- maintenance
- etc.

System personnel
- drivers
- crane operators
- utility personnel
- etc.

System hardware
- casks
- trucks/trains
- cranes
- etc.

SOURCE: (17)

From this broad perspective, failures caused by "human errors" occur when a system goes outside of its acceptable boundaries of behavior due to human-task or human-machine interactions (i.e., they result in undesirable consequences). In many cases, errors can be thought of as the inappropriate match between an individual's mental representation of a task or system and the actual state and dynamics of a task or system. Consequently, there is a need to include subjective reasons, external environmental factors, characteristics of human information and cognitive processing, and task characteristics in any reasonable definition of "human error" in complex technological systems.

One approach for the analysis of behavior in complex human-task systems (such as the transportation of spent fuel) is by the conceptualization of errors as human-task or human-machine "mismatches." Thus, "human error" may be defined as the result of a mismatch between perceived and actual system state and dynamics in human-machine or human-task systems. Events enabled or initiated by mismatches may accumulate to cause system-wide failures or disasters. Mismatches occur as a result of human variability, technical variability or failure, and required interactions that are incompatible with general human cognitive limitations or organizational constraints. This perspective on human error incorporates the important issues shown in Table 3.

TABLE 3

Human error as human-machine or human-task mismatches

- attribution of blame not focused on operators where a task is not well designed
- externally prescribed standards of interaction, procedures, and objectives may differ and lead to failures
- groups and organizations can enable or initiate system failures. through faulty decision-making
- performance-shaping factors affect human-task interactions and human behavior
- human variability and adaptability affect the dynamics of failures and their recovery
- system observability and reversibility affect the dynamics of failures and their recovery

In the case of a frequent mismatch, the cause can be attributed to design error, resulting in an inappropriate match between the content and organization of tasks with respect to human capabilities. For example, misperceptions of system designers can create task requirements that are incompatible with human capabilities, both during normal and emergency operating situations. Design errors can induce failures at a later time because task demands are not matched to human capabilities. Similarly, implementation errors can induce failures at later times because the actual characteristics of the system may end up being quite different from design standards and assumptions.

Infrequent mismatches can be viewed as resulting from variability on the part of the system or of humans during operational activities. Although it is true that there are some failures in system function that can be attributed solely to technical components or to human operators, many result from the interaction of these two worlds. Human variability can affect the probability of errors in two major ways (13):

1) human variability causes system behavior to transcend acceptable boundaries of continued system function; or,

2) human variability is insufficient to maintain acceptable system behavior when the system itself changes.

Thus, mismatches may occur even in systems that have been designed to avoid the occurrence of human errors. Often such mismatches are due to inadequate feedback and excessive demands on human cognitive or motor control capabilities.

TRANSPORTATION RISK MANAGEMENT

When the transportation system is viewed broadly, it is clear that numerous control strategies for improving human reliability exist at all phases of the transportation system and at all socio-technical levels of the system. Ideally such control strategies should entirely eliminate causal chains leading to human-task mismatches through effective design. In many cases, however, this is not feasible, especially in the case of mismatches that cannot always be foreseen or in tasks which are not well-structured or formalized (e.g., decision-making, problem-solving, judgments). The formalization of a task affects the choice of risk management approach. Planning and design tasks, for example, are more ambiguous and their causal sequences less open to analysis. On the other hand, cask handling and loading is completed at a nuclear reactor site where personnel are presumably well-trained in required procedures and to respond to incidents and accidents.

179

FIGURE 2

RISK MANAGEMENT APPROACHES TO TRANSPORTATION INCIDENTS/ACCIDENTS

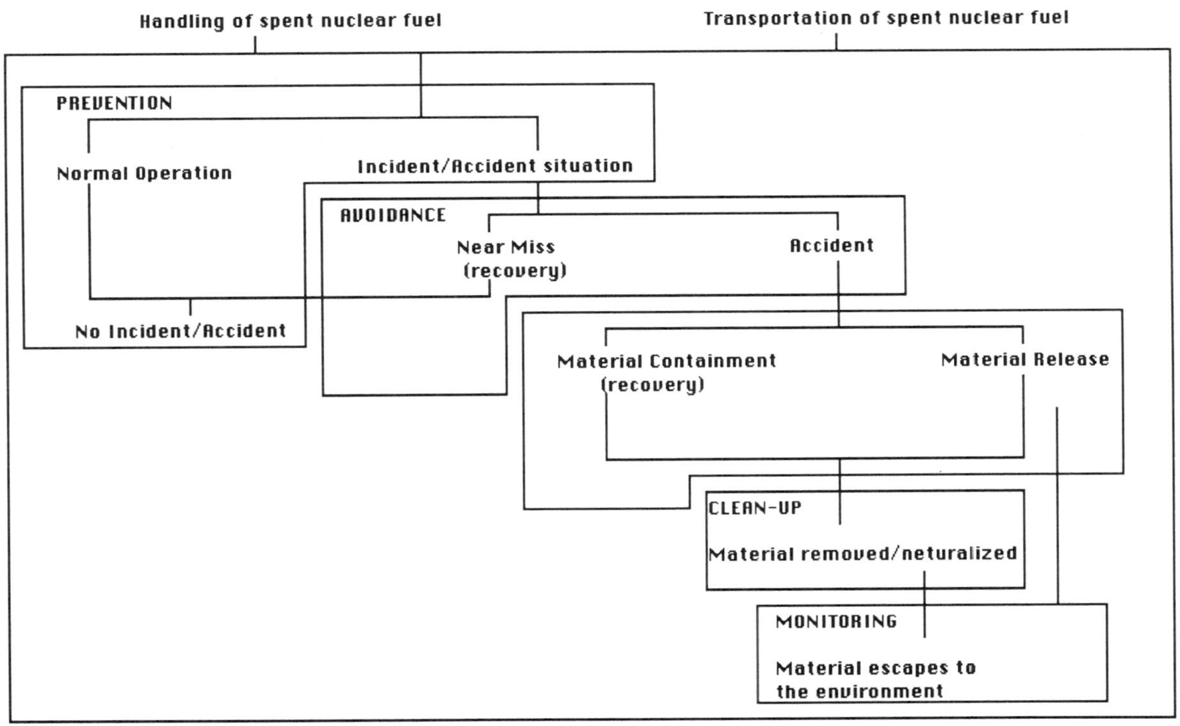

SOURCE: (18)

Accordingly, different activities call for different types of transportation risk management approaches. Consequently, transportation risk management programs should also focus on increasing the observability and reversibility of human-task mismatches and mitigating their adverse consequences. The focus on mitigation and recovery strategies are on incident and accident control, clean-up, and monitoring. Figure 2 illustrates the relationship between these transportation risk management approaches and a generalized transportation incident or accident sequence.

Table 4 provides a suggestive list of possible transportation risk management control options. They are divided roughly into socio-technical levels, although it should be noted that many control strategies can appear at more than one level, affect more than one phase, or affect the interactions among phases. A broad view is essential in that it suggests a number of possible interventions in causal event sequences leading to failures. This broad view for identifying transportation risk management strategies is even more important because the system in question is a new one. Thus, risk can be affected not only at system hardware and personnel levels (as is the most common approach), but also in infrastructural and social levels that may be more effective in eliminating risks rather than mitigating their consequences.

Three strategies in particular are important because of the general perspective that they provide for the identification and evaluation of potential human-task mismatches. They may greatly influence the effectiveness of transportation risk management strategies at other phases and socio-technical levels. They are:

1) job and task analyses that assist in the pre-identification of potential errors and in the design of tasks in transportation related activities. Such analyses may also be used to support evaluations and modifications of transportation risk management programs;

2) an integrated process of risk assessment and risk management that assists the identification of discrepancies between design assumptions and actual operational behavior; and,

3) effective systematic human error data collection and analysis programs to support job and task analyses and post-accident investigations. This risk management program is critical because

of its fundamental contribution to all other risk management options.

TABLE 4

Transportation risk management options

SYSTEM HARDWARE
 Choice of technology (e.g., mode)
 Design of technology (e.g., automation, manual, maintainability)
 Quality control

SYSTEM PERSONNEL
 Procedures and protocol development
 Training
 Staff qualifications, including management
 Job analysis
 Task analysis
 Incentives/discipline (e.g., motivation)
 Quality control

ORGANIZATIONAL AND INSTITUTIONAL INFRASTRUCTURE
 "Culture of safety"
 Data collection and analysis
 Organizational structure (e.g., decision protocols, communication
  channels)
 Safety committees, quality circles
 Labor union/employee management relations
 Enforcement

SOCIO-ECONOMIC FACTORS
 Enforcement
 Coherent and comprehensive regulations
 Economic and political incentives and constraints
 Risk communication

Risk management programs may also be specific to phases in the development and operation of the spent nuclear fuel transportation system. For example, management programs during design activities can reduce human-task mismatches by formally incorporating human factors considerations in the development of regulatory requirements and making equipment and procedures "goof proof." These strategies are important because errors are frequently a direct result of defective designs.

Control strategies during implementation can do much to ensure proper fabrication of equipment and effective training of personnel. Control strategies should include thorough review and inspection before casks and other critical equipment become operational. Similarly, human factors considerations should assist in the implementation of effective and reliable decision protocols.

Control strategies during the operations and maintenance phases should emphasize effective human error data collection and analysis and quality assurance inspections to evaluate actual performance. Similarly, human errors may be reduced by improving the quality of the work environment and by promoting a higher sense of professionalism. Control options include greater employee participation in planning activities, increased work incentives, and the establishment of a "culture of safety."

Control strategies for ensuring effective and reliable accident recovery occur during design, implementation, and actual response activities. They may affect ultimate recovery performance by ensuring proper maintenance of response equipment, training of response personnel, and timely access to equipment. Interagency coordination and well thought out decision protocols can also affect accident response capabilities.

HUMAN RELIABIITY MATRIX

Our approach to the identification of effective transportation risk management programs to improve performance is to systematically relate the risk management options to transportation activities (Figure 3). The nature of human-task mismatches suggests that their total elimination is not possible because of human and system variability and designers' inability to predict all potential situations. Thus, although attempts should be made to eliminate human-task mismatches wherever possible, attention must also be focussed on making the effects of human-task mismatches more benign, controllable, and reversible.

FIGURE 3

HUMAN RELIABILITY MATRIX

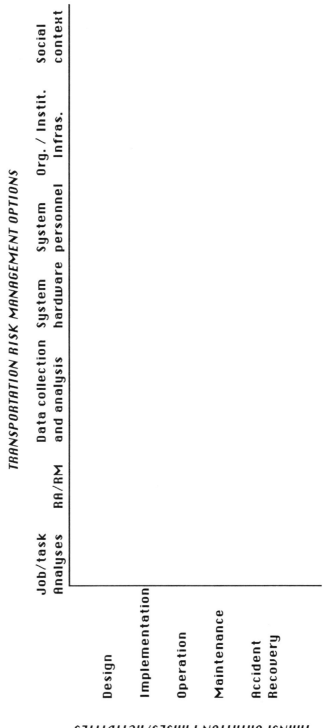

TRANSPORTATION RISK MANAGEMENT OPTIONS

Job/task Analyses · RA/RM · Data collection and analysis · System hardware · System personnel · Org. / Instit. Infras. · Social context

Design · Implementation · Operation · Maintenance · Accident Recovery

TRANSPORTATION PHASES/ACTIVITIES

The approach developed in our research explicitly allows error producing conditions for each transportation activity to be related to error reduction and control methods at all socio-technical levels. The vertical axis identifies the various activities of the transportation system from Table 1. The horizontal axis identifies the types of transportation risk management options available; the figure only shows major categories from Table 4. A fundamental component of this approach is the development of "task-error taxonomies." These are developed through job and task analyses and consist of a set of possible human errors during particular tasks that can seriously affect system performance.

When an incident is analyzed and potential mismatches identified, their sources or causes in earlier system phases need to be identified. In this process, a "stop-rule" is required to identify how far back in time and activity analyses should stretch. We propose stretching the analysis back to the point at which the mismatch occurs. Then, if possible, the source of the mismatch can be removed. If its elimination is not possible, intervention points may be identified which can mitigate consequences or reverse the process of divergence between perceptions and actuality. Moreover, it may lead to the identification of unexpected couplings and other potential effects of the mismatches and strategies chosen to control them.

MISMATCH PRE-IDENTIFICATION

This section discusses the application of our methodology to pre-identify potential human-task mismatches and potential risk management programs. To highlight our approach, an example scenario is discussed: the task of shipment pre-departure inspection of truck braking systems. Prior to the departure of each truck shipment specific inspection activities must be performed on both the vehicle and the cask. One component of the inspection focuses on the quality of the vehicle braking system. If problems exist, they are supposed to be rectified before the shipment can depart. To apply our methodology to particular situations, the following three steps should be preformed for the pre-identification of potential human-task mismatches.

The first, step is to perform a comprehensive analysis of all tasks related to the inspection of the brake system. Job and task analyses can assist in the identification of potential <u>critical errors</u> in each task. Because not all human-task mismatches have the potential for affecting performance of human-task systems they do not all need to be evaluated. Thus, critical errors refer to those errors that have the potential for initiating or contributing to severe accidents or incidents in the transportation system. Attention must be given to the potential for human errors to:

1) initiate risk events (e.g., improper reassembly of parts after inspection leads directly to brake failure);

2) contribute to risk events (e.g., inspection failed to find brake problems);

3) affect the frequency of risk event sequences (e.g., inspection failures lead to increased frequency of accidents from failure to stop quickly);

4) affect the structure of risk event trees by changing points of reversibility or recoverability (e.g., inadequate brakes can lead to driver inability to avoid accidents because he/she cannot stop the vehicle quickly); and,

5) affect couplings and interactions between subsystems and components (e.g., brake fluid leakage may lead to failures in other parts of the vehicle during transport).

The final result of these analyses should be the identification of "task-error taxonomies" for each activity. In other words, the specific set of critical errors that could affect human-task performance should be classified. Frequently, they will fall into a generalized taxonomy:

• errors of omission (i.e., required action not performed),

• errors of commission (i.e., performing action incorrectly),

• extraneous acts (i.e., performing action that should not have been performed),

• errors of sequence (i.e., performing action out of sequence), and

• errors of timing (i.e., too early, too late, or not within specified time constraints), and

• errors of communication (i.e., during sending, receiving, and transmission of messages).

It must be stressed, however, that by itself such an error taxonomy is inadequate to substantially improve human reliability. A model based approach is necessary to related error forms, human information processing capabilities, and cognitive functions (4). A model is necessary to understand how certain cognitive functions fail and errors occur as opposed to just identifying external error forms. Only with the deeper understanding provided by a model can effective, reliable, and cost-effective error prevention and recovery and consequence mitigation strategies be implemented.

The task-error taxonomies must reflect the various dynamics by which errors can arise. For example, they must distinguish between diagnostic errors of omissions that could result from failure to follow specified procedures (i.e., recall failure) and from inadequate strategies to solve problems (i.e., inference and problem-solving failures).

In addition, task-error taxonomies assist:
- the identification of clusters of human-task mismatches in transportation activities,
- the analysis of system sensitivity to actual (as opposed to designed) task characteristics and demands, and
- the evaluation of the effectiveness of various transportation risk management options.

When performing such analyses, the impossibility of identifying all possible problems and error modes in each task must be recognized. In fact, their identification is only limited by the imagination of the analyst. Thus, the composition of the analytical team and the knowledge of the assessors is of critical importance. Accordingly, the investigative team should be inter-disciplinary, including human factors specialists, cognitive psychologists, technical specialists, management personnel, system designers, and experienced workers. The importance of worker participation in the analytical process should not be underestimated as they are the ones who both know how the task is actually performed and the constraints under which they actually operate. For example, when inspecting truck brakes, inspectors may be able to identify design problems that inhibit their ability to efficiently and reliably perform the required tasks (e.g., bolts that are hidden behind other parts and are difficult to remove). Moreover, error modes and conditions that occur in other systems with similar conditions (e.g., heavy truck transportation) may suggest underlying causal factors behind failures in the transportation system for spent fuel.

Second, after critical error types are identified by a task-error-taxonomy, risk management programs for their elimination or for the reversibility or mitigation of adverse consequences need to be identified.

The human reliability matrix suggests the range of risk management control strategies that may be used for each case, although only a subset will actually be relevant or efficient to implement. Figure 4 provides an example of how the human reliability matrix can be used in this example. The figure suggests different risk management options available at different times that can prevent truck brake failures due to improper pre-departure inspections.

Specific risk management options will be suggested by the analyses of the first step. In particular, questions related to the effects of performance-shaping factors and the cognitive and motor requirements of workers will suggest how to eliminate "bad" performance-shaping factors and to reduce individual or group cognitive and physical workloads (e.g., ensure that procedures are easy to follow, brakes are easy to inspect, and that adequate resources and time are available to inspectors). Inferences as to the best options to use should be based on experience and empirical data where available. Where such information is not available, in spite of the predictive problems associated with human information processing models, they may be used (carefully) to identify error mechanisms in relation to cognitive functions. For example, in the scenario under consideration, risk management programs could include:

- improved training and refresher courses for inspectors;
- elimination of time constraints due to scheduling requirements;
- improved design of brakes, tools, and procedures;
- managerial incentives to improve reliability of inspectors;
- simplified reporting mechanisms for inspection reports; and,
- increased number of inspectors.

As can be seen, options exist at all levels of the socio-technical system and at all phases of the transportation system (this example is meant to be illustrative and additional options may exist that are not listed). Our proposed "stop rule" identifies three sources of mismatches:

1) inadequate worker participation in the design of equipment and procedures to ensure their reliability and effectiveness;
2) inconsistent and incomplete regulations that ensure proper inspections of all spent fuel shipments; and,
3) unrealistic scheduling that creates pressures for shipments to proceed without adequate inspections.

FIGURE 4

BRAKE INSPECTION FAILURE

TRANSPORTATION RISK MANAGEMENT OPTIONS

TRANSPORTATION PHASES/ACTIVITIES	Job/task analyses	Data collection and analysis	System hardware	System personnel	Org. and Instit. Infrastructure	Socio-economic context
Design	inspect. procedures		ease of brake inspect.	inspect. proced.	worker participation	
Imp.		reporting incentives		resources and training		coherent regs.
Oper.		feedback of actual exper.	INSPECT. FAILURE			
Maint.	evaluation of procedures		freq. of inspections	number of inspectors		scheduling
Accident Recovery			back-up brakes			

Third, before selected risk management programs are implemented or redesigned for the activity under analysis, the potential effects of proposed modifications need to be determined for the entire system. In our example, potential effects on the design process, maintenance and inspection activities, and emergency response procedures should be assiduously assessed. This step is important to ensure the coherence between risk management options during all activities in the transportation system. Examples from our scenario include the effects of greater demands on resources (e.g., simulators, training programs) and logistical scheduling due to increased inspection duration and frequency.

Finally, specific risk management program options identified from the previous steps should be implemented. Their final selection should depend on a variety of factors including perceived effectiveness, costs, resource constraints, and difficulties of implementation. Specific decision criteria need to be developed to provide assurance that controls will be implemented and justification to budgetary and regulatory agencies and to the public.

POST-INCIDENT ANALYSIS

To ensure effective transportation risk management for spent fuel, on-going evaluations of task and risk management performance are essential. A necessary component in the evaluation process is the analysis of human-task mismatches and incidents during all stages of the transportation system. Ideally, part of the transportation risk management strategy should be to investigate all incidents, accidents, and errors because important knowledge may be gained from even minor events. Practically, however, such an approach is impossible due to resource and time constraints. Thus, it is important to develop formal criteria for the types of events to investigate. For example, one approach might be to investigate all errors or incidents identified in the task-error taxonomies or which might contribute to the social amplification of risk.

The four steps in the process of post-incident evaluation are similar to those of pre-identification; they are described in the following paragraphs. To highlight the methodology, the hypothetical example outlined in Figure 4 is used as the cause of a truck accident during the transportation of spent fuel to the federal repository. The truck accident occurs because the driver was unable to avoid a car that swerved suddenly on a highway. The truck and car driver are both killed during the accident. In addition, a fire erupts and a cask valve seal ruptures allowing small amounts of radiation to escape.

The first step in post-incident evaluation involves an accident or error investigation. Methodologies and issues relating to such investigations have been discussed elsewhere (9, 14, 15, 16). In particular, methods should be based on structured descriptions of events, including the sequence of cognitive functions and human behavior prior to, during, and in response to the event. Questions that should be asked in the investigation relate to what specific events occurred and how they happened. They directly depend upon the task-error taxonomies developed during pre-identification analyses. In the above example, answers might include driver fatigue, brake component failure, defective quality control, and poor vehicle design that made inspections difficult. Each of these possible causes should be evaluated further to identify their root cause--in this example, the failure to identify faulty brake components during the pre-departure inspection.

The second step is to identify the set of control strategies that directly affected (or should have affected) the cause of the accident. The human reliability matrix assists in this process by relating risk management control strategies to the activities in the transportation system. Control strategies may affect the impact of performance-shaping factors, task characteristics, or even cognitive performance. In this case, they might include inspector hours-of-service regulations, shipment scheduling and time available to complete inspections, inspector training, and pre-departure inspection reporting mechanisms.

Third, because sources of mismatches may occur during activities other than those where the actual failure occurred, previous activities that affect the design, implementation, and operation of the task should be evaluated. In particular, relevant control strategies that could block a causal chain leading to the incident should be identified. This process is assisted by an accident investigation analyzing how the failure occurred and the causal sequence of events (the causal "chain" of hazard) leading to the actual failure. The focus at this stage should be on how to eliminate the sources of mismatches and how to make system dynamics more observable and reversible. Effective control strategies in our example might include improved vehicle inspection and maintenance procedures, brake system design for maintainability, quality control during brake component manufacture, scheduling requirements, promulgation of regulatory standards (e.g., frequency of inspections, responsible agency, number of inspectors), and reporting mechanisms for employees to report management abuses (e.g., not repairing brakes when minor problems exist because supervisors do not want the shipment to be delayed). This process suggests that effective and reliable communication processes among individuals at different socio-technical levels and different phases of the transportation system are key ingredients to effective risk management in the transportation system.

Similarly, activities that might have controlled the consequences of the accident should be identified, and control strategies that could improve their effectiveness evaluated. In this way, methods to mitigate consequences to recover effectively from failures can be identified. In our example, these might include back-up brake systems, escorts for shipments, and effective emergency response systems.

Fourth, the most appropriate control strategies for eliminating errors during the activity should be assessed. The potential effectiveness of the control option, as well as related political, economic, and social factors, should be addressed. As the transportation system becomes more established, for example, modification and implementation of control strategies at outer socio-technical levels (e.g., organizational infrastructure and socio-economic factors) will become more difficult.

Human factors research suggests that it may be intrinsically difficult to eliminate all human-task mismatches at their source. As a result, methods should be identified for improving the effectiveness of potential transportation risk management control strategies and developing new ones for event detection, exposure reduction, consequence mitigation, and recovery.

CONCLUSION

We believe our approach provides a powerful tool for the pre-identification and post-error investigation of human-task mismatches. As such, it can assist the evaluation and improvement of human reliability in the transportation system for spent nuclear fuel. In particular, it provides:

1) a comprehensive approach that allows both broad and deep evaluations into the sources and consequences of human-task mismatches and methods for their control and mitigation;

2) an easy to implement management strategy that can be used by all organizations involved in the transportation system at different periods of its design, implementation, and operation;

3) a "modular" approach that allows a variety of state-of-the-art methodologies to be used and modified as improvements occur in human factors knowledge and human reliability assessment methods; and,

4) a substantial step beyond the usual focus on equipment, training, and task procedure relationships to human error by specifically incorporating organizational, institutional, and social factors in analyses.

REFERENCES

1. Battelle Pacific Northwest Laboratories, An assessment of the risk of transporting spent nuclear fuel by truck. PNL-2588, Richland, WA: Battelle Pacific Northwest Laboratories, 1978.

2. Nuclear Regulatory Commission, Transportation of radionuclides in urban environs: draft environmental assessment, U. S. Nuclear Commission, NUREG/CR-0743, Washington, DC; USGPO, 1980.

3. Nebraska Energy Office, A review of the effects of human error on the risks involved in spent fuel transportation, Lincoln, Nebraska: Nebraska Energy Office, 1987.

4. Tuler, S., Kasperson, R. E., and Ratick, S., The effects of human reliability on risk in the transportation of spent nuclear fuel. Unpublished manuscript, Worcester, MA: CENTED, Clark University, June 1988.

5. Kunita, R.K. and Wallace, A.R., Interstation transfer of spent nuclear fuel. In Fifth International Symposium on Packaging and Transportation of Radioactive Materials, Las Vegas, NV, 7-12 May, 1978.

6. Rasmussen, R.W., Duke Power Company spent fuel storage and transportation experience, Nuclear Safety, 1986, 27(4):512-518.

7. Ruska, M. and Schoonen, D., Virginia Power and Department of Energy Spent Fuel Transportation Experience. Report (EGG-2491) prepared for the Department of Energy by EG&G Idaho, Idaho Falls, Idaho, 1986.

8. Kasperson, R. E., Renn, O., Slovic, P., Brown, H. S., Emel, J., Goble, R., Kasperson, J. X., Ratick, S., The social amplification of risk: a conceptual framework, Risk Analysis, 1988, 8(2):177-188.

9. Rasmussen, J., What can be learned from human error reports? In Changes in Working Life, K. Duncan, M. Gruneberg, D. Wallis, eds., NY: John Wiley and Sons, 1980.

10. Bellamy, L., Neglected individual, social, and organizational factors in human reliability assessment. In Proceedings of the Fourth National Reliability Conference 6-8 July, 1983, Volume 1, National Centre of Systems Reliability, Birmingham, England, 1983.

11. Miller, D.P. and Swain A.D., Human error and human reliability. In Handbook of Human Factors, G. Salvendy, ed., NY: John Wiley and Sons, 1987.

12. Office of Technology Assessment, The Transportation of Hazardous Materials, OTA-SET-304, Washington, DC: US Government Printing Office, 1986.

13. Rasmussen, J., Definition of human error and a taxonomy for technical system design. In New Technology and Human Error, J. Rasmussen, K. Duncan, and J. Leplat, eds., NY: John Wiley and Sons, 1987.

14. Bainbridge, L., Diagnostic skill in process operation. Paper presented at the International Conference on Occupational Ergonomics, Toronto, Canada, 7-9 May, 1984.

15. Johnson, W.G., MORT Safety Assurance Systems, NY: Marcel Dekker, Inc., 1980.

16. Lucas, D., Human performance data collection in the nuclear industry. Paper presented at the Conference on Human Reliability in Nuclear Power, London, Englan, 22-23 October, 1987.

17. National Research Council, Human Factors Research and Nuclear Safety, Committee on Human Factors, National Research Council, Washington, DC: National Academy Press, 1988.

18. Martin, M., Matthews, M., and Rucker, L., Developing a plan for R&D in dangerous goods transport. In <u>Recent Advances in Hazardous Materials Transportation</u>, Washington, D.C.: Transportation Research Board, National Research Council, 1986.

PIPELINES ONCE BURIED NEVER TO BE FORGOTTEN

REIN BOLT and THEO LOGTENBERG
R.Bolt: Technical Operations Department
N.V. Nederlandse Gasunie, PO Box 19, Groningen, NL
M.Th. Logtenberg: Department of Industrial Safety
Technology for Society TNO, PO Box 342, Apeldoorn, NL

ABSTRACT

The availability of buried pipelines is a function of preventive and corrective maintenance.

Gasunie's current pipeline maintenance regime was evaluated to determine how far incident frequency and cost could be optimised. The study revealed that closer attention needed to be paid in particular to the monitoring of unreported excavation activities. After assessing the effectiveness of the surveying procedure, three other alternatives were considered. Of these, fortnightly aerial surveys proved to be the most efficient. With a view to limiting the consequences of an accidental escape of gas, a study was made of available detection systems and the desirability of combining such a system with remote valve operation. In Gasunie's opinion, direct combination is not feasible at this stage, but future developments in this field will be given the required attention.

The availability analysis methods as commonly used did not generate the most substantial contribution in this project. The findings of this study are mainly the outcome of structured thinking, data analysis and discussion.

INTRODUCTION

In conjunction with the Industrial Safety department of TNO (the Dutch institute for applied scientific research), Gasunie carried out a number of projects concerned with optimising the maintenance needed to ensure the safe and reliable supply of gas to power stations, large industrial users and public gas utilities.

The procedure employed for optimising the maintenance regime was virtually identical for all the projects, comprising system analysis, analysis of recorded malfunctions and defects, maintenance analysis and construction of a maintenance model. This model was then evaluated on the basis of expert opinion. The procedure is described in detail in [1]. The results of the projects are summarised in [2].

The parts of the gas transmission system covered by the study were the fixed installations and the pipeline systems forming the main transmission grid and the regional grid. Details of the pipeline system are given in table 1.

TABLE 1

Some details of Gasunie's main transmission and regional grid

	MAIN	REGIONAL
Pressure (bar)	> 40	⩽ 40
Diameter (inch)	12 < D < 48	⩽ 16
Material	X56, X60	API 5L gr. B
SMYS (N/mm^2)	415	240
Wall thickness (mm)	6 - 20	4 - 10
Length (km)	4,400	6,000

With regard to the pipeline system, it was found that it was not possible simply to base the desired level of maintenance on a reliability model derived from malfunction and defect frequency, because most defects were the result of unauthorised actions by third parties. The study therefore concentrated more on an analysis of possible alternatives for providing the desired level of preventive maintenance to avoid damage to pipelines and possible measures to limit the consequences. This was partly a reliability problem and partly a safety problem, and the two parts are very close related.

PREVENTIVE MAINTENANCE

Gasunie's preventive maintenance programme is in fact based solely on the technical insights and experience gained over the past 25 years. The maintenance procedures applied to the pipeline system can be divided into:
1. condition-related maintenance;
2. supervision of third-party work;
3. monitoring of unreported excavation activity.

Condition related maintenance
Condition-related maintenance comprises the checks and inspections carried out to detect any changes in the condition of the pipeline. Examples of this type of maintenance include the selective use of an intelligent pig to measure material defects (only possible with the main transmission system), detection of coating damage (by excavation or Pearson testing),

inspection of samples of pipe cuttings, functional checks on the
cathodic protection system and tests to detect pipeline
settlement.

Supervision of third party work
The maintenance personnel are responsible for supervising third
party work whenever excavation work has to be carried out in the
vicinity of a Gasunie pipeline. Their responsibilities include
marking the position of the pipeline and supervising the
excavation work to ensure that no damage is caused to the
pipeline. In practice, it is found that not all excavation work
in the vicinity of the Gasunie pipelines is reported to Gasunie.

Monitoring of unreported excavation activity.
The unreported excavation activities are detected by regular
walking, mobile or aerial surveys of the pipeline route.

Terms of reference for maintenance optimisation
Gasunie management established the following terms of reference
for the optimisation of the maintenance procedures by adopting
alternative forms of maintenance:
"A change to the maintenance procedures is permissible only if
this:
1. reduces the incident frequency for the same annual
    maintenance cost ($5 million) or less, or
2. achieves a significant reduction in maintenance costs with
    no deterioration in incident frequency".

By "incident" is understood pipeline damage, whether or not
accompanied by the escape of gas.

Incident frequency related to form of maintenance
The number of incidents which could be related to pipeline
condition has been negligible in recent years (averaging less
than one a year for the entire pipeline system). A conclusion
which might be drawn from this figure is that the condition-
dependent aspect of maintenance could be given less emphasis,
thereby yielding a cost-saving. This point will be studied
further by Gasunie experts on cathodic protection.
Condition-related maintenance would also be served by a model to
predict when a pipeline coating or the pipeline itself needed to
be replaced.

The number of incidents occurring during the supervision of
third-party work is likewise negligible. In this case, a
significant cost-saving can only be achieved by withdrawing this
supervision entirely - there is no halfway house. Since the
incident frequency would certainly rise if there were no
supervision, this form of maintenance must be retained.
Incidents of pipeline fracture as a result of unreported
excavation activity, on the other hand, average 20 a year. This
number has remained virtually constant over the past 10 years.
The effectiveness of this form of maintenance was therefore
investigated more closely and changes were proposed.

Effectiveness of monitoring of unreported excavation activity

To analyse the effectiveness of monitoring of unreported excavation work, a scheme was drawn up as shown in figure 1.

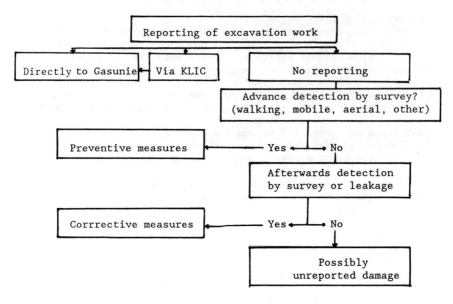

Figure 1. Reporting and detection of excavation work.

This diagram differentiate between reported and unreported excavation work. The following scenarios were defined:
1. Excavation work is reported to Gasunie directly or via a central reporting system (KLIC), so that the necessary steps can be taken.
2. Where the excavation work is not reported, it is discovered by surveying (walking, mobile or aerial) that excavation work is about to commence, allowing Gasunie to take the appropriate action.
3. Excavation work is detected subsequently, whether or not as a result of pipeline damage.
4. The excavation work is not detected by a survey, in which case it comes to light only if damage is caused (revealed by coating condition tests or leakage).

Formulae were constructed to provide an approximation of survey detection effectiveness. These indicate the probability of a specific type of survey discovering unreported excavation work. The formulae were based on the following assumptions:
1. Unreported excavation work can broadly be subdivided into work involving a long preparation period (over 14 days) and work with a relatively short preparation period (2-4 days, such as drainage).
2. Surveys are carried out on 250 working days in the year.

The formulae are:

Probability	Dk.E $\leqslant$ 250	Dk.E > 250
Dg.E $\leqslant$ 250	$\dfrac{\text{Fg.Dg.E + Fk.Dk.E}}{250}$	$\dfrac{\text{Fg.Dg.E}}{250} + \text{Fk}$
Dg.E > 250	$\text{Fg} + \dfrac{\text{Fk.Dk.E}}{250}$	Fg + Fk = 1

where:

Fg = proportion of unreported excavation works with a long preparation period (major works)

Fk = proportion of unreported excavation works with a short preparation period (minor works)

Dg = number of days during which evidence of major works is detectable in advance

Dk = number of days during which evidence of minor works is detectable in advance

E = Survey detection effectiveness.

The effectiveness of the survey schedules was calculated separately for the main transmission system and regional transmission system using these formulae. The following values were used in the calculation:

$$\text{Fg} = 0.3 \qquad \text{Fk} = 0.7 \qquad \text{Dg} = 14 \qquad \text{Dk} = 4$$
$$E_{walking} = 0.8 \qquad E_{mobile} = 0.6 \qquad E_{aerial} = 1.0$$

It should be noted that there is a significant difference between the survey schedules for the two systems: the main transmission system is surveyed by air 26 times a year, with no mobile surveys, whereas the regional grid is covered by 4 mobile surveys a year with no aerial surveys. The walking survey is for each system two times per year. The cathodic protection survey can also be considered as a walking survey of 1.5 times per year. An overview of the frequency of the surveys is given in table 2.

Table 2
Overview surveys main transmission and regional grid
(frequency per year)

	MAIN	REGIONAL
$f_{walking}$	2	2
f_{mobile}	0	4
f_{aerial}	26	0
$f_{cath.pr.}$	1.5	1.5

The percentage of unreported excavation works is approximately 25%. This percentage is based on observations made by aerial surveys of the main transmission system. The total number of excavation works in the vicinity of the main transmission system and the regional grid averages 1,100 and 2,000 per year, respectively. The results of these calculations are given in figures 2 and 3.

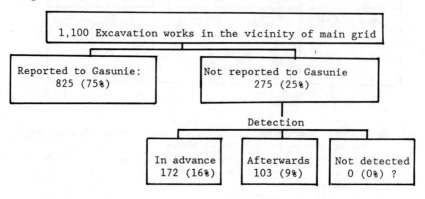

Figure 2. Calculated results for the main transmission grid

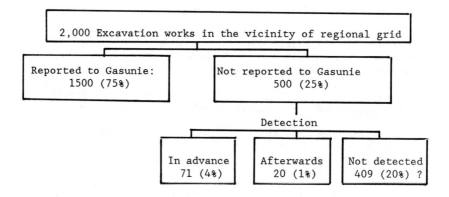

Figure 3. Calculated results for the regional grid

These calculations revealed that around 9% (103 of the 1,100) of excavation works in the vicinity of the main transmission grid were only detected afterwards, assuming the number of not detected is 0%, since all excavations work could be reported by aerial surveys. The percentage of afterwards detection for the regional grid is 1%. This percentage relates to the number of leaks per year caused by excavation works. The percentage of not reported works is according to the used calculation method around 20%. It should be noted that failure to detect excavation work does not necessarily mean that the pipeline will be damaged, nevertheless unnoticed superficial (coating) damage might be possible at a relatively large number of points. Provided the cathodic protection system is functioning properly, this need not, within certain limits, cause a problem.

The conclusion is that the surveys carried out on the regional grid are not particularly effective. The surveys carried out on the main transmission system are significantly more effective, but are not yet optimal in reporting in advance. A reassessment of the desired maintenance effort is therefore considered appropriate.

Alternative methods for checking on unreported excavation work
On the basis of figure 1, maintenance effort can be directed towards:
1. increasing the percentage of excavation works which are reported to Gasunie (from 75% to 100% if possible) directly;
2. early detection of all unreported excavation works by surveys;
3. subsequent detection of all unreported excavation works by aerial surveys.

The level of reporting of excavation works in the vicinity of pipelines can be improved by giving greater publicity to the potential hazards of damage to pipelines. This might take the form of regular advertisements or articles in trade journals aimed at the target groups in question. Another possibility is to constantly remind the owners of land on which pipelines are situated of the presence of the pipeline and that supervision can be provided by Gasunie (free of charge). The latter alternative would appear to be the more effective, although this would first have to be established experimentally. This approach may well be cheaper than the current system of inspection surveys. This form of maintenance can only be applied if it is truly effective and if the present walking, mobile and aerial surveys for this reason can be discontinued.

Early detection of all unreported excavation works means a survey frequency equal to the shortest preparation period for excavation work. This would involve surveying the entire pipeline system every day, or at least once every 2-4 days. The cost of this intensive survey, even using the cheapest survey method, would be significantly higher than the present maintenance cost.

Subsequent detection of excavation works would mean carrying out a survey at least once every 14 days (signs of excavation work usually remain detectable for 14 days after completion). The cheapest and most effective method would be an aerial survey. One disadvantage, however, is that only 60% of the regional grid can be covered by an aerial survey, because of the numerous branch pipelines. According to the formulae which have been constructed, this survey frequency would reduce the number of incidents by around 30%. The total cost will certainly not be higher than the current maintenance procedure, provided that aerial surveying replaces mobile and walking surveys.

Conclusion

Within the terms of reference governing optimisation, the option of a fortnightly survey of the total grid appears to be the best alternative. This alternative will be considered in more detail, as will an experiment in making a direct approach to landowners/caretakers.

CORRECTIVE ACTION

Each year Gasunie has to deal with around 20 incidents which require corrective action. The main consideration for every prudent operator will be to act as swiftly as possible to eliminate or minimise the consequences of the incident. This can be achieved most efficiently by means of a leak detection system combined with a remote control system. Gasunie started to develop a system of this kind in 1974 and initiated research into gas leak detection systems. At the same time, a project was launched to convert the manually operated isolating valves in the main transmission system to remote control over a period of ten years. A second reason for installing remote control was to enable Gasunie's Central Control Room (CCR) to optimise day-to-day operations by intervening at several points within the main transmission grid (process control).

Leak detection systems used/researched by Gasunie

As a general rule, remote valve operation can shorten the duration of gas escape in the event of a pipeline incident. Remote control for this reason is only worthwhile, however, when it can be combined with a reliable gas leak detection system. Various leak detection systems have been developed in the past, usually based on one of the following principles:
1. local observation;
2. local leak detection;
3. pressure monitoring;
4. wave alert;
5. corrected volume balance
6. dynamic modelling.

Local observation

Virtually all incident reports received by Gasunie originate from local observers, whether Gasunie personnel or third parties (the person responsible for the incident, police, fire service etc.). In many cases the extent of the leak and the geographical location are fairly accurately described.

Local leak detection

In 1967, ahead of the plans for a complete remote control system control system for the main transmission grid, Gasunie decided to start by protecting ten major waterway crossings with local leak detection systems employing Line Break Controls (LBCs). When it detects a pressure loss per unit time exceeding a local set value, the LBC shuts down the relevant valve. The last LBCs were taken out of service in 1972, because it was found in practice that they could for example be tripped by the shutdown of a compressor station. A survey among eight other gas transmission companies revealed that they had also had poor experience with LBCs.

Pressure monitoring
Pressure sensors were installed in a number of sections of the gas transmission system, initially at the beginning and end of the section. This system was also found to be unsatisfactory because it was not possible in many cases to locate the leak with sufficient accuracy and inadequate information was provided on the size of the leak.

Wave alert
As soon as a leak occurs in a pipeline, non-recurring expansion waves are created in the form of a sudden velocity increase and a pressure and temperature drop, which propagate at the speed of sound. Instant detection of these expansion waves is still posing many problems.

Corrected volume balance
Small leaks can be traced approximately by means of a mass balance calculation. However, this method cannot give an unequivocal answer on whether a discrepancy is caused by a physical leak or is due to line packing.

Dynamic modelling
Dynamic modelling involves using a computer model to determine whether the measured values (flow and pressure) are consistent. Any inconsistency is translated into an indication of the size and location of the leak. The range and accuracy of the instrumentation are extremely important. Areas which are still unclear are:
1. the precise relationship between measurement accuracy and accurate determination of the size and location of the leak;
2. the required standards of leak detection threshold and response rate.

Conclusion
Despite a great deal of intensive research, it has not yet proved possible to develop a reliable leak detection system which can rapidly and unequivocally determine both the size and geographical location of the leak, nevertheless Gasunie remains active in finding an acceptable solution.

COMBINED LEAK DETECTION AND REMOTE CONTROL

Alternative actions in response to gas leaks
The following table presents various alternative approaches and the associated response times in the event of a gas leak.

TABLE 3

Alternative actions in response to gas leaks

ALTERNATIVE		RESPONSE TIME (minutes)
A.	FULLY AUTOMATIC SYSTEM Leak detection system identifies leak and isolates section automatically	1-3
B. B.1	SEMI-AUTOMATIC SYSTEM Leak detection system identifies leak and CCR isolates section	1-10
B.2	Incident reported by telephone, CCR isolates section	15-30
C C.1	MANUAL SYSTEM Incident reported by telephone, field personnel isolate section with _actuator_	45-90
C.2	Incident reported by telephone, field staff isolate section _manually_	60-120

The response times given in the table are based on the
following assumptions:

1. The fully automatic system (A) will respond immediately to
    any change in the flow. The time needed to shut off the gas
    flow is a function of the system response time. The time
    taken to close valves with remote actuators varies from 0.5
    to 4 seconds per inch of pipeline diameter, i.e. a maximum
    of 2.5 minutes for a 36" pipeline. If the action is taken
    in response to a calculation made by a simulation program,
    the calculation time also has to be added.

2. In the case of the semi-automatic system (B.1), there is
    also the response time of the dispatcher at the CCR and
    the time taken for consultation at the CCR. The
    response time is determined by the frequency with which
    reports are automatically transmitted to the CCR. This
    is currently every two minutes. However, the dispatcher
    will wait for several readings before he takes action.

3. In the case of alternatives B.2 and C.1, the important
    factor is the time taken for the telephone message to
    arrive. It has been assumed that this will take at least 15
    minutes, again followed by internal consultation within the
    CCR.

4. The field personnel must be on the spot within one hour of
    notification from the CCR. If the valve has to be closed
    manually, the time taken to isolate the section will be
    increased by 15-30 minutes.

Functioning of the current system

On the basis of table 3, we can now establish which alternative corresponds to the current system. The following points need to be taken into account:

1. In the event of a pipeline incident involving the accidental, uncontrolled escape of gas, at this moment Gasunie will not act to isolate the pipeline section until a local assessment has been made of the situation (in principle by Gasunie personnel).
2. A remote control system is desirable both for process control and for action in the event of an incident where there is no time for local assessment.
3. A fully automatic system (alternative A) is not available, nor is it desirable in view of the requirement for local assessment.
4. At present the CCR receives virtually all incident reports from outside sources. When it receives a report the CCR will almost always adopt a "wait and see" approach until the position is clarified.
5. In the absence of clear indications to the contrary, maintaining the gas supply will take priority over isolating the pipeline section.
6. The use of a remote control system on safety grounds will impair the availability of gas supply.

In the beginning, efforts were concentrated on developing a remote control system corresponding to alternative A (fully automatic system). This was dictated largely by safety considerations based on the hazards as perceived at the time, such as crack propagation followed by fire and/or explosion. On the basis of an internal Gasunie study [3], however, crack propagation is no longer seen as a potential hazard. The effects of fire and/or explosion have been limited by an appropriate choice of pipeline materials and the legal requirements relating to distances between pipelines and buildings. The remote control system as currently installed, including the leak detection system, corresponds to alternatives B.2 and C.1 in the table. This means that Gasunie's minimum response time, i.e. the time elapsing until the pipeline section is isolated, is around 15 minutes from the start of the incident.

Safety with respect to the surrounding area

One of the reasons given for using remote control is improved safety with respect to the surrounding area. However a communication by Ruhrgas [4] and a report by TNO [5] state that the main hazard (ignition and fire damage) exists only for the first few minutes, and that the hazard presented by burning gas decreases sharply within the first few minutes, even if the gas flow is not shut off. In view of the relatively low frequency of occurrence, the loss of gas is regarded as a second-order problem. Gas transmission companies are in general agreement that excavation activities are the major cause of leaks and that adequate measures have to be taken to prevent them.

The safety of the surrounding area in the event of a gas leak has been carefully analysed and described by TNO in a study commissioned by the government [5]. This study indicates very narrow fire and explosion hazard zones. For fire the safe distance is given at 52 metres (48" pipeline, 60 bar) and for explosion 14 metres (peak pressure 0.1 bar). On the basis of the calculations carried out, it is not necessary to fit remote control to the isolating valves in the main transmission system in order to limit the effects. If this were necessary, then it would also be necessary in principle to fit remote control systems to the valves in the regional transmission system. Remote control operation is not a cost-effective investment in terms of reducing gas losses. It is important, however, to make local provision for rapid closure of the valve (for example with an actuator for large diameter pipelines).

The TNO study referred to above [5] showed that the gas escaping from a pipeline fracture falls to around 20% of the initial exit flow rate within one minute. It follows that, in the event of complete pipeline fracture, the time taken to isolate the pipeline section (response time) would have to be less than one minute to minimise the initial effects. It also has to be borne in mind that the quantity of escaping gas will be greater than the volume of the isolated section, which may make it less important to shut down rapidly in terms of minimising the initial effects. In practical terms, it is considered impossible to locate a gas leak and take the appropriate action within one minute.

Conclusion
Several actions have been undertaken to improve the availability of pipelines in combining leak detection and remote control as part of a corrective action plan. From a safety point of view such a system may not be necesssary, however, Gasunie will continue, possibly in collaboration with other gas companies, to look for a more satisfying solution.
One fact which has also come to light was that time is often lost in reporting the leak to Gasunie. Further studies are therefore being carried out to determine whether communications can be improved between local gas distributors, local authorities, alarm centres and Gasunie.

REFERENCES

1. Logtenberg, M.Th., Bosman, M, and Van der Horst, J., Reliability based maintenance of gas supply stastions, Seminar: Data collection and analysis for reliability assessment, The Institution of Mechanical Engineers, 1986, Londen, UK.

2. Bolt, R, and Logtenberg, M.Th., Maintenance optimisation by reliability engineering or by experience from the field? In proceedings 6th International Conference on Reliability and Availability, 1988, Strasbourg, France.

3. Rietjens, P.H.A., Scheurpropagatie in Gastransportleidingen, Rapport Technische Veiligheid

4. Letter from Ruhrgas to Gasunie (confidential)

5. LPG-integral, TNO-report for the Ministry of Housing, Planning and Environment, Part 14, Number 1128, May 1983

LBL - A COMPUTER SIMULATION PROGRAM FOR RISK EVALUATION OF LIFEBOAT EVACUATION

HELGE S. SOMA & K. HARALD DRAGER
A/S Quasar Consultants
Munkedamsveien 53B
0250 Oslo 2, Norway

ABSTRACT

LBL (LifeBoat Launching) is a PC-based computer program which simulates evacuation of an oil platform during severe weather by use of conventional lifeboats.   The program simulates the motion of the boat with respect to the collision hazard until the boat is at a safe distance away from the platform. Both fixed and floating platforms can be evaluated.

In doing so, the program is handling both the launching operation to the sea and the maneuvering of the boat when it is seaborne.   To perform the simulation, data about wind and waves, the course of the boat to avoid a collision with the structure, the distance to the structure, the initial location of the boat and lifeboat particulars are required.   A probability distribution with respect to time required for release of the boat when seaborne is also needed as well as the motion characteristics of floating platforms.

During descent the twist and pendulum motions are calculated, as well as the distance to the rig structure to identify collisions. The motions are also of importance as to where the boat will reach the sea.

When the boat is seaborne the initial speed, impact from waves, thrust and manoeuvering affect the escape operation.

If the displacement always is less than the distance to the structure, the launching is considered successful.   Otherwise collision speed is calculated.

The program is based on a stochastic model as wave and wind component phase angles are drawn at random when simulation starts.   Wave component amplitude data is obtained from a Newmann wave energy spectrum, and correspondingly a Davenport spectrum is applied with respect to wind component amplitudes.

A Monte Carlo simulation technique is applied. One to five hundred simulations for a given set of input data are required. Given a scenario, the probability of collision and statistics with respect to collision speed, slamming etc. are presented.

The approach fully demonstrates the efficiency of Monte Carlo simulations on this type of problems.

The impact of several parameters with respect to the collision probability can be calculated. Even by giving conservative data for uncertain parameters like time to release, it can be identified whether such parameters have impact on the collision probability.

The results may also efficiently be used to decide location of lifeboat on the rig and possible need for additional boats in case of unfavourable weather conditions.

The evacuation process can be shown graphically on the computer screen. Thereby problems with respect to such operations are highlighted. As interactive input with respect to launching and release can be given, the program also can be used in training situations.

INTRODUCTION

To highlight problems experienced with evacuation with lifeboats, the Alexander L. Kielland (ALK) accident can be taken as an example.

Due to list of the unit during the accident some boats were unavailable or even submerged. Only about 60 persons out of 212 appear to have embarked the lifeboats as they feared the probability of successful launching to be low.

None of the boats were successfully released when seaborne.

Several boats collided with the rig structure during descent and when seaborne, partly as a result of the release problems. Due to the water ingress through damage, capsize accidents also took place.

However, one remarkable fact should be recognized. In spite of the failures, 40 out of about 60 persons were saved in the boat originally embarked. This fact indicates robustness with the concept, after all.

The lifeboats on ALK could only be released with slack wire falls, to avoid premature release of the boats. The system did not work during severe weather.

Todays lifeboats can be released on-load if hydrostatic pressure is provided.

Another severe problem relates to the collision hazard, in particular when the boat is launched on the windward side. The pendulum motion with the boat during descent may result in collision with structural members. When seaborne, the boat may be swept back by a high wave and collide with the structure.

After ALK, it was attempted by Norwegian Authorities to overcome this problem by requiring a clearance of at least 5m between boat and rig, for the rig in listed condition. The 5m requirement was based on rough assumptions.

The background for QUASAR to be involved with this problem, was that oil drilling outside Northern Norway in the Barents Sea was initiated. In this hostile area rescue resources like helicopters would be remote, and the capacity limited, as compared to the North Sea area. The primary evacuation means, would be the lifeboat, and the reliability of the lifeboat concept would be of vital importance.

A risk assessment project was initiated by Esso Norway. The project showed that the reliability of the lifeboat evacuation operation would be of utmost importance. Esso Norway and NTNF supported then QUASAR in the development of a computer code for simulation of lifeboat launching. Such a simulation was necessary for an in depth evaluation of lifeboat launching reliability. The computer code developed by QUASAR was named the LBL-program (Lifeboat launching).

MODELLING THE ENVIRONMENT

In the LBL-program a Monte Carlo Simulation technique is applied. Wind gusts and waves are calculated from a stochastic model. Each individual launching operation is modelled as relastically as possible with respect to physical effects involved.

The simulation of a launching operation starts when the launching operation is initiated. The displacement of the boat as well as the clearance to the rig structure are calculated for each time step until the boat is at safe distance away from the rig. Discrete events like collision with the structure and impact of the sea surface are recorded.

For each launching operation different simulation results are obtained, because the model is stochastic. By performing some hundred simulations, statistics with respect to clearance, collision probability and speed, slamming speed etc. can be obtained.

Modelling of the sea surface
When the frequency (or period) of a sea wave is known, the wave speed as well as the wave length can be calculated. The wave speed increases when the wave length increases.

In wave theories frequently applied, the sea surface is considered to result from a summation of several wave components with different frequency.

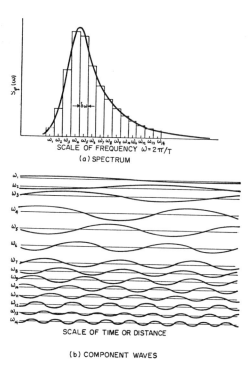

$S_\rho(\omega)$

SCALE OF FREQUENCY $\omega = 2\pi/T$

(a) SPECTRUM

SCALE OF TIME OR DISTANCE

(b) COMPONENT WAVES

Figure 1.   Typical   wave spectrum   with corresponding harmonic
components.

Figure 1 shows individual wave components at a certain
time. By summing the components, the resulting sea surface at
that time is obtained. A short time later, the long waves have
travelled a longer distance than the short ones, and the sea
surface will therefore be different.

At a certain time the relative position of the wave
components shown on figure 1 is as likely as any other
position. If a certain position is selected, however, the sea
surface at any position for succeeding time steps can be
calculated.

When the simulation of a launch operation starts, a phase
angle between 0 and 2π is drawn at random for each wave
component.

The amplitude of each wave component is obtained from a
Newman wave energy spectrum.

Wind Speed Modelling
Wind gusts as well as the mean speed are important regarding
lifeboat motions during descent.

The mean wind speed as a function of height above sea is calculated according to a mean wind speed profile corresponding to rough sea.

The wind gust profile is calculated according to a Davenport wind gust spectrum. Phase angles are drawn at random when the simulation starts.

MOTION OF FLOATING UNITS

The motion of a floating rig causes the fall wire suspension points to move.

For mobile units, Response Amplitude Operator (RAO) curves are prepared. Taking the roll motion as an example, the relation between the maximum roll angle and the maximum slope of a wave of unit height are plotted for different regular wave periods.

There is a strong correlation between the rig motion and the surface elevation below the lifeboat. In order to account for this, the rig motion is derived from the wave model. Phase angles for rig motion relative to the wave components therefore must be known.

By adding the roll motion with respect to each wave component and using above phase angles, the resulting roll motion of the rig in irregular seas is found.

By doing the same for the other rig motions, the resulting motion of the fall wire suspension point is found.

Wind induced lifeboat motions during descent

The pendulum motion in the plane corresponding to the wind speed will be considered. The twist (yaw) motion of the boat also will be included. Motion perpendicular to the wind direction is disregarded. Except for the wind force, which is a function of twist angle, the two motions are independent of each other.

Pendulum motion

This motion can be calculated comparatively accurately for the wind spectrum in question. If the boat is launched from a floating unit, the motion of the fallwire point of suspension is included. Most uncertainty is associated with the drag coefficient, however. Due to the yaw motion, the projected cross-section area perpendicular to the wind direction is a function of the twist angle. The drag coefficient is assumed independent of twist angle.

Yaw motion

A calculation model based on elementary flow theory is developed.

The calculations are uncertain. However, the approach yields results that reasonably correspond to the steady wind test results available.

In TABLE 1, a correction factor to the lift force of 0.85 is applied to calibrate the test results, and the linear relationship for the lift coefficient as function of attack angle is assumed to hold until 80 degrees.

TABLE 1
Comparison between calculation results and test results

Test results (Watercraft Ltd.)			EDP-program results	
Launched distance r (m)	Wind speed (m/sec)	Observed yaw am- plitude	Calculated yaw	Wind speed that creates the test yaw amplitudes
30	27.5	± 45	± 36	28.0
30	34	± 90	± 83	36.0
40	26	± 45	± 62	24.5
40	33	± 90	± 96	32.0

THE RELEASE OPERATION

If the boat becomes seaborne close to the crest of a high wave, only a fraction of a second may pass until the wave has passed, and the boat is hanging by the fall wires again.

Even if the boat becomes seaborne a considerable distance from the crest, insufficient time for release may be available. In this case a shock load when the fall wires are tightened occurs.

In the simulation model, the time elapsed until the boat is released, is based on a probability distribution given as input.

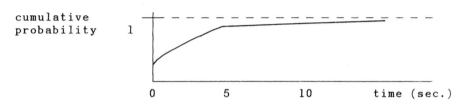

Figure 2. Release time probability curve.

The probability distribution regarding release time may be chosen as shown in Figure 2. In some cases particular release problems might occur. It might for example be necessary with emergency release due to technical failure, or the man doing the operation may fall and loosen the release lever due to excessive wave impacts when the boat becomes seaborne.

The curve can partly be based on test results. According to lifeboat manufacturer HARDING, the release operation during tests often is completed before the boat is fully seaborne.

The boat may be pulled out of the water by tight wire falls when the wave has passed. In the LBL-program, the pendulum motion of the boat when it is retrieved to air from a position behind the wave crest, is calculated.

When the boat is pulled out of the water, the lowering operation can be continued. Thus, inclusion of the probability that time may be unsufficient for release, will also in general lead to lower position of the boat when it finally becomes seaborne.

LIFEBOAT - WAVE INTERACTION

The principle assumption is that the boat is exposed to impact from water particles, thrust and wind when seaborn.

The relative motion between boat and wave has to be found in order to calculate forces. A longitudinal and transverse velocity component results.

The horizontal dynamic drag force D (Newton) is calculated for each wave component as follows:

$$D = 1/2 \cdot \rho \, V^2 \cdot C_D \cdot A_P$$

ρ = Specific gravity of water.

V = Relative speed between wave and boat in longitudinal, respective transverse direction.

C_D = Drag coefficient.

A_P = Projected transverse/longitudinal area of the submerged part of the boat.

The propeller thrust is assumed constant when seaborne. It acts in the forward direction. The turning operation is obtained by assuming a constant angular acceleration. Both thrust and angular acceleration are given as input.

The wind acts on the boat above sea level.

When the forces on the boat are found, the acceleration and speed components are easely obtained as the lifeboat mass is known.

Wave/Wind-Rig interaction
The basic assumption in the program is that the wave or the
wind is not influenced by the rig. With respect to slender
strength members on jackets and bracings on semisubmersibles
this assumption is fairly correct. In the vicinity of the main
columns on semisubmersibles, gravity platforms or ships hull
the displacement results obtained by the above assumption will
be conservative.

THE LIFEBOAT LAUNCHING PROGRAM SYSTEM

The progress of the launch operation is shown on the PC-screen.
Unfortunately the calculations are far too large to allow real
time presentation on a PC. The graphic presentation, however,
greatly facilitate program testing. Some errors that may be
hard to identify through columns of figures, are easily
identified through the graphic presentation.

Input data to the program is structured as follows:

Simulation Particulars

-    Number of simulations, time step etc.

Scenario Particulars

-    Wind direction, rig orientation, lifeboat height above sea
     etc.

Lifeboat Particulars

-    Length, breadth, projected areas etc.

Wave data

-    Significant wave height, number of components etc.

Wind data

-    Mean speed, number of components etc.

Rig structure

-    Coordinates defining planes to be given.

Release time

-    Probability distribution to be given.

Motion of floating units

-    RAO and phase data.

The following figure shows the LBL-system layout:

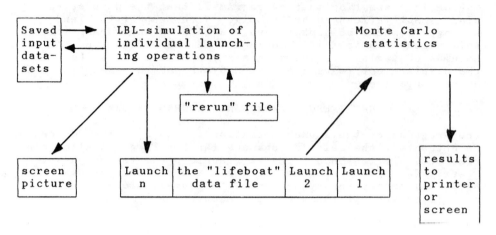

Figure 3.   LBL system layout

LBL
The LBL-program simulates stochastically individual launching operations. If desired, the launching progress is shown on the data screen. For each launching operation simulation, results are stored in the data file "lifeboat". Input data is easily obtained by reading and editing on previously saved input data sets.

Monte Carlo
The program Monte Carlo reads the data file "lifeboat", and presents a result printout on printer or screen.

"Lifeboat" file
The "lifeboat" file contains data from the last performed LBL-run, which may involve some hundred launching operations. When a LBL run is completed, Monte Carlo has to be run, as the next LBL-run will overwrite the data.

"Rerun" file
The stochastic values from the last performed launching operation can be restored from this file, and the simulation repeated.

In the figure 4 and 5, a screen picture when the boat is hanging in wire falls, and a picture when the boat is seaborne are shown.

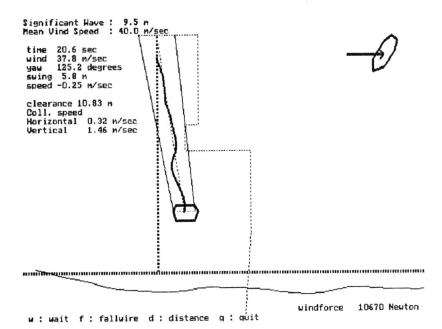

Figure 4.   The lifeboat is hanging in wire falls.

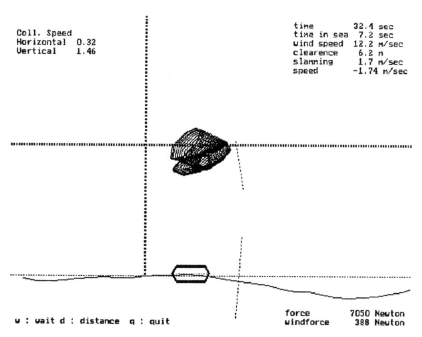

Figure 5.   The lifeboat is seaborn.

SIMULATION RESULTS

In figure 6 a comparison between lifeboat launch from a fixed and floating unit with identical structure, is shown.

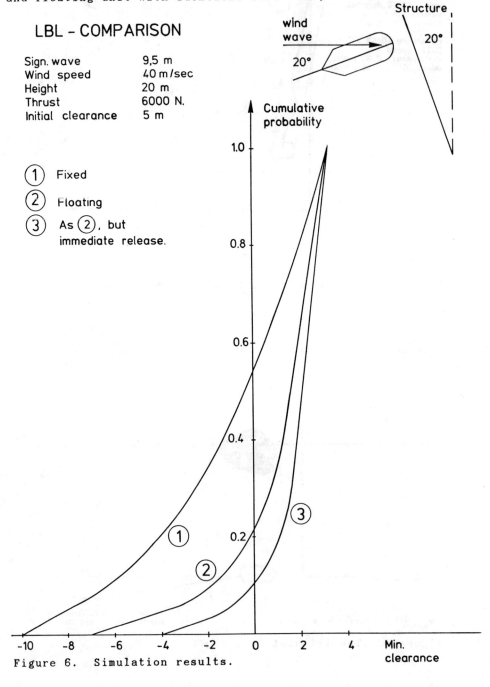

Figure 6. Simulation results.

Curve 1 for the fixed unit as well as curve 2 for the floating unit are based on a release time distribution as shown in figure 7.

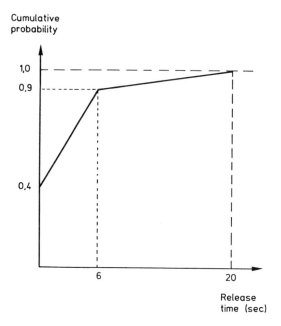

Figure 7.   Release time distribution

The reason that the collision probability is considerably less for the floating unit than for the fixed one, is that the wave that carries the lifeboat towards the rig, also carries the floating rig away.

Curve 3 shows that immediate release is favourable (as compared to curve 2).

When the boat was launched from the fixed unit (curve 1), it was pulled out of the water by tight wire falls in 30 percent of the simulated cases. Corresponding results for the floating unit (curve 2) was 42 percent.

CONCLUSIONS

The LBL-program approach fully demonstrates the efficiency of Monte Carlo simulations on this type of problems.

The impact of several parameters with respect to the collision probability can be calculated. Even by giving conservative data for uncertain parameters like time to release, it can be identified whether such parameters have impact on the collision probability.

The results may also efficiently be used to decide location of lifeboat on the rig and possible need for additional boats in case of unfavourable weather conditions.

Because the launching operation is shown graphically on the computer screen, problems with respect to such operations are highlighted. As interactive input with respect to launching and release can be given, the program can also be used in training situations.

ACKNOWLEDGEMENT

The LBL-program development was financially supported by Esso Norway and NTNF (Norwegian Council for Scientific and Technical Research), and Esso Norway's contribution and support was fundamental for initiation and the success of the project.

REFERENCES

1. Report from the Investigation Commision appointed by the Norwegian Ministry of Justice:
   "Deep Sea Driller's" capsizing by Fedje March 1st. 1976.

2. Report from the Commision appointed by Royal Decree March 28. 1983:
   "Alexander L. Kielland" - accident, Nov. 1981.

3. Pedersen, K.S.:
   The risk picture, fire and explosions risks offshore.
   SINTEF report STF 88 A83012.

4. Westergaard, Rich. H.:
   All About Blowouts
   Norwegian Oil Review 7.8.1985.

5. Kristiansen, Svein:
   Marine traffic and platform collision risk.
   Marine Technology Center of Norway Report 1982.

6. Moan, Torgeir:
   Loads and safety for marine structures accidents loads.
   NTH, Trondheim, Norway 7.-9. January 1985.

7. National Transportation Safety Board Bureau of Accident Investigation Washington, D.C. 20594:
   Marine Accident Report - Capsizing and Sinking of the U.S. Mobile Offshore Drilling Unit OCEAN RANGER, off the East Cost of Canada 166 Nautical Miles East of St. John's, New Foundland, February 15. 1982.

8. Risk assessment of emergency evacuation from offshore installations.
   Technica, London, 1983.

9. Principles of Naval Architecture.
   The society of Naval Architects and Marine Engineers.
   1967.

10. Roland, Ivar et.al.:
    Safety of structures under dynamic loading.
    Tapir NTH 1977.

11. Davenport, A.G.:
    Wind structure and wind climate.
    Article in reference 11.

12. LBL Users Manual.
    Quasar Consultants 1988.

13. Soma, Helge et.al.:
    Risk Analysis regarding Lifeboat evacuation.
    QUASAR Report No: 0-36-86-1 Rev. 2.

14. Soma, Helge et.al.:
    The lifeboat launching (LBL) program system.   Theoretical
    aspects.
    QUASAR Report No: 0-36-86-2 rev. 0.

MONTE CARLO SIMULATION TO ASSESSING THE RISK ASSOCIATED TO THE NAVIGATION IN CHANNEL-PORT

Romano Santucci[1] and Paolo Vestrucci[2]

1. NIER, Via S. Stefano 16 - Bologna (ITALY)
2. Laboratorio Ingegneria Nucleare, Via dei Colli 16 - Bologna (ITALY)

ABSTRACT

Aim of this paper is to present a semi-probabilistic, semi-deterministic methodology to evaluate the risk of dangerous spills, and related public and environmental hazard, associated to the navigation in a narrow channel-port.

Our model uses the Monte Carlo method with variance reduction techniques, such as forced collisions and linear extractions to calculate the probability, location and consequences of several kinds of accidents.

A crude Monte Carlo technique is used to choose the tipology of the ship, the route followed, the substances carried and the gross tonnage.

We apply the conditional probability principles to assess the frequencies and the impact of the accidents occurring to moored ships (whose location is known).

In this way, using the Monte Carlo technique, we can simulate the spatial distribution of incidents along the channel, starting from global information about it.

Moreover, variance reduction techniques yield an acceptable error value with a number of histories much lower than using the Crude Monte Carlo. The simulation of the system in study can be performed automatically by a package of two programs: the first (input module) accepts the topological and traffic information about the port; the second (simulation module) simulates the port and the traffic using the inputs created by the first. The simulation program can handle sensitivity analysis.

Finally, we present the results of the application of our model to an idealized but realistic situation of channel-port.

1. INTRODUCTION

The assessment of the risk associated to the navigation in ports is a very important step in the framework of evaluation of the overall hazard for many industrial sites. [1÷4]

The main difficulties encountered in this kind of analysis arise from:

- the spatial extension of the area to be studied;
- the wide variety of situation to be considered.

Usually a port has a very complex geometry, moreover the ships can follow a rather large number of different routes within it: the assessment of the accident consequences implies the knowledge of several details, first of all where the event takes place.

The goods transported have a wide range of properties, so the characteristics of the carriers and of the quays structures (e.g. loading/unloading equipments) are very different: the incidental sequences and consequences must be assessed for a large number of situations.

2. THE METHODOLOGICAL APPROACHES

The analysis of a port area is always a challenging goal, due to the number of variables, the complexity of the system and the large set of events to be considered.

Of course a simple method will ignore most of the details, so yielding general results, while a complex method will require a more consistent amount of data, a proper computer program, and will generate specific information on the port associated risk. Three main classes of methods can be recognized:

a - methods based on historical accident data, [1,2]

b - deterministic methods, [3,4]

c - simulation methods.

The type (a) approach consists in the direct use of historical data of accidents and movements relevant to several and hopefully similar situations to infer the probabilities of accident occurrences in the case under investigation.

The simplicity of this approach is apparent, and this feature is the attractive advantage of it. The drawback of methods (a) is the impossibility to take into account the real characteristics of the port examined and to yield significant suggestions for optimization and recovery actions. Only rough and global evaluations should be expected by using this approach.

The second class of methods (b), which we called "deterministic", removes some of the previous limitations using phenomenological models in order to filter the historical data adapting them to the specific situation.

For example in Ref. [3,4], a model based on the ship flux entering a (large) port zone and on ship cross sections (calculated as functions of ship lengths and widths), together with historical data properly adapted, is used for predicting collision events.

Despite those efforts, these models seem sometime over complicated in the sense that the mathematical structure does not add new information, reproducing with minor improvements the input data.

Methods belonging to class (c) avoid some of the previous problems.

The bottom line is to use basic event probabilities to originate accident sequences taking into account geometrical and physical port characteristics and traffic distribution. In this way apparent advantages are obtained:

-   the basic event probabilities, which are based on historical data, work as initiating events of accidents sequences which can be absolutely new and ignored by historical accident data;

-   the location of the accident can be predicted in a much more precise way;

-   the interaction of the ship(s) with port structures, other ships and physical characteristics can be deeply studied;

-   specific optimization criteria can be grasped in respect to port physical configuration and regulation.

Of course, the application of these methods requires always a computer supported tool, certainly more complicate than in case (a), not always than in case (b). Depending on the study-case objective, one is preferable to the others.

In the next paragraphs the simulation via Monte Carlo method is presented.

3. THE MONTE CARLO METHOD

The Monte Carlo Method (MCM) is very attractive for the simulation of complex systems. [5,6]

It is rather simple to use, flexible and allows an in-depth analysis of the results (i.e. a more immediate understanding and acceptance by the customer and public opinion).

Unfortunately its wide application to reliability and risk assessment has been prevented by the extremely low values of the probabilities to be evaluated [7,8]: in fact, it can be seen that to evaluate a low probability P, i.e. rare events, with an error; $\epsilon[\%]$ it is necessary to run

$$n = 10^4 / (\quad P \quad \epsilon^2) \text{ event simulations (i.e. histories).}$$

It is apparent that for $P \sim 10^{-4}$ and $\epsilon \sim 10$, a very large number of simulations has to be performed, with an impracticable computer time consumption.

A variety of so called "variance reduction" or "biasing techniques" have been developed to make MCM applicable to rare events study. [8,9]

In our model, we choose to use the so called "forced collisions" techniques (FC), coupled with a linear extraction of the mismanoeuvring point along the channel.

This choice follows from the results of a comparison of various biasing methods in human reliability problems. [9]

In this way, the distribution of mismanoeuvre events along the channel can be evaluated with a practicable number of simulated histories.

The fundamental idea of the forced collision approach is to divide each history in two parts: in the first the (rare) mismanoeuvre event occurs in the second the event does not occur. In doing so, we force a mismanoeuvre for each history (or ship entering the port).

In order to take into account this effect, we give appropriate weights to the two parts of the original history.

The linear extractions techniques consist in extracting, via the introduction of another weight, the distance travelled by the colliding parts of the ships, from a linearized probability density function. This not only allows a saving in calculation time (if the number of simulations is large), but also has an important effect in reducing the variance of the results. [9]

4. THE CHANNEL - PORT MODEL

4.1 Topologic Description of the Channel

We represent the channel as a set of segments of equal length (Figure 1). To evaluate the propagation and the effects of a spill it is important to know the land use around the port (Table 1); to assess the consequences of a mismanoeuvre, we must know the characteristics of the sides of the channel. To do this, we assign, for each segment, the lengths of the various jetty features, listed in Table 2.

Figure 1. Example of geometric model of a channel-port.

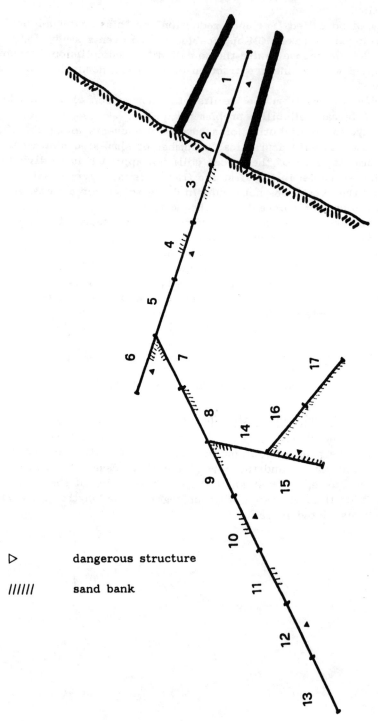

▷   dangerous structure

//////   sand bank

TABLE 1

The kinds of shore use considered on our model

Shore feature	Description
Free Area	No problems of accidents propagation
Built-up Area	Hazard of public exposure
Presence of Dangerous Substances	Hazard of domino effect on dangerous plants and/or ships
Built-up and Dangerous Substances	Hazard for people exposure and for domino effect

TABLE 2

The kinds of channel sides considered in our model

Jetty features	Description
Sand bank	The consequence of a manoeuvre error is a grounding without release
Dangerous structures	If a ship strikes such a feature, a spill occurs
Moored ships	If a ship strikes a moored ship, the Minorsky model is used to evaluate if the struck ship rupture occur
Free jetty	If a ship collide with a portion of free jetty, there is a given release probability

From these information we obtain, for each port segment, the probabilities for various scenarios descending from a manoeuvre error. In this way a lot of physical details are considered.

Knowing the location of the active quays in the port, we can built up the routes followed by the ships in the channel (Table 3); e.g. (with reference to Figure 1), to reach all the quays in the segment 7, a ship will follow the route given by the set of segments (1,2,3,4,5,7).

In our model, we consider every segment as represented by its mid point.

TABLE 3

Example of routes composition for the Port in Figure 1

ROUTE DESCRIPTION		
ROUTE NR.	ROUTE COMPOSITION	ROUTE LENGHT [km]
1	1 2	3.0
2	1 2 3	5.0
3	1 2 3 4	7.0
4	1 2 3 4 5	9.0
5	1 2 3 4 5 6	11.0
6	1 2 3 4 5 7	11.0
7	1 2 3 4 5 7 8	13.0
8	1 2 3 4 5 7 8 9	15.0
9	1 2 3 4 5 7 8 9 10	17.0
10	1 2 3 4 5 7 8 9 10 11	21.0

4.2 Ship Classifications

To assess the probability and the consequences of a release event, it is important to know the dimensions of the involved ship.

From statistical analysis of the ships, it is possible to find simple and reliable correlations (Figures 2a , 2b), which allow to classify ship dimensions in classes of tonnage only (see Table 4).

Figure 2a. Correlation between ship gross tonnage and length
for a Channel-port.

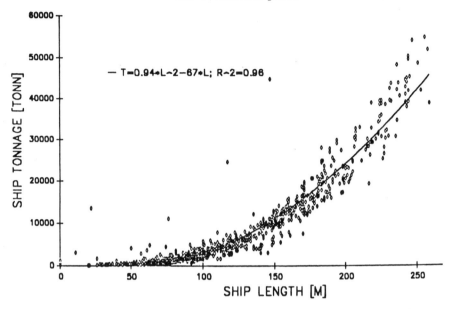

Figure 2b. Correlation between ship width and length
for a Channel-port.

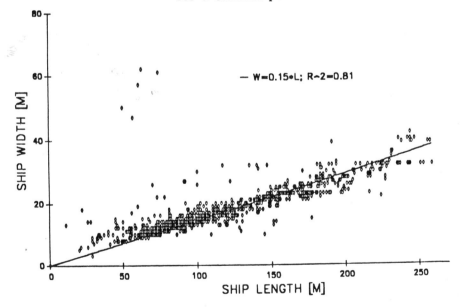

TABLE 4
Example of tonnage classes

Class	Tonnes
1	0 - 999
2	1 000 - 4 999
3	5 000 - 9 999
4	10 000 - 50 000

The correlations should be calculated using the data relevant to the particular port in analysis.

Obviously, it is important to know the characteristics of the transported goods.

We grouped the various substances into a given number of categories (like in Table 5, for example) from the point of view of the hazard due to a spill.

In summary, a ship entering the port (i.e. a simulated history) will be specified through the gross tonnage class, the category of the transported substance and the route followed in the channel, i.e. the quay to be reached.

TABLE 5
Example of substance classes

Class	Substance
1	GENERIC
2	FLAMMABLE TOXIC
3	FLAMMABLE GAS
4	FLAMMABLE LIQUID
5	TOXIC

4.3 Traffic Description

The traffic in the port is described by means of the historical navigation data, i.e. by the frequencies at which the ships (of each dimensional class) entering the channel travel along each route transporting a particular substance category.

We consider here a one-way regulation for the traffic flux.

This information is available in (or easily inferred from) the port registers. Obviously it is necessary, at the present, to assume some simplifications in order to simulate the traffic in the port:

- we suppose that each ship is loaded with substances of only one category (typically the more dangerous one);

- we assume each ship reaches its arrival quay and exits the port following the same path, without any further berthing;

- we assume that usually the ships enter the port loaded and come out empty;to take into accont that a small number of ships have some load during the return travel, we apply to the ships a probability, inferred by traffic data, that they leave the port with some load. These assumptions are not real constraints for the method: depending on the case in study they can be removed and substituted with others more acceptable.

4.4 Basic Events Data

We choose the following basic events as those leading to a dangerous spill:

a.   mismanoeuvre;   (for moving ships)

b.   fire / explosion;

c.   loading / unloading accident;   (for stationary ships)

d.   berthing / unberthing accident.

The probability for each of this initiating events has to be given as input to the model.

To evaluate the spill probability, we must assign, via historical analysis, the release probabilities due to a ship / jetty collision (derived from a mismanoeuvring event), to fire / explosion, to a loading / unloading accident and to a berthing / unberthing accident.

We note that these input data are not affected by the drawbacks outlined for the models mainly based on historical data.

In port documents a relatively large number of events due to mismanoeuvre is registered; only a few of these events leads to serious releases (often none of them): so, while the statistical data about releases due to mismanoeuvring are very poor, the probability of the initiating event "manoeuvre error" is confidently known, even for small ports.

On the other hand, the data about fire / explosion, loading / unloading and berthing / unberthing accidents are quite general (procedures and equipments are rather standardized), so that the related probabilities can be obtained from bibliographical information as well assessed values.

5. THE SIMULATION OF THE SHIP HISTORY

The assessment of the spill probability for the channel port, is performed by following the evolution of a large number of ships entering in the system, storing the results of each history and statistically analyzing the stored data.

With reference to the schematic flow chart of Figure 3, we can see that the first step of the calculation is to select, via Crude Monte Carlo (CMC) method and using the traffic data, the route followed by the ship, the substance category of the load and its gross tonnage class.

Then, we force a suitable fraction of the ship to have a mismanoeuvre and by means the FC method we select the point (segment) of the channel where the event occurs.

According to the characteristics of the segment, by applying the conditional probability principle, we can infer the occurrence rate for various events: ship / ship collision, ship / jetty collision, ship / port dangerous structure collision or grounding.

In the case of a ship / ship collision, we apply a simplified version of the Minorsky model to assess the occurrence of a struck ship rupture; the deviation angle θ (respect to the route direction), to evaluate the collision

speed, is extracted with a CMC method from a $\cos \theta$ distribution, with $\theta \in [0°, \theta_{MAX}°]$ Normally we assume $\theta_{MAX} = 40°$. [2]

This choice is due to the narrow width of the channel with respect to the ships dimensions; in this way we have a suitable large probability to select a little deviation angle.

In the case of a rupture, a spill occurs if the collision involves the hold of the struck ship.

We note that, due to the one-way nature supposed for the port, we do not consider collisions between moving ships. This limitation can be removed too, in the case of two-way navigation.

A spill can arise from a ship / jetty collision with an assumed probability given as input.

We consider as "dangerous" a structure that can cause a spill if struck by a ship.

Finally, if a grounding occurs, we suppose that the kinetic energy is entirely dissipated by friction between the sand bank and the ship bottom.

At the same time the fraction of ship without manoeuvre error is arrived to the quay, where we apply the conditional probability principle to assess the occurrence of fire / explosion, loading / unloading and berthing / unberthing event and related releases.

The aim of this semi-stocastic, semi-deterministic approach is to obtain a distribution of events a long the channel, without loss of reliability in the final results due to the fragmentation of the statistics.

Figure 3. Schematic flow chart of the typical ship history.

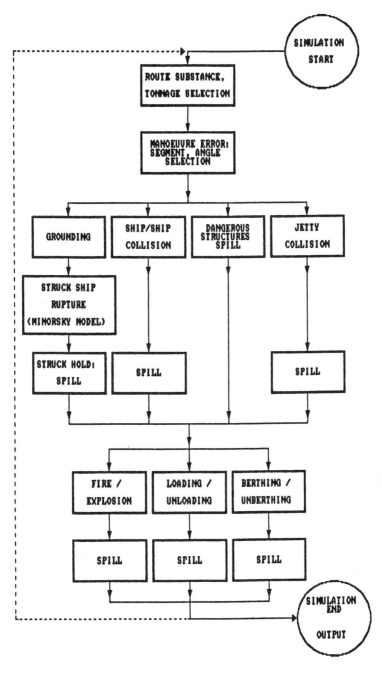

6. THE SIMULATION PACKAGE

A simulation package to automatically perform the above operations has been developed.

The package is written in Microsoft FORTRAN 77 ver. 3.2, and runs IBM MS/DOS compatible PCs.

It consists in two separate modules:

-       INPOR, which is the input program,

-       PORTO, which is the simulation program.

The input module accept the main data of the problem, performs some preliminary elaborations and write a file in a suitable format table used as input file for the PORTO program.

The traffic data can be read from an ASCII file (obtained processing the port data).

The other quantities are inserted interactively from the keyboard, answering to appropriate questions.

The file generated by INPOR can be modified by the user, via a word processor program, to evaluate the effect of the variation of some parameters, without rerun the entire module.

The simulation module after reading the file generated by INPOR, performs the operations outlined in the previous section for the number of histories selected by the user.

Some data must be inserted interactively in this module (e.g. the speed in the channel, the probabilities of fire, explosion, of loading / unloading events, of berthing / unberthing events and the associate release frequencies, etc.), so that it is easy to perform some sensitivity analysis in a single run of the program.

At the end of the simulation the program performs the calculation of the tallies for the events listed in Table 6.

TABLE 6
List of the events Analyzed by the package PORTO

NR	EVENT
1	Manoeuvring Error
2	Grounding
3	Ship/Ship Collision
4	Rupture Due to a Ship/Ship Collision
5	Release Due to a Ship/Ship Collision
6	Ship/Jetty Collision
7	Release Due to a Ship/Ship Collision
8	Fire/Explosion
9	Release Due to Fire/Explosion
10	Loading/Unloading Accident
11	Release Due to a Loading/Unloading Accident
12	Berthing/Unberthing Accident
13	Release Due to a Berthing/Unberthing Accident
14	Ship/Dangerous Structure Collision
15	Release Due to a Ship/Dangerous Structure Collision
16	Dangerous Spill

Finally an output file is produced in which, after some general information about the simulation, the probabilities for the identified events are written, for the port, and for each substance and segment.

7. AN EXAMPLE OF CALCULATION

As an example of the results obtained from the package, we report some part of the file generated by INPOR (Table 7) and of the output produced by the program PORTO (Table 8), for the reference channel-port (see Figure 1, Tables 3,4,5).
In Table 7, we have a summary of the main information about the port (Table 7a).

TABLE 7a

Example of the file generated by the program INPOR

GLOBAL SIMULATION PARAMETERS	
Nr. of Routes in the Port	15
Nr. of Substance Classes	5
(first 1 are NOT dangerous)	
Nr. of Tonnage Categories	4
Nr. of Segments in the Port	17
Segment Length [km]	1.0
Nr. of Ships Entering Yearly	3650.0
Mean Nr. of Ships Moored	57
Mean Ship Length [km]	.100
Mean Length Travelled [km/sh.]	17.184
Nr. of Analysed Man. Err.	10
Man. Error Probab. [ev/ship*km]	1.531E-05

Then a description of the port segment is given (Table 7b); in the second column, we have the shore description (for example, segment nr. 3 is close to built-up areas, while segment nr. 12 has also dangerous substances).

TABLE 7b

SEGMENT DESCRIPTION - OCCUPIED FRACTIONS -					
SEGMNT	SHORE	SHIP	SAND.B.	DGR.ST.	FREE
1	1	.000	.750	.250	.000
2	1	.031	.700	.250	.019
3	2	.009	.250	.000	.741
4	3	.023	.150	.050	.777
5	3	.049	.000	.000	.951
6	1	.177	.150	.100	.573
7	1	.054	.050	.000	.896
8	3	.148	.050	.000	.802
9	3	.583	.200	.000	.217
10	1	.754	.050	.050	.146
11	3	.080	.100	.000	.820
12	4	.191	.000	.050	.759
13	2	.620	.000	.000	.380
14	1	.000	.050	.000	.950
15	1	.006	.500	.100	.394
16	1	.031	.500	.000	.469
17	1	.094	.500	.000	.406

In the others columns, we can see the fractions of the segments sides occupied by the various features. In particular, we note that segment nr. 1 has a fraction of 25% (i.e. 0.5 km of 2 Km) occupied by dangerous structures: this is a way to take into account high occurrence of accidents at the channel inlet, leading to a collision with channel head.

In Table 7c, the route manoeuvring accidents probabilities are reported.

TABLE 7c

MANOEUVRE ERROR PROBABILITY BY ROUTE	
ROUTE	M.E. PROB.[EV./SHIP]
1	8.157E-05
2	9.605E-05
3	1.105E-04
4	1.519E-04
5	1.664E-04
6	1.664E-04
7	1.808E-04
8	1.953E-04
9	2.554E-04
10	2.699E-04
11	2.843E-04
12	4.198E-04
13	2.098E-04
14	2.098E-04
15	2.243E-04

In the complete file generated by INPOR, we can find also the segments manoeuvre error probabilities and the traffic frequencies by route, substance and tonnage, which are not included for space problems.

A selection of the results for 10^5 simulated histories is reported in Table 8.

After some input parameter values (Table 8a), some global results are shown (Table 8b); for the various selected events, we give the probability values in [event/ship] and in [event/year] referred to the assumed yearly traffic flux (see Table 7a).

TABLE 8a

Example of the output file generated by the program PORTO

SIMULATION PARAMETERS		
Nr of Simulated Ships		100000
Max Speed in the Channel	[knots]	5.000
Max Deviation Angle	[deg]	40.000
Normalization Factor for D. A.		2.865E+00
Scale Factor for D. A.		2.250E+00
Probability for Fire/Explosion	[ev./ship]	6.000E-05
Probability for Load/Unload. Acc.	[ev./ship]	3.000E-05
Probability for Berth./Unb. Acc.	[ev./ship]	3.000E-04
Prob. a Ship Exit Empty	[%]	90.000
Probability for Spill due to S/J Coll.	[%]	15.000
Probability for Spill due to F/E	[%]	15.000
Probability for Spill due to L/U	[%]	10.000
Probability for Spill due to B/U	[%]	10.000
Probability to Strike the Hull	[%]	60.000

TABLE 8b

GLOBAL RESULTS		
Manoeuvre Error Frequency	[ev./ship]	2.503E-04
Manoeuvre Error Frequency	[ev./year]	9.135E-01
NOT Man. Err. Frequency	[ev./ship]	9.999773
SQM related to M. E. F.		7.987E-07
SQMR related to M. E. F. (Rel. Error)	[%]	.319

RESULTS BY EVENTS				
NR.	EVENT	SIM. NR.	[EV./SHIP]	[EV./YEAR]
1	Manoeuvre Error	100000	2.503E-04	9.135E-01
2	Grounding	100000	6.878E-05	2.511E-01
3	Ship/Ship Collision	100000	5.541E-05	2.022E-01
4	Rupture <- S/S Coll.	339	7.797E-08	2.846E-04
5	Spill <- S/S Coll.	339	4.678E-08	1.708E-04
6	Ship/Structure Coll.	100000	2.197E-05	8.018E-02
7	Spill <- S/St Coll.	100000	1.318E-05	4.811E-02
8	Ship/Jetty Collision	100000	1.041E-04	3.801E-01
9	Spill <- S/J Coll.	100000	1.562E-05	5.703E-02
10	Fire/Explosion	100000	6.005E-05	2.192E-01
11	Spill <- F/E	100000	9.000E-06	3.285E-02
12	Load/Unload	100000	3.002E-05	1.096E-01
13	Spill <- L/U	100000	3.000E-06	1.095E-02
14	Berthing/Unberthing	100000	2.998E-04	1.094E+00
15	Spill <- L/U	100000	3.002E-05	1.096E-01
16	Dangerous Release	103034	1.408E-05	5.138E-02

In the output file are recorded the results by substance and segment; as an example we give in Table 8c a sample of these values for the substance "FLAMMABLE LIQUID" and for the segment nr. 9.

TABLE 8c

RESULTS BY SEGMENT AND SUBSTANCE CLASS						
N.B.: Results with occurence probability .LE. 10.E-30 are not reported.						
***** SUBSTANCE FLAMM. LIQ.						
** SEGMENT NR 9						
EVENT	600.0	2500.0	8000.0	20000.0	.0	TOTAL SIMUL.
1	1.4E-03	2.7E-03	9.4E-05	2.9E-04	.0E+00	4.5E-03 949
2	2.8E-04	5.4E-04	1.9E-05	5.7E-05	.0E+00	9.0E-04 949
3	8.2E-04	1.6E-03	5.5E-05	1.7E-04	.0E+00	2.6E-03 949
4	.0E+00	.0E+00	.0E+00	5.9E-06	.0E+00	5.9E-06 2
8	3.1E-04	5.9E-04	2.0E-05	6.2E-05	.0E+00	9.8E-04 949
9	4.6E-05	8.8E-05	3.1E-06	9.4E-06	.0E+00	1.5E-04 949
10	1.1E-03	5.1E-03	2.1E-04	6.0E-04	.0E+00	7.0E-03 3177
11	1.6E-04	7.6E-04	3.2E-05	8.9E-05	.0E+00	1.0E-03 3177
12	5.4E-04	2.5E-03	1.1E-04	3.0E-04	.0E+00	3.5E-03 3177
13	5.4E-05	2.5E-04	1.1E-05	3.0E-05	.0E+00	3.5E-04 3177
14	5.4E-03	2.5E-02	1.1E-03	3.0E-03	.0E+00	3.5E-02 3177
15	5.4E-04	2.5E-03	1.1E-04	3.0E-04	.0E+00	3.5E-03 3177
16	7.8E-04	3.6E-03	1.5E-04	4.2E-04	.0E+00	5.0E-03 10587

We note that while the whole probabilities of the basic events are in accordance with the input values, we obtain information about incidental sequences for which a-priori probabilities are unavailable.
Another result is the spatial distribution of the accidents given according to the traffic and incidental historical data for the port.

8. CONCLUSION AND FURTHER DEVELOPMENTS

The above mentioned results confirm that our simulation based on MC approach is able to yield sufficiently detailed and reliable results to be used in the framework of risk assessment of the marine traffic in a portual area.
Actually, we are working to insert in our computer programs a section for the automatic calculation of the spill amount.

Furthermore, most of the limitations and assumptions (e.g. the "one-way" navigation constraint) made in this application can be easily removed, in virtue of the great flexibility of Monte Carlo simulation. Much different situations could be analyzed with minor changes and efforts.

9. ACKNOWLEDGMENTS

This methodology has been developed in the framework ARIPAR Project for the evaluation of the risk associated with the industrial and dockyard area of Ravenna (Italy).
ARIPAR is a project sponsored by the Regione Emilia Romagna, the Italian Civil Minister and other local Authorities. Dr. Amendola, Dr. Egidi, Dr. Boattini, Prof. Foraboschi, Prof. Zanelli of the Project Direction and Cap. Caricato of Ravenna Port are greatly acknowledged for interesting discussion and cooperation; Mr. A.S. White of Lloyd's Register of Shipping is also acknowledged, for his comments and suggestions during the development of the analysis.

REFERENCES

[1]   Canvey: an investigation of potential hazard from operations in the Canvey Island/Thurroc area - Appendix 11 -; Health And Safety Executive, London, 1978.

[2]   Study into the risk from transportation of liquid chlorine and ammonia in the Rijnmond area; Technica Consulting Scientist And Engineers, London, 1984.

[3]   LNG facility risk assessment study for Nikiski, Alaska,; Science Application, Inc., La Jolla, 1976.

[4]   Risk assessment study for the Cove Point, Maryland LNG facility; Science Application, Inc.; La Jolla, 1978.

[5]   Rubinstein, R.Y.: Simulation and the Monte Carlo method; J. Wiley And Sons, New York, 1981.

[6]   Spanier, J. and Gelbard, E.M.: Monte Carlo principles and neutron transport problems; Addision - Wesley Publishing Company, Reading, 1969.

[7]   Dubi, A., Goldfelf, A., Leibowitz, A. and Sasson, D.: Aspects of evaluation of reliability of complexed systems by the Monte Carlo method; Ben-Gurion University In The Negev, Beer Sheva, 1986.

[8]   Dubi, A. and Goldfeld, A.: AMIR, a multipurpose performance and reliability analysis code; Malchi Science Ltd., Tel Aviv, 1985.

[9]   Vestrucci, P., Santucci, R. and Calderan, R.: Monte Carlo simulation of crew responses to accident sequences; Submitted For Publication.

RELIABILITY ASSESSMENT OF THE PROPULSION MACHINERY, STEERING GEAR, ELECTRICAL SUPPLY AND FIRE SYSTEMS OF IRRADIATED FUEL SHIPS

ROGER CHESHIRE
TRANSPORT APPROVALS AND SAFETY MANAGER
BRITISH NUCLEAR FUELS PLC
FLEMING HOUSE, WARRINGTON
CHESHIRE WA3 6AS

ABSTRACT

Pacific Nuclear Transport Ltd a subsidiary of British Nuclear Fuels Ltd owns and operates five purpose built ships for the carriage of irradiated fuel from Japan to France and the UK. The installed systems on board these vessels have been assessed for reliability and where appropriate recommendations made for modifications to the ship systems or for institution of appropriate maintenance or testing. No significant deficiencies existed in the design of the vessels but minor modification to engine control systems resulted in substantial improvements in reliability.

1. Introduction

   Pacific Nuclear Transport Ltd, a subsidiary company of British
   Nuclear Fuels plc own and operates five purpose built irradiated
   fuel carriers. The vessels transport irradiated nuclear fuel
   assemblies from Japan to France and the UK. Each vessel is 110m
   long, 15m beam, gross weight 3000 tonnes and can carry up to 26
   flasks. Depending on the type of fuel flask carried the number
   of assemblies per flask varies from 5 to 17.

   The design of the vessels evolves from a number of different
   requirements.

   (a) The size of the Japanese reactor port facilities which
        limited the draught to 7.5m and the length to 110m.

   (b) The rules of the Japanese Ministry of Transport which
        require duplication of generating machinery, anti-collision
        systems, post accident stability and fire fighting systems.

   (c) BNFL's commitment to the highest possible standard of
        vessel consistent with an economically viable operation.

   The objective of the reliability study was to assess and
   wherever possible quantify the probability of failure of those
   items of the ships machinery and equipment, the individual or
   combined failure of which could put the vessel in a potentially
   hazardous situation. Clearly the nature of the design of the
   flasks carried (IAEA Type B Packages) means that for any
   conceivable marine accident there is a negligible possibility of
   release of radioactive material. The assessment was therefore
   intended from the outset to minimise risk to the crew and
   prevent adverse publicity in the event of a marine accident
   involving an irradiated fuel carrier.

   The following items were covered in the report:-

   (a) Steering Gear
   (b) Main propulsion machinery
   (c) Electrical Power Supply Installation
   (d) Bow Thrust Unit
   (e) Fire Detection and Fire Fighting Installation

   Sailing conditions fall mainly into two types, open water and
   confined waters. The study took this into account and
   quantified the reliability performance for the two conditions
   where necessary. The assessment included both engineering and
   human error type failures, the latter mainly in a qualitative
   manner which attempted to emphasise those areas which are
   particularly sensitive to failures of that type.

2. Guide to the assessment

The assessments have been based on the fault-tree type of analysis. Given a particular failure, termed the "top event", e.g. stoppage of main engine, the fault-tree model is used to identify the various combinations and sequences of other failures within the system that ultimately lead to and result in the failure of the top event. The generic failure data that have been used in the fault trees have been obtained from a number of sources including the Systems Reliability Service Data Bank, Lloyd's Register of Shipping, James Fisher & Sons Ltd. and the Institution of Electrical Engineers. For those items of equipment for which failure data were not avaiable, "best estimate" values based on engineering judgement have been used.

The work was carried out under contract to BNFL by the Systems Reliability Service of the U.K.A.E.A.

3. Steering Gear Installation

The vessels are fitted with twin rudders, mechanically linked and driven by four double acting cylinders. A block diagram of the steering gear system is given in Fig. 1 The fault tree for the steering gear installation is shown in Fig. 2. The assessment predicted that the probability of installation failure due to engineering type faults during a voyage of 45 days duration (Japan-UK) is 2.4×10^{-3}. Assuming $2^1/2$ return voyages per year this corresponds to a failure on average once every 83 years. The only identified common mode fault was a rupture of the isolating valve housing which causes a gross leak of oil from both port and starboard circuits but the probability of this event has been calculated to be $< 10^{-5}$. As a result of the assessment it was recommended that the automatic isolation valve system is proof tested on a 3 monthly basis and it is confirmed that the valves have closed.

4. Main Propulsion

The main propulsion units of the vessels are twin diesel engines rated at 2000 BHP at 600 RPM. The engines drive their associated propellers through a reverse reduction type gearbox fitted with two hydraulically operated clutches, one for ahead and one for astern movement of the ship.

Assessments were carried out for two conditions.

(i) simultaneous failure of both main engines or associated machinery or control equipment.

(ii) the failure of a single propulsion unit or control equipment which would render the ship unsteerable if there was simultaneous failure of the steering gear. Diagrams of the main engine systems and associated fault trees are shown in Figs. 3-7.

Complete Loss of Propulsion

It was assessed that the probability of complete loss of propulsion due to engineering type failures is in the order of 1.3×10^{-2} or once every 77 voyages or once every 15 years. This loss of propulsion is dominated by failure of the air driven control system and by modification of that system the probability of failure was reduced to once every 213 voyages or once every 85 years. In this area alone the value of a detailed reliability assessment can be clearly seen.

Stoppage of a Single Engine

Stoppage of a single engine was assessed to have a probability of 0.97 or once every voyage or five times per year. This was again dominated by control system failure and modification of that system resulted in a similar improvement to that for complete loss of propulsion.

The main engine system was also assessed for human error and as a result procedures were adopted for testing and witnessing of completed maintenance in key areas.

5. Electrical Power Supply Installation

The power supply has six 415v 3 phase 50HZ diesel driven alternators. Two sets are designated to supply the normal loads and the remaining four sets supply the cargo cooling system. Interconnecting arrangements are such that the ships normal loads can be supplied by any one generator. A 100kw diesel driven generator is situated in the bow and this unit can supply all essential loads. Diagrams of the supply system and fault tree for the main electrical supply are given in figures 8 and 9.

The object of the assessment was to ascertain

(a) the reliability performance of the main power supply provided by the two generators installed for the purpose with back-up provided by the four cargo cooling sets.

(b) the reliability performance of the overall power supply under circumstances in which there is a sudden failure of the main supply duty generators and power to the essential loads is maintained automatically by the emergency generator.

It was assessed that the probability of failure of the main electrical power supply due to an engineering type fault is 8.7×10^{-4} per voyage or once every 1150 voyages or once every 230 years. This is mainly influenced by the presence of 6 generators each capable of sustaining the full electrical load. The only recommendation to come from this part of the assessment was the provision of a spare circuit breaker on board the vessel to replace the single circuit breaker which connects the cargo plant generators to the main supply bus bar.

The probability of failure of the two main generators and the emergency generator has been assessed to be 1.6×10^{-2} per voyage or once every 63 voyages or once every 13 years.

Recommendations for testing and maintenance of the emergency generator were made since statistically 56% of failures to start for such generators are due to starter, battery or fuel failures.

6. Bow Thrust Unit

The bow thrust unit is only of use in steering at low speeds and hence assessment of the unit was restricted to a 2 hour operating period typical of harbour manoeuvring operations.

A diagram of the system and the system fault tree are given in Figs. 10 and 11. It was assessed that the probability of failure due to an engineering type fault is of the order of 2.26×10^{-3} or on average once every 44 demands. The availability of the unit on demand is largely dependent upon the successful starting of the engine and recommendations have been made and adopted to test the unit before it is required.

7. Fire Detection and Fire Fighting Installations

The fire-detection installation consists of zones of detectors connected to an AFA-Minerva Type T880 control and alarm unit in the wheelhouse. A Type 280 repeater unit is situated in the engine-room machinery control room. Ionisation smoke-detectors and infra-red flame detectors are used in the engine room and diesel-generator rooms, and heat detectors are installed in the accommodation areas.

The fire-fighting installations are Halon systems discharging into the holds, engine room and diesel-generator rooms, sprinkler systems in the holds, and hosepipes in the accommodation areas. A diagram of the fire detection and fire fighting systems and fault trees for the system are shown in Figs. 12 and 13.

The assessment concentrates on those engineering-type failures of equipment that will prevent the installed fire-detection and fire-fighting installations from being available on demand. Human factors, e.g. failure of the crew to take the correct action, have not been assessed. Similarly the availability and use of other fire-fighting equipment such as portable extinguishers has not been taken into account.

The probabilities of failure of detection and operating systems are given in Table 1 below.

TABLE 1

Area	Installation	Probability of Failure to Operate on Demand
Holds	Detection	1.2×10^{-3}
	Halon	1.7×10^{-3}
	Sprinkler	4.3×10^{-5}
Engine Room	Detection	9×10^{-4}
	Halon	1.7×10^{-3}
Generator Rooms	Detection	9×10^{-4}
	Halon	1.7×10^{-3}
Crew Accommodation	Detection	1.6×10^{-2}
	Hosepipes	1×10^{-4}

It can be seen from Table 1 that the probability of detection-system failure to operate on demand has been assessed to be in the order of 10^{-3}, i.e. one failure on average every 1000 demands. In the accommodation areas only one detector is fitted in each unit of accommodation, whereas in other areas, e.g. engine room, holds, detectors are duplicated, and these single detectors reduce the reliability of the detection system by a factor of approximately ten.

It is noted that the detection system in the engine and generator rooms has detectors wired in duplicated circuits so that failure of one circuit will not inhibit detection in these areas.

Conclusions

The assessment of the reliability of ships systems in detail did not reveal any major deficiencies in the design, installation or operation of the vessels. However in various areas significant improvements were possible by the implementation of minor modifications, particular in the area of the engine control system and by instituting appropriate maintenance and testing of key components.

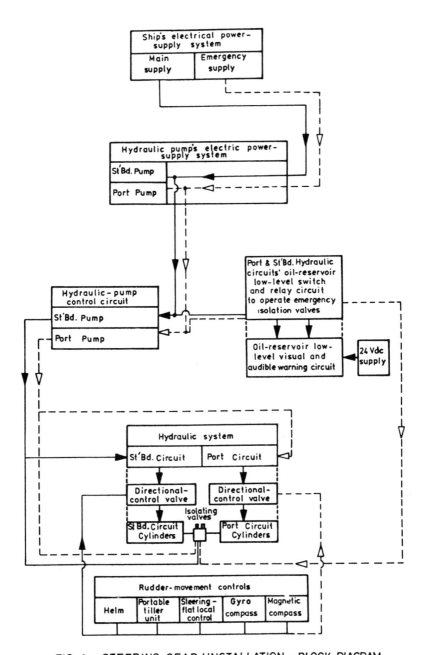

FIG. 1   STEERING-GEAR / INSTALLATION − BLOCK DIAGRAM

248

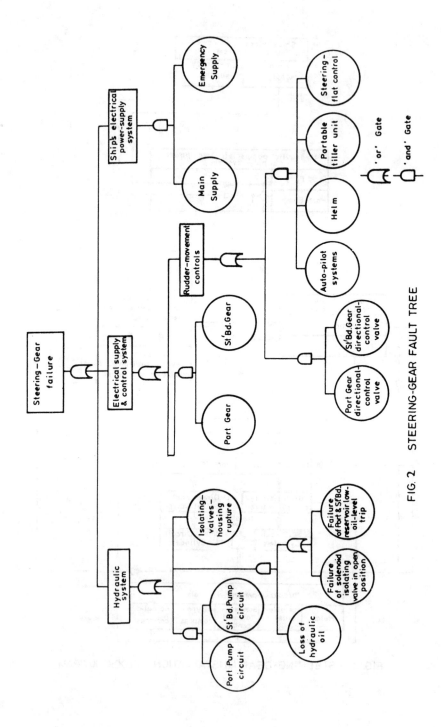

FIG. 2   STEERING-GEAR FAULT TREE

249

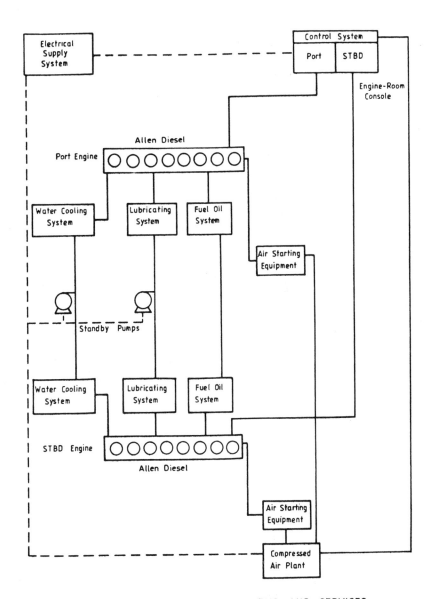

FIG. 3 MAIN – ENGINES SUB-SYSTEMS AND SERVICES-
BLOCK DIAGRAM

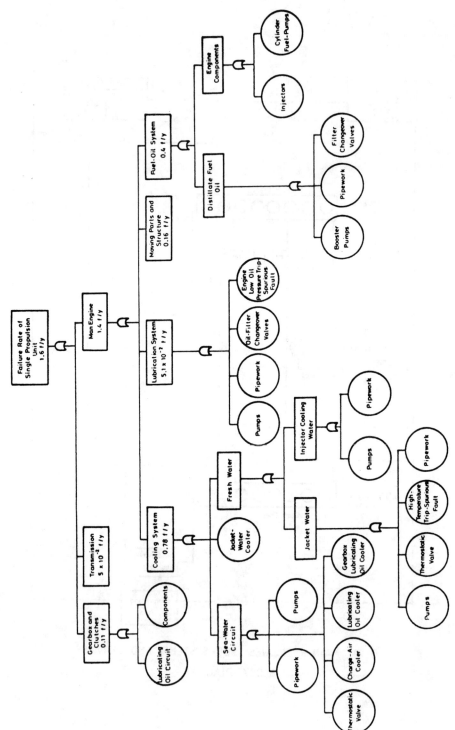

FIG. 4 SINGLE PROPULSION UNIT FAILURE. FAULT TREE

251

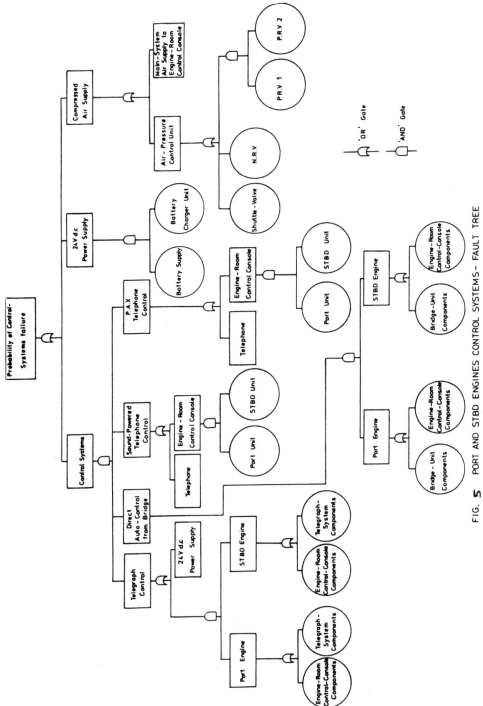

FIG. 5 PORT AND STBD ENGINES CONTROL SYSTEMS- FAULT TREE

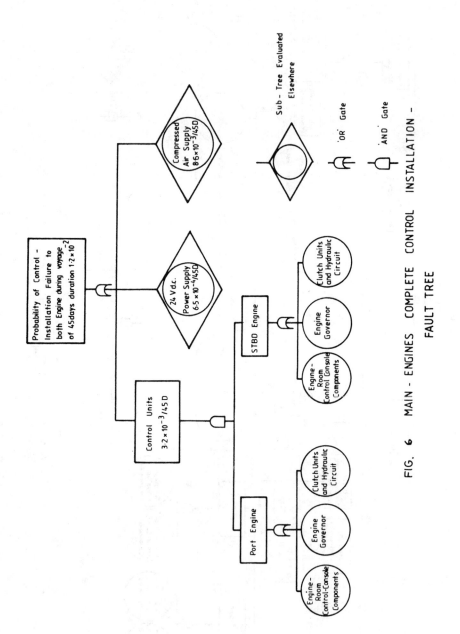

FIG. 6   MAIN - ENGINES COMPLETE CONTROL INSTALLATION -
FAULT TREE

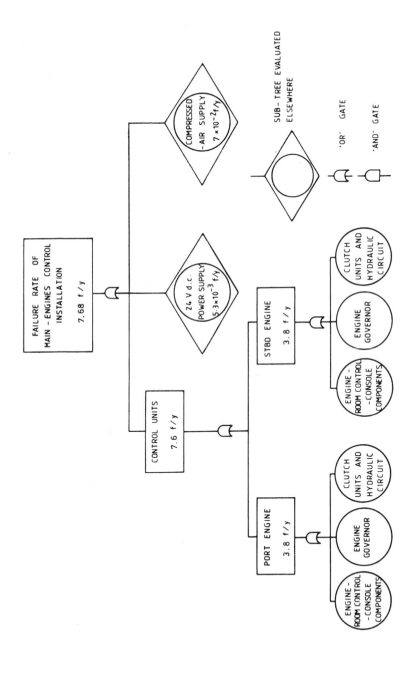

FIG. 7 FAILURE RATE OF MAIN - ENGINES CONTROL INSTALLATION - FAULT TREE

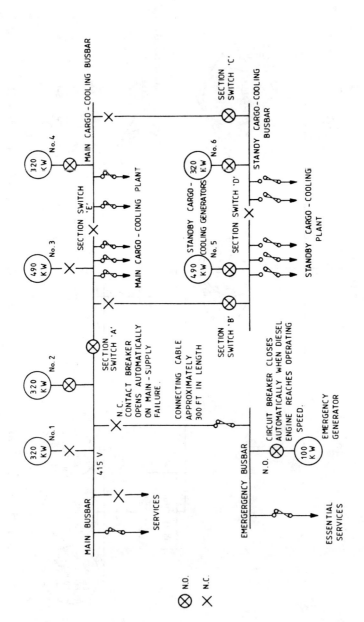

FIG. 8 ELECTRICAL POWER - SUPPLY INSTALLATION

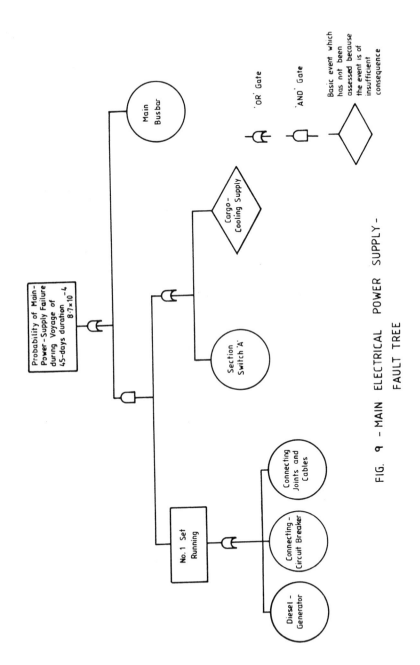

FIG. 9 – MAIN ELECTRICAL POWER SUPPLY –
FAULT TREE

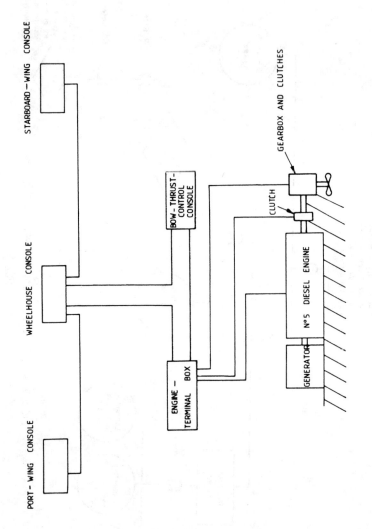

FIG. 10 BOW THRUST UNIT - BLOCK DIAGRAM

257

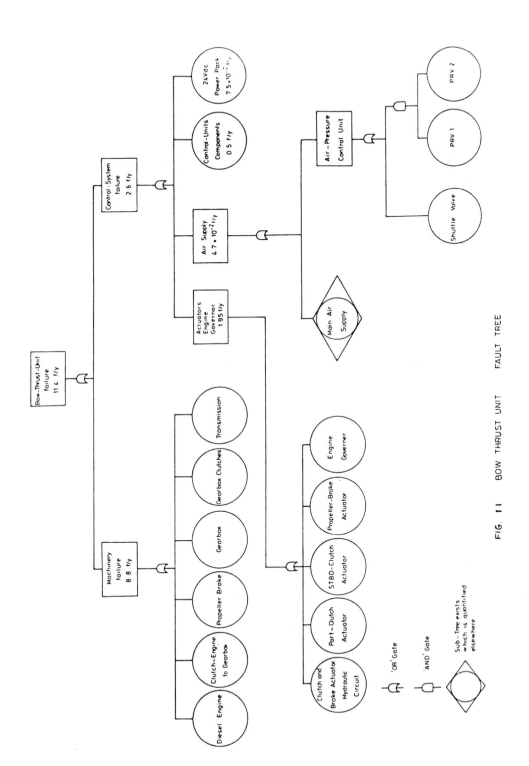

FIG. 11   BOW THRUST UNIT   FAULT TREE

258

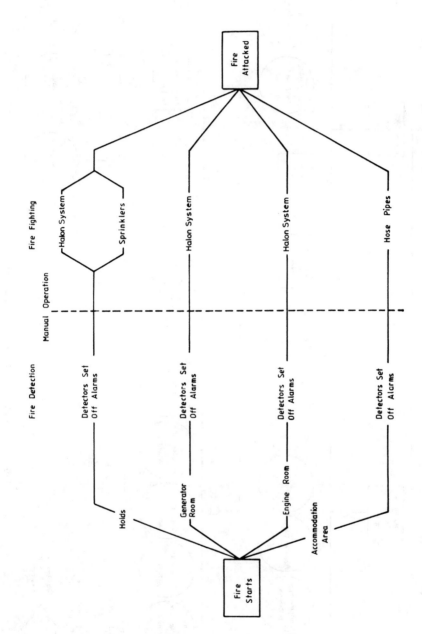

FIG. 12   INSTALLED FIRE - DETECTION AND FIRE-FIGHTING EQUIPMENT

259

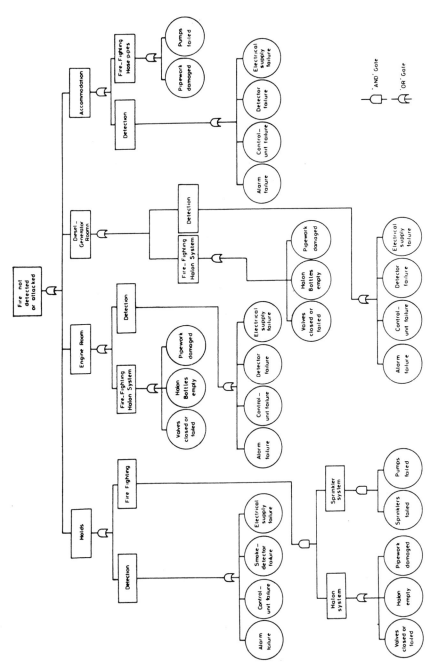

FIG. 13 FIRE - DETECTION AND FIRE - FIGHTING SYSTEMS - FAULT TREE

BAYESIAN AND TIME SERIES MODELLING TECHNIQUES IN TRANSPORTATION RELIABILITY

N Davies, J C Naylor and C McCollin
Department of Mathematics, Statistics and Operational Research
Trent Polytechnic Nottingham

ABSTRACT

We give an introduction to how existing methodology in Bayesian time series and Bayesian modelling can be applied to transportation data. We show how modifications to traditional Weibull plotting and modelling, hazard plotting and proportional hazards modelling can be made with resulting superior flexibility in the applicability of these techniques.

INTRODUCTION

Many reliability engineers employ graphical approaches to fitting models to their data. Typically, even assuming a single probability model such as the Weibull, a number of different plots, analyses and interpretation are possible.

These will involve traditional Weibull plotting and modelling, hazard plotting [1] and more recently proportional hazards modelling [2] and numerical Bayesian statistical methodology [3]. Reliability engineers prefer to employ graphical approaches to 'fitting' models to their data. Apart from the obvious disadvantage of subjective inaccuracy in drawing these graphs, interpretations very often involve 'estimating' various imposed model parameters.

Reliability engineers should be aware of the possibility of a dynamic, or evolving relationship amongst observable data, and consequently among model parameters. This is especially the case for any data collected consecutively or over time.

Examples in transporation data are : times between engine overhauls, milages to mechanical breakdowns and numbers of faults discovered during specified times in service. All these data sets would involve observations either through time or with the data collected consecutively. In this paper we show how the classical models, inherent in graphical reliability plotting, can be extended from time static regression assumptions to the much more flexible formation where all parameters are allowed to evolve with the data.

Another alternative to graphically based methods is to use the likelihood function. This is well defined in the case of the Weibull distribution for both observed failure times and censored values (i.e. items which have not yet failed) but there are problems in its use. Bayesian methods can be demonstrated to have advantages over traditional maximum likelihood methods.[3] We also demonstrate these methods as an alternative to traditional Weibull modelling.

CLASSICAL MODELS FOR RELIABILITY DATA

For some years the reliability literature has reported many successful applications of the well known Weibull distribution

$$f(t) = ab^{-1} t^{a-1} \exp(-(t/b)^a), \tag{1}$$

where t is the random variable that can represent time between failures of an item, distance to wearout etc and a and b are termed the shape and scale parameters. Graphical procedures (Weibull plotting) used to estimate a and b are usually implemented using appropriate transformations of the Weibull reliability

$$R(t) = \exp(-(t/b)^a), \tag{2}$$

the Weibull hazard rate

$$h(t) = ab^{-1} t^{a-1}$$

or cumulative hazard

$$H(t) = (t/b)^a. \tag{3}$$

The linear equations assumed in the plotting procedures are thus

$$\log(\log(1/R(t))) = \log(b^{-a}) + a \log t \tag{4}$$

and

$$\log t = \log a + b^{-1} \log H \tag{5}$$

Weibull plotting paper and hazard plotting paper are merely mechanisms to **graphically** estimate the parameters. Equation (5) is usually preferred when censoring occurs in the data, for the hazard estimate conveniently takes this into account. A more consistent way to estimate these parameters can be used by employing linear least squares to transformed data modelled by (4) or (5).

BAYESIAN MODELS FOR RELIABILITY DATA

Time series Bayesian models

The simplest form of the dynamic linear models developed by Harrison and Stevens [4] relates an observation equation for data Y_i

$$Y_i = \mu_i + r_i + v_i \tag{6}$$

where i is an index, μ_i is a level, r_i is a regression variable and v_i is white noise.

Level and regressor variables are allowed to evolve according to **parameter equations**

$$\mu_i = \mu_{i-1} + w_{1i}$$

and

$$r_i = r_{i-1} + w_{2i}$$

where w_{1i} and w_{2i} are independent white noise variables.

If we allow a failure number indexing in (4) and (5), so that we assume, for example time or distance between failures of a component evolves with a dependency between those failures, from (6) we could write, for equation (4)

$$Y_i^{(1)} = [\log (\log (1/R(t)))]_i$$

$$\mu_i^{(1)} = [\log (b^{-a})]_i \tag{7}$$

and

$$r_i^{(1)} = a_i[\log t]_i$$

For (5)

$$Y_i^{(2)} = [\log t]_i$$

$$\mu_i^{(2)} = [\log a]_i \tag{8}$$

and

$$r_i^{(2)} = (1/b_i)[\log H]_i$$

Given this Dynamic Linear Model formulation it is straightforward to apply the Bayesian Analysis of Time Series (BATS) program developed by West, Harrison and Pole [5], to recursively estimate the μ_i and r_i. The advantage of the more flexible Bayesian formulation is that the constant a and b parameter cases implied by (4) and (5) will be a special case of the models for Y_i (1) and Y_i (2) defined above.

Likelihood Based Bayesian Estimates

The likelihood function for a sample with observed failures at t_1, t_2, ..., t_m and units surviving to time or distance t_{m+1}, t_{m+2}, ..., t_n when observations cease, can be obtained as

$$\ell(\underset{\wedge}{t} \; ; a,b) = \prod_{i=1}^{m} f(t_i) \prod_{i=m+1}^{n} R(t_i)$$

For the Weibull distribution f(t) is defined by (1) and R(t) by (2).

The Bayesian approach assumes knowledge about the parameters before the data, i.e. in the form of a prior density p(a,b) and presents the knowledge after as a posterior density p(a,b/t) which may be defined by

$$p(a,b/t) = \frac{\ell(t; a,b) \, p(a,b)}{\int\int \ell(t; a,b) \, p(a,b)dadb}$$

Point estimates of the parameters, on a well defined function $\theta = \theta(a,b)$ of the parameters are readily available as posterior moments:

$$\hat{\theta} = E\,(\theta/t) = \int\int \theta \, p(a,b/t)dadb$$

For comparison with graphical methods we choose $\theta\,(a,b) = -a \log(b)$ which is the intercept of a standard Weibull plot.

To obtain such estimates efficient numerical integration methods are needed, and ones based on iterative application of Gauss Hermite product rules is highly efficient in this context, see for example [3].

APPLICATION TO TRANSPORTATION DATA

Graphical approaches

We analyse data relating to distance to failure of subsystems of buses operating in different environments.

Information on five different environments were supplied, but in this analysis space only allows us to concentrate on just one of those. The information was given on 50 buses in the form of distance to first failure of each of two subsystems on each bus and distance travelled before all other subsequent failures was also supplied.

Our initial analysis involved drawing the Weibull plot corresponding to (4) and the hazard plot corresponding to (5) for each of the two bus subsystems for (i) distance travelled to first failure and (ii) subsequent distance travelled to second failure. Not all buses failed within the distances recorded (at least 100,000 km) and so some censoring exists. Many authors [1] prefer only using the hazard plot in this case, as the method has a limited allowance for censored data. Pressure of space prevents us from presenting the plots, but the general picture is that some evidence exists for a non constant slope (shape) in the Weibull modelling procedure in (4) for distances travelled to first and second failure of subsystem A. Similarly, using the hazard plotting approach via (5) both shape and scale parameters appear to be non constant for both subsystems for first and second distances to failure. The actual parameter estimates are collected later in Table 1.

In figure 1 we present the graphs of the on-line estimates of $\mu_i^{(1)}$ and a_i for the Weibull plotting system represented by (7) for both subsystem A and B, and the corresponding on-line estimates of $\mu_i^{(2)}$ and $1/b_i$ in (8). We restrict ourselves to graphs for distance to first failure. Constancy of the estimated parameters would be indicated by a near horizontal line over the buses as they failed.

For subsystem A the on-line estimate of intercept $\mu_i^{(1)}$ (corresponding to a changing Weibull scale parameter) becomes constant after about the 12th bus has failed. Similarly, the coefficient estimate a_i (corresponding to a changing Weibull shape parameter) also becomes steadier after about the 12th bus failure, although there is some evidence that the shape parameter is increasing over the last few bus failures. Under the same conditions we note that for subsystem B, parameter estimates tend to be constant, but different from those in subsystem A.

Figure 1

Level and Slope Estimates for Models using the Weibull plot

Subsystem A distance to first failure

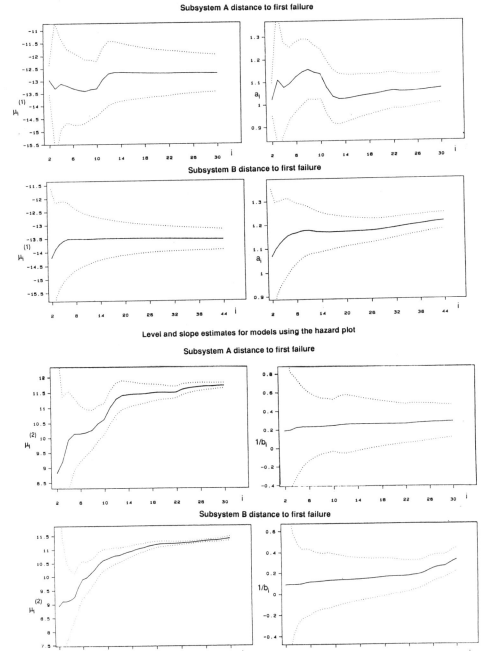

Subsystem B distance to first failure

Level and slope estimates for models using the hazard plot

Subsystem A distance to first failure

Subsystem B distance to first failure

Using the hazard modelling approach and for subsystem A, we again note that $\mu_i{}^{(2)}$ (corresponding to a combination of changing Weibull shape and scale parameter) becomes constant after about the 12th bus failure. For subsystem B after about half the buses have failed parameter estimates settle down.

Parameter estimates

In Table 1 we present estimates of the Weibull shape and scale parameters obtained from the three methods associated with traditional Weibull plotting (LS), Bayesian on-line time series modelling (BTS) and the method based on Bayesian likelihood (BL) for both subsystems for distances to first and second failures.

As has been noted the LS approach assumes parameter estimates are constant for the whole bus - failure period. The hazard approach is better at allowing for censored bus distances, but nevertheless contain some unexpected values for scale parameter estimates.

The value in the BTS approach Is the on-line assessment that is available from inspecting plots of recursive parameter estimates. We therefore present the final (posterior) estimates of the Weibull shape and scale parameters just for completeness. Thus, the BTS estimates presented in Table 1 represent the picture current at the last recorded bus failure. Nevertheless, LS and posterior BTS estimates are in broad agreement in cases where constant Weibull shape and scale parameters are adequate. The biggest discrepancies occur when constancy of parameter estimates are inappropriate over the whole bus - failure period in the subsystems. For example, in subsystem A the intercept term for distance to first failure, modelled from the hazard approach, is not constant. This will affect the posterior estimate of shape as well.

The BL results give generally higher values for shape and lower values for scale (characteristic life) than the plotting based methods, though most lie within about 2 standard deviations. The BL results also show smaller changes across the different data sets; this is almost certainly due to the likelihood function giving a better specification of the effects due to censoring.

Clearly a simple Weibull model is not adequate for the whole of this data as the buses fail and extensions should be considered. The distances to failure may well be influenced by other factors not reported here which may be incorporated, via a proportional hazards model, into the likelihood function. Analysis of such a model is relatively straight forward using numerical Bayesian methods [6] and will be reported at a later date.

Table 1

Estimates of shape and scale parameters for the Weibull distribution applied to distance to failure for fifty buses in one environment

Subsystem			Distance to first failure (all buses)		Distance from first to second (those buses that failed at least once)	
			Shape a	Scale b	Shape a	Scale b
			(Sample size 50, 21 censored)		(Sample size 29, 19 censored)	
A	LS	WB	1.08	169602	0.41	2041460
		HZ	1.00	189094	0.39	1859465
	BTS	WB	1.07	814557	0.40	1465922
		HZ	3.45	124244	1.28	194464
	BL		1.45	125817	0.98	132403
			(0.25)	(19028)	(0.27)	(68916)
			(Sample size 50, 7 censored)		(Sample size 43, 10 censored)	
B	LS	WB	1.35	82180	0.89	59935
		HZ	1.31	79778	0.83	60084
	BTS	WB	1.21	71721	0.83	2266
		HZ	3.01	88433	0.74	60597
	BL		1.52	72294	1.14	42178
			(0.20)	(7568)	(0.16)	(6802)

Note: LS - indicates estimates after transforming back from least squares estimates of slope and intercept of the Weibull plot.

BTS - indicates estimates obtained after transforming back from the posterior estimates of level and the regression coefficient.

BL - indicates estimates from the Bayesian likelihood approach (with standard errors in brackets).

WB - using the Weibull plotting model.

HZ - using the Weibull cumulative hazard plotting model.

CONCLUSIONS

We have shown that the traditional Weibull-based plotting approach may be extended to allow for a failure number dependency in parameter estimates for transportation data. This Bayesian time series approach permits a graphical judgement about the appropriateness of parameter constancy in the underlying Weibull model. Taking proper account of censoring can only be achieved using Bayes likelihood methods and in general the resulting parameter estimates seem 'sensible' overall. Where the Bayesian time series method gives 'unrealistic' posterior estimates, we have found that that is mainly due to weaknesses in the underlying assumptions behind the Weibull plotting approach.

Censoring is a time dependent effect and so the time series approach may well provide guidance on the magnitude of the censoring problem during the collection of transportation data.

REFERENCES

1. O'Connor, P D T Practical Reliability Engineering Second Edition, John Wiley, 1985.

2. Wightman, D W and Bendell, A Proportional Hazards modelling of software failure data. Software Reliability, State of the Art Report, 14 : 2, 230-242. Pergamon Infotech, Oxford.

3. Smith, R L and Naylor J C A comparison of maximum likelihood and Bayesian estimates for the three parameter Weibull distribution. Applied Statistics, 1987, 36, 358-369.

4. Harrison, P J and Stevens C F Bayesian Forecasting (with discussion). J R Statistic Soc., 1976, B, 38, 205-247.

5. West, M., Harrison, Jeff and Pole, A. BATS : A User Guide. University of Warwick, 1988.

6. Naylor, J C and Smith, A F M Applications of a Method for the Efficient Computation of Posterior Distributions. Applied Statistics, 1982, 31, 214-225.